MW01049795

Malachite Lion
A Travel Adventure in Kenya

by

Richard Modlin

Bloomington, IN

Milton Keynes, UK

AuthorHouse™
1663 Liberty Drive, Suite 200
Bloomington, IN 47403
www.authorhouse.com
Phone: 1-800-839-8640

AuthorHouse™ UK Ltd.
500 Avebury Boulevard
Central Milton Keynes, MK9 2BE
www.authorhouse.co.uk
Phone: 08001974150

First published by AuthorHouse 3/28/2006

ISBN: 1-4033-7333-7 (sc)
ISBN: 1-4033-7334-5 (dj)

Printed in the United States of America
Bloomington, Indiana

This book is printed on acid-free paper.

IN PRAISE OF *MALACHITE LION*

". . . written about a unique topic with such passion that it is hard to put down this book . . . friendly, conversational tone and eloquent scenery descriptions make readers feel like they are traveling with him [the author]. . . " — *Writer's Digest.*

"For those of you who have spent any time in Kenya or East Africa in general, I can recommend *Malachite Lion* . . . if you haven't, you will enjoy this piece of armchair travel." — Patty Eby, *Union Jack.*

". . . attention to detail of the daily activities of life in Kenya, on safari and just traveling there in general is superb. Written in a style that is very descriptive of the subtle and obvious sights and trials encountered. This book will be a great primer for anyone planning a trip to East Africa." — William Chapman, author and photographer, *Face of Tibet.*

"You my never get the chance to travel to East Africa, but you may be an armchair traveler. If so, this is the book for you Not that it is limited to the category of travel." — Sara McDaris, *The Huntsville Times.*

". . . charming book. It's a remarkable mix of storytelling, exploration and education." — Rusty Bynum, author and playwrite, *Legacy of Galileo* and *Legacy of Michelangelo.*

". . . the author samples the culture of Kenya in a way that a tourist rarely achieves." — Mema, *Amazon.com.* Reader's rating, 5 stars

"I read this book while traveling alone for the first time in a foreign country. It was inspirational to me as a traveler, especially one who travels alone, to have a companion (even if it is just a book) understand what it means to discover a place on your own (and all the fears that go with it). — Carechemist, *Amazon.com.* Reader's rating, 5 stars

". . . knowing little of Africa and intrigued by the "real life suden trip" aspect, I decided that *Malachite Lion* could be fun. And it is quite fun to read." — W. Doug Bolden, *Amazon.com.* Reader's rating, 5 stars

DEDICATION/ACKNOWLEDGMENTS

This book is dedicated to my wife, colleague, friend, and fellow explorer, Marian L. Lewis, who, as a matter of fact, visited Kenya the same year I did, in 1987. Although we traveled many of the same paths, we did not meet until three years later and a few thousand miles from Kenya. Her encouragement, support, comments and suggestions on this work are greatly appreciated.

I would like to express my gratitude to Bill Chapman, Rusty Bynum and Karen Murphy whose comments and suggestions greatly improved the text of this book.

Cover design by Carrie Alderfer.

Author portrait by Marian L. Lewis

PREFACE

A question I'm often asked when I discuss my book, *Malachite Lion*, is, "What prompted you to travel to East Africa in the first place?" Especially curious are those colleagues, friends and acquaintances that knew me prior to the trip. To them I was a quiet, somewhat shy biology professor not overly endowed with confidence. Although I had traveled widely, my apprehension in the face of the unknown had never materialized because either someone I trusted, or myself, had planned the details of the trips that I took. Likewise, this venture to East Africa also began as a highly organized, itinerary-specified, well-defined research trip. I had applied for a grant from the Smithsonian Institution and, because of my expertise in marine biology; I was awarded a slot on an international expedition to the waters off Aldabra Island in the remote Seychelles Archipelago located in the Indian Ocean. My contribution on this journey would be to survey and collect small marine crustaceans. A dream comes true - I couldn't pass up this opportunity. All that remained for me to do was to get time off from the university and travel to Nairobi where I would join the other members of the expedition. Once there, funding from the Smithsonian Institution and other museums and research institutes in England and France would support all of the expedition's activities for a six-week tour.

About a week before my departure date I watched helplessly as my plans fell apart. With great apologies from my Smithsonian colleagues, I was notified that President Ronald Reagan had frozen all federal funding. Because of this, the Smithsonian Institution could not provide travel support for non-Smithsonian researchers, so my slot on the expedition was canceled.

Dream shattered! Now, what's a poor biologist to do? My leave from the university was approved and I had a non-refundable ticket to Nairobi. Perplexed, I discussed my situation with the dean of my college, a prudent man whose judgment I trusted.

"Go anyway," he said. "Maybe you'll learn something about yourself."

His words propelled me into an unplanned odyssey to a land about which I knew very little.

Table of Contents

THE FLIGHT

The air is still, cool. A slight amount of humidity enhances the musty odor that rises from the great herds roaming the grasslands. I crawl out of the tent on my knees, rise, stretch and watch the genesis of the African day. It brightens from stark blue-black through pastel hues of reds and blues interspersed with bronze, beige, and gold. Thin white clouds on the horizon fracture the gilded sky into beams that radiate from the awakening source and continually stretch upward toward zenith, then outward until the firmament saturates with intense radiance when the sun enters the scene.

But wait! I have the proverbial horse before the cart! First let me tell you how I came to be in Africa.

* * *

"We're now passing out over the Adriatic Sea," the pilot announced over the intercom. He proceeded to chart the plane's course for us. "We'll pass near Athens. Those sitting on the left will be able to see it. Our route over Africa will take us east of Cairo, over Khartoum and Addis Ababa, then we'll turn due south and head into Nairobi. Welcome aboard. Sit back. Relax and enjoy the flight."

His words made me feel a bit anxious. My mind hadn't clicked to the fact that this trip was taking me a long way from home. I'd never before been in this part of the world, and the places the pilot announced had only occurred in my fantasies.

My flight across the Atlantic Ocean had been benign. I had flown from Atlanta, Georgia to London and Paris several times before, but never to Frankfurt. I changed airplanes at Frankfurt's Rhein-Main Airport. This airport just a little deeper in the continent was like all other international airports: large, busy, and crowded with both travelers and airplanes.

Earlier in the month there had been several bomb threats at the Rhein-Main airport. One bomb actually exploded. I had been warned before leaving the U.S.A. that Frankfurt's Rhein-Main International Airport and many other air terminals in Europe were being hustled by terrorists, so security would be especially tight.

The only thing out of the ordinary in Frankfurt was that all passengers had to identify their checked luggage before it would be loaded onto the flight to Nairobi. This we did as we boarded the plane. There was no jetway. Passengers exited the terminal onto the tarmac and climbed a set of stairs to enter the Boeing 747. But before being allowed to climb the stairs, each individual was required to file past the luggage displayed on the ground under the wing and point out to a security officer those pieces belonging to them. The bags were then loaded into containers, which were placed in the cargo hold.

Flight time from Frankfurt to Nairobi was approximately eight hours. Since the flight departed at about 3:00 pm, it would still be daylight when the plane reached Egypt. I wondered if the pyramids would be visible from 35,000 feet. I got my answer a couple of hours later. They were not. But, when I looked down on the Sahara Desert, I saw the most spectacular effect of a sunset I'd had ever seen. Because of the extreme clarity of the atmosphere, the terrain below was sharply visible. It splayed out in irregular rows of long and short, jagged and smooth, straight and sinusoidal black shadows that stretched across the brilliant flame-colored desert. Transfixed on this scene of magnificence, grandeur and ruggedness, I watched the brilliance fade slowly to absolute darkness as we continued south over the Sahara.

Elspeth Huxley, in her travels after World War II, flew on one of the first scheduled commercial flights between London and Nairobi. Although early flight plans were similar to the one I was on, Elspeth's trip took six days to complete. Such a journey required several plane changes, many refueling stops, at least two railroad legs between airline terminals, and overnight stays in remote locations - back then, commercial airliners didn't have the instrumentation that allowed them to fly at night. Although Elspeth wrote that the trips were memorable because of the exotic sites and experiences, she also indicated the discomforts. The flights were bumpy, hot, stifling and nauseous, and the meals served during stopovers were unpalatable and any overnight lodging, Spartan.

I can empathize with Elsepth. In the seventies I made several flights to the Bahamas and other Caribbean locations as a passenger on a commercial airline that still used the DC-3. These were slow, noisy, hot, and poorly ventilated, but my flights never lasted more than a couple of hours. On the other hand, aboard the flight to Nairobi I was wined and dined, enjoyed a movie and fine music, and had partial control of the airflow around my seat. Although exhausting, the experience was one of total comfort.

AN ARRIVAL FRAUGHT WITH UNCERTAINTY

Exhaust blew through the open door. Headlights momentarily illuminated the interior of immigration check-in as Lufthansa's 747 turned onto the tarmac readying for its return to Frankfurt. Acrid odors of exhaust mixed with stale and freshly applied colognes, perspiration, and the fetid breath of the newly arrived, weary silhouettes pressed into the dim, airless room, bewildering my mind with anxious hallucinations.

Travel prolongs time if one cannot find sleep. The journey to Nairobi took thirty hours. My insomnia flared.

This is my first trip to the African continent, and I have taken it on my own and totally unplanned. I have six weeks to do whatever I want. I'm wired, feel like I'm floating. But first, there's a minor obstacle to be overcome: immigration.

Provoked, my body moves, forced to flow with the disordered queue of passengers, toward a wall upon which the words PASSPORT CONTROL - WELCOME TO NAIROBI were painted years ago. Beneath this sign is a row of windowed counters; one is open. All of us are trying to get to this window.

The garlic smelling coat in front of me moves aside. I'm next. I advance. An official, dressed in a military- green uniform, stands behind the window, demands my passport. Automatically, I slide it across the counter. Whatever happened to "Welcome *Bwana*"? I muse. He fumbles through my passport's pages, stops, then turns the pages more slowly, examines more carefully, more critically.

"Is there a problem?" I ask.

"You have no Visa."

"No, didn't think it necessary."

"Move aside," he says. Closes my passport, lays it on a shelf behind him, and makes eye contact with the woman in dark glasses who elbows me aside.

Suddenly the heat in the room intensifies. My palms moisten. My stomach tightens. "Is there a water closet near?" I ask the two official looking guys in plain clothes who escort me through a door in the plywood wall. Neither answers. I'm taken to a room where a single bulb hangs over a lone table. It provides the only illumination. Dark stained walls absorb most of its light. I move into the room without thinking. I'm asked to stand in front of the table. A frightening thought stabs my mind. Is this room to be my prison? The place from which, I will experience Kenya?

A wailing roar passes the terminal. The airliner's return to its element removed any thought of transport home that I might have had. Worried? Yes. My passport is confiscated. I can't go home without it. With no visa, I'm not legal here either. So I'm stuck in this dimly lighted box of plywood cured in cigarette smoke, in limbo, gasping for some fresh air.

A young man appears behind the table. He may have been there all the time. I wasn't aware of him when I entered. He wears a freshly pressed, light colored, short-sleeved shirt with its collar unbuttoned. It hangs loosely about his waist and covers the top of a pair of dark colored trousers. He smirks sheepishly. His hands guard a rubber stamp, ink pad, and a thin stack of mimeographed forms, decorations on an otherwise empty table.

My escorts relax near the sides of the table, but retain a hair-triggered attitude. Escape never enters my mind. Instead I stand at attention, rigid, in front of the table, barely breathing, just as I did long-ago when I was confronted by my platoon commander.

"You must fill this out." He hands me one of the mimeographed forms.

"I need a pencil."

He hands me a Mont Blanc pen. I'm impressed, but it feels thin in my unyielding fingers and eludes my grip. The pen drops onto the table, rolls across the edge of the form. I furl and unfurl my stiffened digits. Shake my hands in an attempt to loosen them enough to pick up the pen. The activity produces little sensation, but the pen is in place. I try to write. Jittery, barely readable symbols appear on lines. Miraculously, they spell-out my name, home address, point of embarkation, port of entry. Passport number? Place issued? "I need my passport to complete this form," I say.

"If your visa is approved, I'll enter that information," the young man says. He takes the form and his pen. "Fee is eight dollars U. S. Do you have the money?"

"I have a ten dollar bill," I say.

"Thank you." He examines his Rolex. "Its one-thirty in the morning, but I'll try to get your application approved tonight. . . ." He disappears through a doorway with my ten dollar bill.

Approval could take hours, days. This would not be a very appealing room in which to enjoy my first dawn on the African Continent.

Imperceptibly, my feet slide. My body wavers. I try to loosen up. My eyes, neck and shoulders, my stomach, thighs and calves ache. The guards perceive my agitations. They smile warmly. Their attempt, I feel, is to reduce my anxiety, which they had originally caused. Across the table the young man finally reappears. He's only been gone five minutes. It seems like hours. His hand, holding two American dollars, extends toward me, but hesitates.

"You don't want these do you?" He makes momentary eye contact with me and the guards.

"No."

A cool waft of air, lightly perfumed with burnt wood, dried grass, barnyard odors, enters the room. Thud! Thud! Thud! The table reverberates with quick sharp beats of the rubber stamp. My passport is handed to me.

"Welcome to Kenya - Alabama - you'll do well here," the young man said, pocketing the money. Three stoic faces brightened to friendly. I'm ushered, amid convivial handshakes and pats on the back, into the bright, neon-signed lobby filled with excited, lost faces of fellow passengers moving in third-world chaos. On the conveyor was my luggage, all of it, bags and backpack. My newfound friends vaporized in wafts of cigarette smoke and auto exhaust.

Blurry eyed and in a trance, I slipped on my backpack. It slapped into position knocking me forward. I stabilized my stance, collected my suitcase and staggered toward the officious line of customs inspectors. They stood next to a group of counters where luggage could be opened and rummaged. But, for bureaucrats, these guys were downright pleasant. All they wanted to know, was if I were bringing in any cigarettes, alcohol, or *Playboy* Magazines. I shook my head at their questions. Assured that I had no contraband, they directed me through the checkpoint into the lobby. Free, rubber stamped, and now legal in Kenya, I stood in a daze contemplating my next move.

After a quick stop at the Foreign Exchange window to buy some Kenyan Shillings, I made my way through the large open doors to the curb. A parti-colored line of taxis, bathed in the warmish tint of sodium lighting, outlined the contour of the street leading to the terminal entrance, their engines running in readiness to transport tourists to desired destinations. There must have been 30 or 40 of them waiting outside the Jomo-Kenyatta International Airport terminal. This was one of the places in Kenya, I suspect, where taxi drivers can secure a fare at two o'clock in the morning. The cabs snaked up a slight incline and disappeared into shadowy darkness.

The coolness of the night condensed the acrid exhaust emanating from the curbside serpent into turbulent vapors that rose through beams of headlights and the reddish glow of taillights. The vapors coalesced into seemingly cone-shaped clouds that caressed the poles supporting overhead security lights, and beyond them, total darkness. But at curbside, cigarette smoke and barnyard odors flavored the exhaust. I overheard someone say that Nairobi National Park surrounded the airport; that explained the fetidness.

A couple of deep breaths of African "fresh air" stimulated a strong sneeze and attracted a mélange of requests in several different languages to transport me to Nairobi. The chaotic medley of taxi drivers, competing for the few remaining tourists not carried away by tour buses, agitated and electrified me.

"Need a Taxi!" They yelled while hanging out of their cabs' driver's-side window. "Take you to Nairobi . . ."

"Fast . . ."

"Soft ride . . ."

"Safe . . ."

Others ran along the curb soliciting. Several even grabbed my suitcase handles and tried to escort me toward their vehicles. For a moment there was one on each side of me, each pulling in a different direction.

"How much to Nairobi?" I asked. This request slowed them down a bit.

"We'll negotiate when you're sitting safe in my taxi. Now I'll help you to it," said the well-dressed guy on my right.

"Two hundred Kenyan shilling," shouted the one on the left.

"One hundred and thirty shilling," said a deep baritone voice in front of me. I look up into the face of a very large man in a soiled T-shirt, faded black pants and tattered sandals. The guy on the right and the one on the left release the suitcase handles and quickly backed away. It was as if the "Godfather" had spoken.

"Sounds reasonable," I said, and allowed him to take my suitcase.

He loaded it into a faded hospital-green early-model 1950s VW van with a cream colored roof sculptured along its right margin as if the bus may have made contact with trees or buildings while angling through tight curves at high speed.

I got aboard, sat in the middle of the seat in the row just behind the driver, in a vehicle the hippie generation would have savored. Its well-worn seats had their stuffing oozing out in surf-like clumps; a small section of the flooring behind my seat, missing; the dashboard was brush-painted maroon with a large hole where the speedometer should have been; and the left side windows were held in place with several strips of Duct-tape. A cardboard flower-shaped air freshener hung from the rearview mirror, its scent vaporized long ago. For two hundred shillings I could have ridden in a Mercedes, but I didn't think it wise to back out of my commitment at this moment.

The driver flung the side-panel door several times along its slide. Each time, it contacted the frame with a ricocheting slam. Frustrated, he really laid into it with all his strength. The panel screamed on its runners. It connected. It locked, but the vehicle rebelled, shuddered. Its windows rattled. Some mysterious object fell from beneath the dash. I hoped that whatever broke wasn't crucial to the trip to Nairobi. Would the panel ever open again? I wondered.

"Where to?" He asked as he slid into his seat.

"Aren't you gonna get some other passengers?"

"Don't need any. I want to get home tonight."

"But, you can't make much money with one passenger. There's room for at least four others."

"You're all I need. I'll get your money. Don't want to take anyone else. Just you." He started the engine and turned away from the curb. "Where you goin'?"

"Ambassador Hotel," I said, loud enough to be heard over the buzz of the engine, then sat back and tried to think clearly.

Strange, I thought these guys were out for a buck. The fare is calculated by the person, so taxi drivers try to pack their cabs to overflowing - more bodies more shillings. Apparently, this guy isn't greedy. I guess he's just in a hurry to get home.

By the time I lifted my head to gaze out the window, the security lights around the terminal were in the background and, except for the dim splay of our headlights, we were enveloped in total darkness. But still being within the confines of airport property, we passed through periodic illuminated circles produced by occasional street lamps.

The van bounced, swayed, and floated onto a freeway. The last street lamp decreased in the rear window. The driver shifted into fifth gear and we zipped toward a pair of electric-green signs, illuminated by our headlights that hung above the highway. Big white letters on the larger sign spelled Nairobi and an arrow pointed in the direction we were headed. On the smaller sign the arrow pointed toward an exit to an unknown destination.

My anxiety flared when the bus dramatically veered to the right and I was jerked to the left. The van whirred into the black velvet aura that engulfed the exit ramp. Barely slowing, the driver turned right and preceded along a narrow, partially paved, two-lane road. The edge of the road, delineated by the beam from our headlights, streaked along in a confusion of fuzzy vegetation. In a 360-degree visual sweep of the ebony panorama surrounding our cruising pod, I saw no other lights, not even a glow nor a reflection. Did the moon shine over Africa? I wondered. Probably it's a new moon. "I need to check this out if I ever get to where I'm going," I mumbled.

The buzz of the engine and the whoosh of air through the cracks in the van lulled me into a drowse. A kaleidoscopic mirage of the day's episodes, some real, others reorganized and chaotic, whirled past my eyes and through my brain. Hypnotically, I relaxed back into the seat. The mohair textured backrest caressed my cheek, tickled my nose as my head rolled against it. Subtle exhaust fumes aroused visions of the recent airport encounters.

"Oh, my God!" I blurted. My body jolted to attention. "I'll get your money. That's what he said," I mumbled. A nauseous impulse spread across my stomach. My heart pounded. My mind screamed. He really did say, he'd get my money. I know I heard him say that. I stared at the back of the cab driver's head. My agitations didn't detract him from his mission. He appeared tranced on the roadway that rolled through the VW's spotlights. What should I do?

I looked out the window. Nothing out there but blackness. And, I'm being driven around by some brute impersonating a taxi driver, and with thoughts of selling my valuables and cashing my traveler's checks.

What a racket. All a crooked taxi driver has to do is pick up a single fare, an unsuspecting, half-asleep stranger lost in a bumping, jostling crowd of tourists that have just arrived and who are trying to out-compete each other for transportation to the city. Then he'd drive his victim out to the boonies, bop him on the head, and take his money and passport. Passports, especially American ones, I'm sure are high on a terrorist's shopping list.

That's right, he's a terrorist. So he'll do me in because he knows how, he's done it before, many times, I'll bet. Then he'll dump my carcass somewhere off the road where vultures can dispose of all traces of me. But, if anyone found me, intact, they'd not know who I was, because he'd have taken my passport, so there'd be no identification. This being a third-world country, he'd get away with it. Laws here, if there are any, are only for convenience. Corruption probably runs rampant in the police department. For a small bribe the authorities would look the other way. Why not, I don't mean anything to them, and they'd make a little extra cash.

I tried to sit back, relax, get rid of the anxiety, but my mind was working overtime.

This guy will no doubt take my clothes too. They're American made, so probably worth something. I'd be lying out there naked, exposed for all to see. That's an unpleasant thought. But, who'd see, who'd care? I sure won't, because I'd be dead. But its cold out there. Naked dead bodies attract things, like mosquitoes and bugs, because they don't have to work through all those clothes. I wonder if mosquitoes bite dead bodies. It would be more comfortable if he'd leave my clothes on when he does me in. I should try to bargain with him.

Nobody knows me in Kenya. I'm 8000 miles from home. Who'd care if some guy's body is found, in the brush, half eaten by the wild animals. I'd just show up as a statistic like all those other lost souls. Probably happens all the time. I bet there's lots of lonely tourists lost each year in Africa. Who knows? The Chamber of Commerce, if such an agency exists in Nairobi, is not going to publish any reports on lost tourists. It's bad for business.

Wow, did I get myself into a fix. My palms began to sweat. I fidgeted. I've got to save myself, but I'm defenseless except for my Swiss Army Knife. I could shove the corkscrew into his ear. Oh, that would hurt and make him madder than all hell. Then he'd really wallop me and I'd be just as dead. I can't really take him out because he's so big. I could stab him. But if I'd killed him, the police wouldn't understand because I don't speak their language. They'd arrest me because I'm a foreigner. Even worse, they probably know this taxi driver personally because he gives them a cut. I'd be tried for murder and hung.

I wonder if murder is a hanging crime in Kenya. More likely they'd execute me with a firing squad. Ugh, that would sting.

I could cause him to slow down, then I'd jump out and run into the bushes. I'm not sure there are any bushes out there, it's so dark. Oh, so what? I'd still get away. But I don't know where I am. And, this is Africa, and there are lions out there that feed at night. They love to go after anything that is running. Seems they enjoy a chase.

Hey, there's a light out there. I see a trio of spotlights illuminating a railroad yard ahead.

Oh, wow! Here it comes. I'm done. When we get to that railroad yard he'll drag me out, sock me in the head, take my money, and throw my corpse across the rails. It'll look like I got run over by a train. Such an event may not be that unusual. Lots of young people hop freights to extend their transportation options.

There are a few more lights down the road past the freight yard. Looks like an all night gasoline station, a vestige of civilization. Maybe I could talk him into making a pit stop. I'll try to negotiate.

I leaned forward. "How much further?" I asked.

"Not far." He maintained his concentration on the road. It began to widen. We rapidly passed the gasoline station. It wasn't open. We passed through more intersections. Streetlights illuminated corrugated shacks. Cottages appeared and disappeared behind broken vehicles and piles of trash. The driver slowed the vehicle and made several turns. We entered a more lighted area of commercial buildings of several stories in height. There were billboards advertising goods and services, automobiles, foodstuffs. We were in a city. Shortly the VW van turned into what appeared to be an alley and stopped.

"We're here, *Bwana.*"

The driver slipped out of his seat and came around the van. I was pushing on the door handle even before he left his seat, but the door was jammed from the powerful slam it received at closing. He gave the panel a good jerk and it slid open.

"I will carry your luggage to the desk, Sir. You follow. You're tired from your long journey. You must rest and then enjoy our beautiful country." He carried my luggage as if it were weightless through a door below the sign identifying the Ambassador Hotel and gently set it down next to the registration desk.

"Thank you." I felt calm, tired, foolish. I handed him 200 Kenyan shillings. It's rare to get an exciting taxi ride from an international airport to the heart of a city for about $12.50.

"Asante sana, Bwana. Hujambo." The taxi driver smiled, turned and left.

"What'd he say?"

"He liked the tip you gave him, thanked you and wished you a good night," the casual, but well dressed, clerk behind the desk said as I filled out the registrations form. "The fares they charge don't pay the maintenance on their vehicles and most of them have families to support. But they're proud, honest and reliable."

"We expected you, Mr. Modlin," the clerk said after I handed him the completed form. "I hope, although tiring, your trip was comfortable. Your agent booked you for two nights. Is that correct?" He rotated the ledger for my signature. Although it was almost two o'clock in the morning, he knew how to handle bleery-eyed arrivals.

"I think so."

"Very well. Your room number is 433. Since the lift does not operate after midnight, go up the stairs to my left, through the door at the landing and up the next three flights and turn to your right. Room 433 is down the hall. Here's your room key."

I nodded.

"Mr. Mjamani - you can call him Jimmy - will carry your luggage and show you to your room." An old man whisked my bags off the floor, put one under each arm and proceeded in front of me.

"Allow me, Sir." With a free hand he opened the glass door at the landing with his key. "Keeps the cool air in and the proletarians out. Your room key will allow you to enter, Sir."

Proletarians. What a proper term for riffraff, I thought. Must be a carryover from British colonial days? "Thank you. Are you sure you can carry all those? They're heavy."

"Oh yes, Sir."

Room 433 contained a single-sized bed, a straight back chair next to a small writing desk decorated with a vase that contained two pieces of dried grass. The room also contained a shower, a lavatory and commode, all within an eight by ten-foot space. Clean, efficient, businesslike, the room definitely was not designed for holding parties. Europeans are more accustomed to these Spartan accommodations than Americans.

"Breakfast is from 6:30 to 10:00, Sir. And, it's served in the restaurant to the left of the lobby." His eyes brightened when he examined the two 10 shilling notes I handed him.

"Asante sana, Bwana." He bowed and closed the door behind himself as he left my room.

"Time to clamp a lid on all those mind monsters," I mumbled, crashed onto the bed fully clothed and immediately fell asleep.

GOOD MORNING NAIROBI

The sunlight blared through the curtained window. It burned the fog from my eyes. I couldn't recall where I was. I rubbed them hard, arose, slid to the foot of the bed, parted the curtains and looked out. Before me materialized a modern city, Nairobi, brightly lighted and strongly contrasted. Across the street, over a clump of low trees, the Nairobi Hilton and several other skyscrapers blocked the skyline. I stood looking down toward the street. Below, a potpourri of costumes worn by the crowds flowing chaotically along the sidewalks formed colorful mosaic borders between which a hodgepodge of taxies, Fiats and Mercedes tried to negotiate their way around smoke-belching, yellow buses, with dirty, gray roofs, nosed at odd angles toward the curbs. The energy on the street excited me, along with the fact that it was already 9:30 AM. If I didn't hurry, I'd miss breakfast.

* * *

I read in Errol Trzebinski's *The Kenya Pioneers* that Joseph Thompson the explorer who is credited with the discovery of the Rift Valley, several of the Rift Valley lakes, and the spectacular waterfall (Thompson's Falls) first described the location where the city was built. This location initially served as a communication point on the frontier between Masailand and Kikuyuland. Some "stepping-stones" in the river allowed women of both cultures a way of crossing to exchange their products. The Kikuyu, the agriculturists, traded vegetables and grains with the nomadic Masai, while the Masai bartered cattle and sheep. While the women of each tribe bargained, the men conducted raids into each other's territories, or guarded against such raids.

An old Arab-Somali caravan route from Mombasa on the coast of the Indian Ocean to the interior of Africa also crossed the Nairobi River near Ngong. This brought additional trading activity to this area. Coastal traders carried a variety of trinket-like products, beads, copper wire, and cloth on the inward trek, and returned ivory and slaves to the coast. Because of the availability of food stuffs, livestock and water, the Nairobi area, a series of marshy flatlands known as the Athi Plains, served as a primary supply station for the caravans. However, in those times no permanent structures were built because business was transient on this plain where different cultures converged to trade. More permanent development was initiated in the early 1890s, when Britain decided to build a railroad from Mombasa to Port Florence (now the City of Kisumu) on Lake Victoria. What started as nothing more than a way station to warehouse materials for the construction of the Uganda Railroad became the City of Nairobi.

Dr. Henry Albert Boedeker, one of the earliest Kenyan pioneers, immigrated in 1896 to Africa to plant roots in an area free of the bigotry and scandal that plagued him in Scotland. Boedeker, although fluent in the English language and educated at the University of Glasgow, was of Indian descent, thus dark complected. His marriage to a daughter of a British aristocrat did not sit well with the local gentry.

After arriving in Mombasa, Boedeker and his wife, along with the Wallaces and McQueens, all seeking an adventuresome holiday in East Africa, trekked inland along the proposed route of the Uganda Railroad to Fort Smith, a remote outpost on the Athi Plains. This was an arduous trip, but it took Boedeker and his friends past the location which was to become Nairobi.

In 1896, mile 327 of the Uganda Railroad was nothing more than a collection of tents, dilapidated tin shacks and cattle corrals. Sir Joseph Whitehouse in 1897 earmarked the site for the railroad's headquarters.

The Masai called the place *Engore Nyarobe,* the place of cold water. Whitehouse thought the location would be ideal for base camps and the storage of supplies for railroad construction as it continued toward Lake Victoria. What faced construction beyond this point was the Rift Valley. The railroad line would have to descend the Kikuyu Escarpment, a nearly sheer plunge of about 2000 feet, to the floor of this arid valley.

The site Whitehouse identified was actually miserable. In the rainy seasons the soil turned into a spongy, black cotton-like substance that formed part of the base of embryonic Nairobi. It became a swampy quagmire full of mosquitoes carrying malaria and pestilence. At other times the soil dried to the fine dusty powder responsible for a malady that came to be known as "Nairobi Throat." Although railroad officials realized these problems, this site was not moved. Construction of habitat buildings and warehouses had already begun and considerable supplies sequestered. Dr. Boedeker initially thought the site attractive, but after being appointed temporary medical officer for the railroad, he realized that the site was "the worst possible choice by virtue of the swamps." However, through the perseverance and commitment of pioneers, railroad builders, and settlers from Britain and other nations, and the help of native Africans, these initial problems were overcome. In a little less than one hundred years, Nairobi became the capital of Kenya and one of the most modern and progressive cities in East Africa.

* * *

I arrived for breakfast near the end of the serving time, but the restaurant was still crowded with customers. Businessmen in suits, casually dressed tourists, and several elderly ladies seemed to be enjoying the morning's repast. The patrons represented several nationalities, but I was the only American.

No one took notice when I entered. A comfortable feeling, but my mind seemed to work overtime; it generated anxiety. Today's apprehensions were budgetary. Although I thought I had brought sufficient funds, they were limited. A room at a four-star hotel would quickly reduce my cash. Throw in food, I'd soon reach a poverty level long before my six-week stay was completed. One satisfying thing, I had already paid for transportation back to the U. S. A. Many of the early settlers to Kenya came with only the clothes on their backs. Today one needs some money. You'd be expected to tip the man on the wharf who told you he saved your luggage from being absconded, even though the only luggage you're carrying is strapped to your back.

The Maître'd snapped my thoughts back to reality. I'd just have to be frugal, the original plan for this trip anyway.

Another distressing thought troubled my mind. What do they eat in Nairobi? I'll bet the food here is probably not what I'm accustomed to. This country is really foreign. Hemingway wrote about fried hartebeest kidneys for breakfast. Elspeth Huxley was served rancid mutton during stopovers in her travels between Nairobi and London. The Masai drink the blood of a cow mixed with unpasteurized milk. Other tribes eat grubs and grasshoppers. Americans eat shrimp and crabs . . . "insects of the sea." Get real! Relax! This is what I came to Kenya to experience.

"You may serve yourself from the bar, Sir." The Maître'd said.

I looked in the direction of his extended his arm. A bar covered with plates upon which lay slices of pineapple, watermelon, orange, mango, and papaya - called papaws I soon learned - bacon and sausages, and a variety of rolls, biscuits, and toast. In the midst of the room a waiter - he was more a chef - fried eggs over a small gas flame on a cart he wheeled next to a customer's table. He maneuvered the cart beside my table. "How would you like your eggs, Sir?"

"Oh. Yes. Sunny-side up."

At a four-star hotel in Nairobi, I wondered just what this was going to cost me. My room was about $100 a night. Add to that this elaborate breakfast. Oh, what the hell, I concluded. Splurge today - starve tomorrow.

The chef smiled. "Your first trip to Nairobi, Sir?"

I nodded.

"You'll enjoy Kenya. There's much to do and see. We're very exotic."

My breakfast was excellent. To my amazement, its price was included in the room rate. I was in Kenya and on my way to a six-week adventure.

* * *

After breakfast I stood outside the Ambassador Hotel to absorb the activity and energy, the hustle and bustle emanating from the crowds that moved along Moi Avenue. People in large cities seem always to be in a hurry to get off the street and find safety and solace behind concrete walls. Not all though, because some individuals hang out near sides of buildings, in doorways and alleyways, watching the street migrants like predators scrutinizing their prey. Then there are the groups, aggregated along the curb, stemming natural flow, thwarting escape, waiting for buses to whisk them away from street jeopardy. Travel books mention that the streets of Nairobi are infested with pickpockets and con men. There's a certain sense of exhilaration and attentiveness stimulated by the knowledge that "Faginism" did not die with the rescue of Oliver Twist.

I strolled around the corner where I found a young man selling paperback books. The books were neatly displayed on a blanket that covered a portion of the sidewalk next to the curb; an ideal marketing arrangement since all pedestrians had to carefully maneuver around his transient store. It amazed me how oblivious pedestrians abruptly stopped, turned, avoided the edge of the blanket kiosk. No one seemed to pay much attention. There were no dirty looks or curses. No one said, ". . . get this crap out of the way, I'm walking here! You broke my stride! My lawyer will contact you!" or what you'd normally hear on a crowded sidewalk in an American city.

Among this loosely organized mosaic, I saw some familiar names and recognizable covers. Romance novels of Danielle Steel added most to this pattern. They intermingled with Louis L'Amour and Zane Grey western sagas, Robert Ludlum mysteries, *The Hobbit, The Catcher in The Rye, Of Mice and Men,* and about one hundred other books of lesser known fame. I felt excited when I found a copy of *Snows of Kilimanjaro* and one of *The Green Hills of Africa.* What an opportunity to read Hemingway's most famous works on Africa, in Africa. Maybe even be able to see Kenya the way he saw it? Not a chance. Hemingway's days and those of the "Great White Hunters" don't exist anymore.

The sale came to about fifty cents. The vendor smiled. "If you are interested in more books," he said, "many of my friends have their collections displayed on the street in the next block." I passed on his offer and ambled back to Moi Avenue with my purchases securely in hand.

MOI AVENUE

Traffic on Moi Avenue in the heart of Nairobi moves at the pace and confusion of a herd of turtles searching for a pond. When movement nearly comes to a stop, taxis, tour vans, and buses burst ahead, continuously competing for any vacant space available in front or to the side. Pedestrians seem oblivious to the cacophony of horns, bells, shouts, and whistles. This tepid, exhaust flavored atmosphere resounds with the pandemonium of accelerating engines and screeching tires. It's a wonder that passengers and foot-travelers reach their destinations in a timely fashion.

Rickshas, the earliest privately owned commercial vehicles that plied Moi Avenue, were two-wheeled, human powered carts made from woven cane or wood. For a couple of rupees rickshas transported visitors between the railroad station and what was then downtown Nairobi. When motorized vehicles appeared on the scene, rickshas gave way to the box-body cars, assembled from a salvaged, dilapidated frame around which a wood and canvas box was built to house passengers. These box-body cars were probably the ancestors of the Matatu, a modern form of transportation unique to Kenya, used primarily as conveyance to towns and villages outside Nairobi. These colorful vehicles are privately owned and, for the most part, are beat up and poorly maintained. Except for the windshield, some are windowless. Old or new, Matatus show considerable wear. Many are nothing more than a truck with a wood and wire box built onto their beds. The passenger box is fitted with internal planks for seating, a canvas roof, and canvas drapes that can be unrolled along the sides and back in case of an unexpected shower.

Matatus are a very cheap way of getting to and from distant locations. In fact, the word Matatu originated from *tatu,* Swahili for three, because the original fare to anywhere was three Kenyan shillings per passenger. To make any money drivers had to pack their vehicles to capacity and beyond. Often, the load also included boxes, crates, animals, backpacks, luggage and any other paraphernalia. All this extra stuff was tied on top the roof.

Matatus are driven at the fastest speeds destiny allows. On the streets of Nairobi, a Matatu can easily be identified as a vehicle that erratically swerves in and out of traffic. And when the roadway ahead clears, it races away at top speed while the passengers literally swing out windows and pitch about to and fro.

Because buses are slow or nonexistent to many destinations, and their fares unaffordable to some, Matatus have become a primary means of transportation for most common folks, as well as for venturesome or uninformed tourists.

I wasn't adventurous enough to ride in a "take your life taxi" when I learned that most Matatu drivers were not trained or licensed, and were extremely reckless. There were at least one or two fatal accidents per week during the six weeks I was in Kenya. It's a cheap means of transportation and for some, a necessity. Though it beats walking in the heat and dust, I passed up the experience. I like to arrive at my destinations with all my parts attached and functioning. Besides, riding in a bonafide Nairobi taxi is itself a thrill.

Moi Avenue, a beautiful divided, tree-lined boulevard, is laid out along one of Nairobi's original dirt thoroughfares, Station Road. Station Road ran south from the primary crossing point of the Nairobi River to the site of the Uganda Railway yard and station. In the early nineteen-hundreds it became known as Government Road because government offices, and houses where the country's officials resided, were located on or very near the road. Additionally, a variety of corrugated tin shacks called "dukas" flanked the road. These were the stores run by Indian merchants. Government Road was renamed Moi Avenue in honor of Daniel Toroitich Arap Moi who assumed the presidency of Kenya after the death of Mzee Kenyatta in 1978. President Moi still successfully presides over Kenya.

Government Road, the main drag of Nairobi since the city began, is a thoroughfare steeped in history. Had I strolled along it in the early nineteen hundreds, on a day when the local gentry assembled for some celebration, I might have encountered Karen Blixen and her husband Baron Bror von Blixen sorting out the drawbacks between coffee farming and cattle ranching. She may have been telling Bror how much of her money he had squandered. Not far away among a group of men, a roguish white-hunter by the name of Denys Finch Hatten, Karen's famous lover, might have been overheard discussing the price that an elephant tusk would bring on the wharfs of Mombasa. Interestingly, Finch Hatten and Bror von Blixen remained friends even after the Baron and Karen had divorced and Bror remarried. Together Denys and Bror entertained the Prince of Wales on a hunting expedition in the wilds of Kenya. No doubt in this gathering of rogue aristocrats frequenting Government Road I might have encountered the legendary Lord Hugh Cholmondeley Delamere, the "George Washington" of Kenya, shaking hands with his constituents, thanking them for making him President of the Colonists' Association, the unofficial parliament of British East Africa before self-government was initiated. Lord Delamere, or "D" as his friends called him, was a strong advocate for the establishment of self-rule and he was very much involved in the politics of this developing country. He was also a close comrade of the Masai and one of the largest land owners in what is now Kenya.

This early festival may have been held in recognition of the Under-Secretary of State for the Colonies, a young upstart statesman named Winston Churchill on his official visit in 1907, or in honor of President Theodore Roosevelt's visit to Nairobi in 1909. Both of these dignitaries influenced the development of Kenya.

Had I wandered into one of the dukas along Government Road during this early time, I might have encountered a young woman attempting to obtain supplies for the farm owned by her parents Jos and Nellie Grant near Thika. Their daughter Elspeth (Grant) Huxley would have been accompanied by her father's Kikuyu headman, Njombo. Elspeth's experiences and observations on Government Road provided material years later for *Out in the Midday Sun,* one of her many books on Kenya.

More recently, because of several large international hotels on or near Moi Avenue, celebrities are often seen walking nearby. I might catch glimpses of Robert Redford, Meryl Streep, and others from the cast of *Out of Africa.* Earlier, probably in the nineteen sixties and seventies, William Holden and Stephanie Powers may have strolled along the avenue. These latter two celebrities heightened awareness of the plight of African wildlife and stimulated efforts toward its protection.

*   *   *

On my visit I did have an opportunity to observe President Moi in a motorcade that came down Moi Avenue. When I learned of this event, I hurried to the curb only to find it barricaded by a line of very heavily armed, intimidating policemen. I gained permission to stand between two of these large guards, but I had to stash my camera in my backpack and keep my hands free and exposed, and not make any sudden changes in activity. The motorcade consisted of several motorcycles in front of, and behind, a single long limousine. The President sat by himself in the middle of a very large back seat. He appeared small and lonely.

President Moi was the only person of note that I encountered on Moi Avenue. Some more obscure individuals that I met along this avenue included several Peace Corps volunteers, the head of the African Division of the U. S. Food & Drug Administration, and one of the demigods from the American Embassy. Other than that, Moi Avenue was occupied with very stimulating, everyday people doing the things they normally do.

A SCAM WITH ACRONYMS

It wasn't that I didn't want to talk to him. But on my first day in Nairobi, all I wanted to do was to get comfortable in this new place. And, still wrapped in the confused, lethargic cloud of jet lag, I just wasn't in a mood to engage in inquisitive chitchat with a local, especially a determined, fast-talking one.

When I arrive in a city where I've never been, I need to adjust to its cadence, set my tone. I gain composure by strolling, bumping into the crowds, hearing shouts and whispers, breathing the smog, playing tag with traffic, and listening to honks, squeals, and sirens. I want to see the city's glitter, feel its excitement, its rhythm.

There's a period of anxiety, of intimidation, I must overcome before I feel comfortable, gain confidence and can appreciate a new city. This is especially so when I travel to some remote place and my well-wishing friends, in their concern for my welfare, charge my mind with their preconceived notions of disease, dangerous animals, robbers, muggers and prostitutes. I appreciate their apprehensions, but Africa to them is as unreal as Sindbad's Baghdad.

Africa is a place my friends have only experienced through Discovery Channel documentaries, CNN stories, and Tarzan movies. It doesn't really exist as part of their world. It's a place in fantasy. Most of them have rarely traveled beyond the security of their own hometown; some haven't even been farther than their grandmothers' backyards. Television, movies, and newspapers are their primary sources of knowledge about the world. The media, in their quest for viewers, readers, and high ratings, strive for realism, but communicate sensationalism. The daily news is flavored with iniquities, villainies, and disasters. It's no doubt my friends' views of the world are hooded in anxiety, concern, and distrust. So, when this young African man eased to my cadence and attempted to intrude further into my space with, "I beg your pardon, but aren't you from France?" I remembered my friends' warnings and became unnerved and suspicious.

I had just walked out of the Ambassador Hotel after a relaxed breakfast of eggs fried to my liking. Bacon, croissants, pineapple slices, orange juice, and tea served on silver-plated tableware topped off the meal. My course lay across Moi Avenue; my destination, the Information Bureau in front of the Hilton Hotel. While crossing Moi Avenue, I got caught in the crowd dodging taxis, limos, and lorries creeping and cramming onto the busy boulevard. Vehicular and pedestrian traffic paid no attention to the red and green traffic lights swinging above the streets, probably hung there only to satisfy some safety law. People streamed, like water, through fissures that appeared between slow moving and stopped vehicles. Likewise, vehicles accelerated forward, weaved into adjacent lanes, filled open spaces, in an apparent attempt to stem the flow of human tributaries. Although I had only had about six hours sleep since leaving Atlanta two days ago, a bright sunny morning and all this human excitement energized me. I crossed the intersection without incident with this fellow attached like a remora.

Instinct warned. The length of my step increased. A jog to the right, I crossed Luthuli Street. A twist to the left, I coursed for the Hilton Hotel. Its lobby, I delusively hoped, had a security guard, maybe a U.S. Marine. My commensal hung tight. I sped up. So did he, persistent, but not threatening.

"You from France?" He asked again. "Been there once, . . . few years ago. Love that city." He took a breath, ". . . and the people, too. Maybe you'd talk to me of Paris, its museums, cafés . . . what's happening there. I really miss the place."

I'm sucking air, almost out of breath. I check him out. He's breathing normally. Probably works out, jogs, I thought. He's right next to me. I'm almost running. Could this guy be for real? On his way to the office perhaps? Maybe he's a bank teller, a shopkeeper. He's dressed in a casual plaid sport shirt, dark gabardine slacks, and black Italian-styled loafers. A mildly handsome guy in his mid-twenties, definitely doesn't look like a bum. His light framed body is slightly shorter than my five feet, eleven inches.

Could Nairobians be so hospitable? Maybe. But, they probably never develop acquaintances with Americans. We're a wary group, so how could they?

We Americans crave protection. We'd rather sightsee from soft seats of tour buses rather than stroll along crowded streets. Protected by steel and glass, we feel safe in our bus; we're in the country, but not really; we view, but don't engage. It's as if we were watching a film.

If this guy really does just want to talk, I could spare him a few of my precious, paranoid minutes. Maybe he does miss France . . . or has a fondness for Paris? I've been there. I can talk to him about Paris. But, it might be that he just wants to practice his French? Anyway, I'm running out of breath and I'm not shaking him.

Besides, we've passed the Hilton several blocks back.

We arrive at another large boulevard. This one is divided by a median. It's busy, has the appearance of a mini Fifth Avenue or Michigan Avenue. Barriers restrict pedestrian crossings and focus them toward guarded intersections in an attempt to control traffic flow.

I grab the barrier. Stop. Catch my breath. In a voice that distinctly lacks a telltale French accent I finally acknowledge his presence. "Where are we?" I ask.

"You're not from France," he said with an incredulous look.

"No. You made a mistake."

"But, you look European."

"Maybe. I'm American. First generation."

"That's good," he said. "I love America, too. But, we must stop running. We should sit; talk of America. I am going to go to America . . . to the university."

We relaxed next to the barrier.

"Where are we?" I asked again.

He leaned against the barrier, looked up and down the boulevard and turned, faced the traffic. "Kenyatta Boulevard," my remora said with pride. "But, we should take it easy. You are winded. You tire fast. Nairobi is about twenty five-hundred meters above sea level. One could pass out if he's not adapted to the altitude."

A good piece of advice, I thought. My breath came in short controlled gulps. Coolness from the steel rail that I gripped permeated my body, relaxed me. My vision emerged from the tunnel contracting around it. I forgot that Nairobi sat on a high plateau. Back home, I live almost at sea level.

I was vaguely aware of department stores, specialty shops, travel agencies, high-rise hotels lining this boulevard. A diversity of humanity flowed past us, gentlemen mimicking the Wall Street look, young women in tailored suits, others sporting Levis, T-shirts, Nike sport shoes, and baseball caps. Several tall, thin, spear wielding men clothed in bright red print robes crossed at the intersection. "Masai," he said. Inquisitive folks, outfitted in new-looking khaki-colored attire, cautiously peered at the native warriors. "Tourists," he called them, grinning slyly. Caftan-clad men, sporting a fez or turban, displayed their wares and haggled a price. And, hidden in the shadows of alleyways and boarded doorways, the decrepit, diseased, desperate, begged for shillings.

"Catch your breath. Then we'll stroll up the block to the New Stanley Hotel. You can buy me a coffee . . . for saving your life," he said confidently.

"Yeah sure."

We walked, this time at a more casual pace. Maybe he's OK. Seems concerned, I thought.

A growth of tropical shrubs isolated the patrons in the sidewalk café from the street and taxiways to the entrance of the New Stanley Hotel. The vegetation emerged from a waist-high wall constructed around the café. Customers entered through several openings. Within this café stood the famous mail tree, a large acacia to which explorers of the past, and now tourists, attached messages destined for colleagues. Most messages were dated. Their recipients usually arrived long after the authors returned to the wild, or went home. Actually the tree had a more substantial function. It provided a respite from the equatorial sun, an attractive commodity for a sidewalk café on the streets of Nairobi. My acquaintance and I, although we hadn't introduced ourselves yet, found a table shadowed by the hotel's facade near the rear. We ordered two coffees.

"*Tres bonne*. . . . Oh sorry, I forgot. You're not French," Remora said. "But now you must tell me where you are from in America. We must talk of America. I am so curious."

He seemed eager to talk. Well, why not? Most foreigners want to visit America; many want to live there. But the fact he hadn't provided his name, or even asked for mine, gnawed at me, made me uncomfortable. I knew nothing about him, but he already knew something about me, where I came from.

Pull yourself together. You're really getting suspicious, I thought.

I decided to proceed with care. Give only the information I wanted him to know. Act confident and in control. Listen. If he turns out to be a good guy, I will talk more openly.

By the time I gathered my composure, the coffee had arrived along with two other young men. They seated themselves at our table. Both were casually dressed, in their late twenties or early thirties, but one appeared especially confident, in charge, businesslike. The other, with hair styled in thick, frizzy, reggae braids, was quiet and concerned. Mr. Confident sat opposite me, between Remora and Reggae. He became the spokesman.

"We're students," he said.

More cups of coffee arrived. It was as if the waiters were aware of this situation, because no orders were placed. "We want to hear all about where you're from because we are going to America to study at the University."

"All of you?" I asked.

"Yes. We will all go," Mr. Confident replied.

"Suppose I told you that I'm from North Carolina . . ." But, before I could complete my statement they began to tell me the merits of various universities in North Carolina.

"Duke University. Very good biology . . . marine biology too," Remora said.

"North Carolina. Basketball. In College Park . . . close to Research Triangle," commented Reggae. "What university are you near in North Carolina?"

"I'm not from North Carolina. I only visited there a couple of years ago."

The three of them continued to press me for information about where I lived. Each time I mentioned a city, they knew something about it and some crucial information about the universities in the area. They provided enough information, which, if taken at face value, would convince an unsuspecting listener that they were very familiar with the places they were describing.

Tourists, particularly Americans that travel to Africa or other such mysterious places, become homesick and love to chat with someone who seems acquainted with their hometown. They will even overlook minor inconsistencies in the information they hear, because they feel they've made a connection, a friend. I guess I'm more suspicious, because

I've encountered individuals who attempt to gain my confidence, and if they succeed, throw me a proposition I can't, for reasons of concern or guilt, refuse.

My brain raised a couple of distress flags when I realized that the facts these guys were laying on me sounded, albeit with some confusion, like passages from *Peterson's Guide to Colleges and Universities* and *The AAA Travel Guide to the United States*, so I decided to level with them and tell them where I really live. I wanted to know if they were seriously looking for information about education in the states or had some ulterior motives for befriending me.

"I'm really from Huntsville, Alabama," I said.

"The University of Alabama," Mr. Confident said. "Good university for medicine and law. American football, end run, touchdown, field goal, Bear Bryant . . ."

"Yes, but that university is about two hundred miles from Huntsville," I said. "And its claim to fame *is* American football. But that's not where I live."

"Yes," said Mr. Confident, lifting his head in assurance. "Is it not so that in Huntsville there is also the University of Alabama? Where physicists and engineers study, and farmers learn to grow peanuts and study cotton-ginning. Is this not correct?" His voice threw an inflection.

"Partly." I countered. "Farmers do attend my university, but they come to study science or engineering. They want to get off the farm. Besides, peanuts don't grow around Huntsville, and the farmers from North Alabama already know more about cotton than they want."

Huntsville is also home to Alabama A. & M. University, so Mr. Confident's error is one of confusion. Alabama A. & M. specializes in agricultural research. This university has a very active ongoing recruitment campaign directed specifically at students from the African countries. About a third of the students attending Alabama A. & M. University are visitors from Africa. Consequently, if these fellows know so much about universities in the States, they should be aware of Alabama A. & M. University.

To satisfy my curiosity and learn whether these fellows were who they said they were, I asked them the following question: "What do you know about the other universities in Huntsville?"

My question, after a few minutes, went unanswered. So I said, "I'd like to commend you three for knowing what you do about the universities in the United States and in Huntsville, Alabama. You really put a lot of effort into learning bits of persuasive information, convincing stuff, well almost, but you're missing some very important facts. And," I said nodding and scratching my head, ". . . you're not here to discuss life or educational opportunities in the United States with me. You guys have another agenda."

I straightened up, leaned back in my chair, looked Mr. Confident directly in the eyes. "This is my first trip to Africa, and I just got here. I don't want to sit around wasting my time discussing the qualities of universities. And, I'm here trying to relax and, for at least a short time, forget the academic commitments I left behind. What do you really want of me?"

The group became fidgety. Drank their coffees.

"You're a professor, aren't you?" Mr. Confident put his hands on his cheeks and, for a moment, cradled his head, looked surprised and excited simultaneously. "You'll understand our problem," he said. "You know students. You can empathize with us."

"We are students, but not from Kenya," said Mr. Confident quietly. "We're illegal here . . . refugees." He leaned toward me feigning the divulgence of some deep dark secret. The other two nervously looked around as if the "KGB, CIA and FBI" were about to pop out of the bushes. Except for a couple of Air India flight attendants sitting at the far end of the café and a waiter standing in the doorway to the kitchen, there were no others in the café.

"If we get caught, we'll be put in jail. . . . . Interrogated, then deported to Uganda," Mr. Confident whispered. He looked around. "That's where we're from. Students are not safe in Uganda. We're forced to join the military, be soldiers. If we refuse, they shoot us. Only yesterday. . . ."

"You were there yesterday?" I asked.

"No," Remora interjected. "We met our friend who escaped from Kampala yesterday. He had some major wounds, but he was able to tell us that the soldiers arrested all our professors, lined them up next to the science hall and sprayed them with machine gun bullets. The soldiers then threw all the bodies back into the building and set it on fire. Some of the students were also shot when they tried to run away. That's what happened to our friend. The military doesn't like intellectuals. They're afraid we'll interfere, speak against the rulers. Liberals they called us . . . revolutionaries. The soldiers think we know more than they do. . . ."

"That's a frightening story. I'm surprised that your friend, the wounded one, was able to make it to the border, and alive."

Reggae, distracted from his nervous surveillance of the café, said, "He's dead. He died while we talked to him. We buried him outside the city, covered his body with stones so the baboons wouldn't devour him. . . ." He looked dejected.

Had I heard this story in the 1970s or early 1980s, it would had seemed plausible. The regimes of Milton Obote and Idi Amin were very bloody. They almost destroyed Makerere University and definitely murdered intellectuals. But, this was 1987. The political atmosphere of Uganda, though somewhat wobbly, was not as tyrannical as these three described. Nairobi's newspaper headlines would have screamed of mass murders and other atrocities even before the bodies cooled. No word of this event appeared in the media. In fact, just this morning I overheard several excited American tourists at the Ambassador Hotel talk of taking a train today to Kampala to check the sights. If anything is going on in Uganda, they're going to be in the thick of it . . . but I don't think so.

I really perceived that I was being scammed, but I was not sure. If I were being taken for a ride, these men were doing it very well. They spoke with such sincerity, such finesse, so convincingly. They were probably swindlers, but the experience excited me. I wanted to know their adventure, or their scheme, so I pressed on.

"Tell me about your escape from Uganda. It sounds like a great story," I said.

Mr. Confident made eye contact with Remora, nodded.

Remora, nervous and distracted, disclosed the story of their escape in a low, hidden voice.

Seems that after escaping a military raid on their campus, they had hidden in the basement of the bombed out Serown Hotel. The accommodations weren't great, but the hotel was near the city's market place. This was advantageous because, in case the students were detected, they could escape by losing themselves among the crowds. And the hotel's location was also close to Entebbe Road, an easy, rapid escape route out of the city that led directly to the Kenyan border. But most important, the hotel served as a secret base for members of the ARS, a group that was to help the students in their escape from Uganda. They hid out in a darkened room concealed behind piles of concrete rubble, dust, and large, crushed, twisted metal boxes; from Remora's description they seemed to have hidden in the laundry room. A pawpaw they stole from the market provided their only source of moisture and nutrition. Remora fervently impressed upon us that no ARS members nor any messages were at the hideout when they arrived. He apparently didn't enjoy the way the ARS provided for them, because they had to wait for travel instructions and a vehicle that was to be driven by an ARS sympathizer. This was supposedly arranged to secrete them out of town and into Kenya.

"What's the ARS?" I asked.

"African Students for Revolution," Reggae said. "They rescue students and intellectuals. Really they're militant students, who are trying to overthrow the government."

Two days after they sequestered themselves in the bombed out laundry room a beat-up, nondescript Fiat flatbed truck loaded with straw and old tires arrived just after sunset during the height of market activity. The trio were told to scramble onto the bed of the truck and hide under the cargo. The supposed ARS freedom fighter drove the truck to Jinga, a small town on the Ugandan shore of Lake

Victoria near the Kenyan border. According to Remora, it was touch and go around Kampala. Seems that soldiers took some potshots at the truck as it drove away. Luckily the bullets only imbedded themselves in the tires lying on the bed of the truck and not those attached to the axles.

Jinga had very few soldiers. Those that were in the village could easily be convinced of their sympathy for the ARS with a few schillings. But, for the time being, Jinga was the end of the overland experience for the trio, because without proper paperwork, they could not cross into Kenya. Consequently, to continue the getaway required a cruise on Lake Victoria.

This is where I learned that Uganda actually had a "Navy." The Ugandan navy patrolled their portion of Lake Victoria with a couple of dilapidated German gunboats that survived World War II. When Remora told me this, visions of the patrol boat destroyed by the torpedo rigged into the bow of the *African Queen* passed through my mind.

Jinga harbor contained several Ugandan patrol boats crewed by mercenaries loyal to the Ugandan government's concerns. However, if bribes were large enough or more than what the sailors could pirate from their activity, the ARS could gain their sympathy. The costs were too high, however, so the students had to take to the water secretly.

Remora described their boat, the one the ARS insurgents commissioned to spirit them to Kenya, as an old, leaky, shallow draft fishing boat without a cabin or cargo hold, but with high gunwales. A lateen sail rigged on a 12-meter mast could provide locomotion if the boat could be kept in open water and the winds were from the right direction. Otherwise, it would have to be poled. An important feature of this boat was that the sail and mast could quickly be dismantled. If an escape became necessary the crew could hide in the coastal marshes and the boat could also be poled along tree-lined rivers and narrow marsh channels.

The trip took them eastward to Kisumu, Kenya's town on Lake Victoria. Two local fishermen, ARS sympathizers, were secured to sail the boat. They also lent authenticity, since the trip had to take place in daylight hours. Mr. Confident mentioned that only patrol boats were allowed to sail after dark in Ugandan water. Others, if caught, were considered subversive and sunk along with the crew. Consequently, the crew must give the appearance of fish during the day and the escapees were forced to lie in the bilge covered over by the fishing nets to avoid detection.

"Man. My hair still smells like dead fish." Reggae broke Remora's account on their escape from Uganda.

"Ugh." I grunted, surprised that they tolerated the fetid smell that emanated from the nets and slime in the bilge. Under the heat of the sun it must have been noxious.

"What'd you say?" Asked Mr. Confident.

"Nothing. Just committing something to memory."

Remora continued his narrative. The boat hugged the shoreline. It sailed slowly in the open water near the reed marshes, trailing fishing lines to avoid creating suspicion. Although a lone patrol boat cruised about a kilometer offshore, they were not stopped. They landed slightly west of Kisumu after sunset. According to Mr. Confident, Ugandan fishing boats were illegal in Kenyan waters. But, since old fishing boats tend to look alike, don't fly country flags, or have any apparent markings, and, since there's no revolution going on in Kenya, vigilance was more relaxed. Even so, they had to sneak in. They came ashore by wading across a muddy, mosquito and snake infested marsh. This didn't matter, they said, because now they were in Kenya.

The waiter disrupted Remora's story when he approached the table, unbidden, to refill our coffee cups.

"Tell me more. This is great stuff. You guys had one hell of an adventure. Did the ARS continue to help you get to Nairobi?"

"No. They're only active in Uganda, so we had to contact members of the UGSM or the KSFED" Mr. Confident informed me while Remora drank his coffee and inattentive Reggae nervously scratched his ear and furtively looked around the cafè.

They continued to use acronyms as if I were acquainted with the organizations they identified. I wasn't. In fact, I believed that these factions were probably all bogus. But I wanted to hear their intriguing story, so I encouraged them to continue with a question to learn who the UGSM and KSFED were and what they did.

Mr. Confident appeared impatient with my questions, but supplied names and some information. The UGSM was the Underground Student Movement, a group composed of rebellious young people, not necessarily students, whose plan it was to disrupt any of the government's or the establishment's activities that they didn't like. They did not seem to have any specific focus and, according to Mr. Confident and his two friends, they didn't agree with anything but their own interests. The KSFED, Kenyan Students for Free Education and Democracy, I was told, was a student organization that lobbied for quality and free education. They were supposedly housed at the University of Nairobi.

"The KSFED is full of bourgeoisie and aristocrats," Reggae interjected with a hint of aversion.

Mr. Confident countered that for a price the KSFED would aid refugees such as themselves. But as Mr. Confident, Remora and Reggae had informed me earlier, they didn't have any funds. So they were left to rely on the more subversive UGSM for help.

Mr. Confident then told me that they contacted the UGSM and these rebels gave them a choice of transportation to Nairobi. They could either walk, which wouldn't cost them anything, or hide out in some cattle car being pulled by the nightly freight train. They opted for the train, although it cost them their meager savings.

To avoid getting caught, their contacts in UGSM told them that they had to jump from the train when it slowed for the shanty town on the outskirts of Nairobi. The police always inspect trains that enter the station for stowaways. Mr. Confident told me they followed their orders. Some members of the UGSM met them in the shanty town and provided further assistance, a shower, some food and a flat in downtown Nairobi where they could hide out.

Remora ended the story, sat back, breathed a sigh, and finished his coffee. The lunch crowd began slowly filtering into the café and the three began to fidget. I began to get the impression that they were spending too much time with me, but I still didn't know what their game was, or why they were so insistent on talking to me.

"Well, now that you're here, what are your plans? How are you going to stay in Kenya without passports or any kind of immigration papers? You can't work, or go to the university. You can't even get out of this country without sneaking out." I began to slide my chair back from the table as I finished my coffee. "Its time for me to go, because if the police come by to check you guys out, and find me associated with you, I'd have a lot of explaining to do. We'd all end up cell mates and awaiting deportation. I haven't time to waste sitting around in a jail, especially one in Kenya."

"Relax. Sit, Alabama. The police are not looking for us . . . yet." Mr. Confident's impatience began to magnify. The others seemed more at ease, wanted their coffee cups refilled, gestured to attract the waiter. Mr. Confident shoved his cup toward the middle of the table and took on a more forceful demeanor. "We're not finished with you. You need to know that we are planning to go to America and attend a University. You can help us."

"Carry on. Inform me. But I'll tell you now, I'm one of hundreds of faculty that teach in the United States, and I don't have any influence with my university or any other. So I can't see how I can be of any service to you."

"You're right," said Remora. "We can not do anything in Kenya. But, you Americans can help us get to America. We need your help to continue our trip and reach our goal. Americans are rich. They help many people. We need to get to Dar es Salaam in Tanzania. There we do not need papers. Once there we can move about freely, apply at the university to take tests and, if our scores are good, the Tanzanian government will give us passports and visas to study in America. We are intelligent, we will score high on the tests, and we will go to America, but we must leave here and go to Tanzania."

"But you can't cross the Kenyan-Tanzanian border." I folded my arms across my chest and sat back in the chair. "How are you planning to go over the border, or even get to it?"

"The UGSM will drive us to Mombasa tomorrow. With their connections we will secure work to load dhows in the Old Harbor. There no one checks papers of workers. When the UGSM arranges with a captain sailing to Dar es Salaam, he will take us to be his sailors. Captains own the dhows they sail so they can do whatever they want. And, they like to make extra money."

To go through all this trouble to attend a university in the United States, these fellows have to be really serious and dedicated, I thought.

"So you want me to provide you with money to pay for your boat trip, on which you still have to work, to get you to Tanzania? The Captain should pay you, but instead you pay him and become his slaves. That's not too bright."

"We have no papers and can not stay in Kenya. If we get caught here, they will send us back to Uganda," Remora whined. "We don't need money to pay the Captain. The UNISF has provided us some funds for him."

"And who is this group?"

"The United Nations International Student Fund."

"But you have to have citizenship in some country. And, at this time, you are not citizens of Kenya or Tanzania. If you apply as Ugandans, the Kenyan's will put you in jail as illegal aliens. You fellows are men without a country," I sneered.

"Our money will come to us tonight. The UNISF has an office at the University of Nairobi and a friend of ours is in the KSFED. She will get it for us." Remora looked insecure.

"We need you to help us to pay for our passage from Dar es Salaam to America." Mr. Confident said with authority and control. "It will cost two hundred and fifty American dollars for each of us."

"You've got to be kidding," I asserted. "You want me to give you seven hundred and fifty dollars? And where do you think I should get it? Where did you get the idea that Americans have big bundles of money?" I realized my attitude was becoming aggressive. I wanted their story and they told me their tale. I must now reciprocate. "Sorry guys, I'm only a faculty member," I said in a relaxed controlled voice. "My funds are limited and I must account for each penny I spend. If I gave you $750, I would have to take up begging for coffee. So you see I can't really help you."

Mr. Confident pushed back his chair. "He's of no use. Let's get out of here. We'll try the Hilton." Remora and Reggae followed.

"I'm sorry guys, but here's a hundred shilling for the great story." I stretched out the note and extended it toward Mr. Confident. "I'll even buy the coffees. I think you expect me to do that."

"Keep the hundred shillings. It's only worth seven dollars and fifty cents American, but the coffee you can pay for." My offer exasperated Mr. Confident. He turned and headed for the boulevard followed by his accomplices.

"Does the ARS or the UGSM really exist," I said to their backs.

"Maybe," I heard in return.

I laid the note on the table for the waiter. It paid for the coffees and gave the waiter a two-dollar tip. Not bad for his contribution of quietly serving our little group.

When I reached the boulevard I looked up and noticed that my three new acquaintances got into a large black Rolls Royce that drove away toward downtown Nairobi.

Five weeks after this incident, as I walked through a mall just off Kenyatta Boulevard one Sunday afternoon looking for open stores, a group of animated young men caught my eye. Few people and reduced lighting suggested that all the stores were closed. But this group of men entered through the door at the far end of the mall and began waving. One yelled, "Hey Alabama, how you doing? Good to see you around." They disappeared into another corridor before I had an opportunity to acknowledge their greeting. I did, however, recognize Reggae's hair style. Their nonchalance with the encounter was comforting and suggested that the ARS or UGSM or the other imaginary rebels were not out to get me.

SEARCH FOR AN AFFORDABLE HOTEL

After three days my bill at the Ambassador Hotel climbed to about 2500 Kenyan shillings (Ksh), approximately $167.00 at the rate of exchange in effect during my 1987 visit. This bill covered my room, taxes, and a couple of meals a day. At this rate of spending I'd be, as I mentioned earlier, almost in the poor house before I ended my stay.

My travel agent had done as I asked. She tried to find a reasonably priced hotel in Nairobi; the Ambassador Hotel was the only one close to my price range on her list, but still it was about two times what I could afford to pay if I planned to stay six weeks. Arriving in Nairobi, I had seen many hotels, in all qualities, but my travel agent only had access to the Ambassador and five others, the Inter-Continental, Hilton International Nairobi, Nairobi Serena, and the two Nairobi historic hotels, the Norfolk and New Stanley.

*   *   *

Both the New Stanley Hotel and the Norfolk had entertaining and charming origins and each contributed greatly to the cultural and historic development of Nairobi. Staying at either would have been exciting and inspirational, but unfortunately both were beyond what I could afford.

The Stanley Hotel, the forerunner of The New Stanley Hotel, first appeared on the scene in 1902 as one of the newest corrugated metal shacks along Victoria Street (now Tom Mboya Street, the street behind The Ambassador Hotel). Land for the hotel was purchased by a demure and dainty lady by the name of Mayence Bent.

Mayence arrived in Nairobi during the last years of the Nineteenth Century and went to work as a milliner in Nairobi's first general store. She eventually took charge of the department and, because of her abilities to choose the proper and stylish combinations of dresses and bonnets, Mayence came to be known as a fashion consultant. Unfortunately, her days of keeping the ladies of Nairobi in vogue were shortened by a dispute with the owner of the general store, a Mr. Tommy Wood. Their disagreement must have been terrible. Mayence quit. She bought land down the street, built herself a hotel, and named it after the great explorer, Stanley. Interestingly, the Stanley Hotel was established as Mayence's revenge against Wood.

Wood's general store was located very near the railroad station and a few years before he had employed Mayence at his store, Wood had converted the second story into individual rooms. He named this upper story the "Victoria Hotel." The Stanley Hotel was in direct competition with the ramshackled Victoria Hotel. As a shining new corrugated metal building, the Stanley Hotel presented a more attractive appearance. Also, it was a dedicated hotel, not an afterthought thrown together above a general store. Mayence, no doubt, received a sense of gratification and satisfaction because visitors to Nairobi found the Stanley Hotel more appealing. The popularity of the hotel avenged the consequences that had resulted from her feud with Wood.

Although Mayence is portrayed as delicate and reserved, she had ambition. Behind her misleading appearance hid a self-assured woman. She became one of Kenya's tough, capable, pioneering entrepreneurs.

An interaction between Mayence Bent and Abraham Lazarus Block, a Lithuanian Jew, illustrated the vision, ingenuity and perseverance of the early East African pioneers, and the fortunes gained from their endeavors. In a sense, it also defined the ultimate fate of the Stanley Hotel.

Block, an adventurer, a merchant by trade, but really a refugee from the Boer War in South Africa, arrived in Nairobi penniless about the time Mayence planned to open the Stanley Hotel. But Mayence faced a dilemma. There were no mattresses available in Nairobi. If she were to have a sufficient number, they would have to be shipped to Nairobi. This would postpone the opening, possibly for months.

While trekking about Nairobi in search of work, Block observed that piles of cut grass lay drying along the railroad right-of-way. He had heard of Mayence's problem and observed that dried grass would make a great mattress stuffing. Block obtained permission from the railroad office to collect the grass. He then bundled it, bought some durable cloth from local Indian merchants, and secured the service of a tailor. With the help of the tailor, Block designed a sample mattress and the two prepared to construct it, but a major problem stood in their way. The tailor didn't have any needles strong enough to sew the ticking. Block solved this problem ingeniously by constructing sewing needles from bicycle spokes. A sample mattress was made, shown to Mayence, and she ordered twenty-three. These were delivered within a matter of weeks and the Stanley Hotel opened. Abraham Block bought himself a farm with the profits he made from the sale.

The original Stanley Hotel lasted until a fire devastated it and all of Victoria Street in 1905. Mayence reopened the hotel on Government Road in a building vacated by the railroad. Mayence married. Her surname changed from Bent to Tate. And, she and her husband maintained ownership of the Government Road site until they sold it in 1913 to an ex-postmaster from Nairobi named Dan Noble.

Noble's claim to fame was finding the largest gold nugget during the Kakamega Gold Rush. The nugget, named after Noble by reversing his surname, became known as the Elbon Nugget.

In 1912 the Tates designed and built a new hotel on Delamere Avenue (today's Kenyatta Avenue), which they also wanted to name the Stanley Hotel. But, because of its reputation, Noble wanted to maintain the name "Stanley Hotel" for the lodging he had bought from the Tates. Consequently, Noble obtained a court order that stated the hotel's name could not be used for the Tates' new hotel. Not to be thwarted, the Tates solved the quandary by adding the word "New" to their hotel's name.

About thirty-five years after The New Stanley Hotel opened, the Tates sold it to none other than the individual whose foresight aided Mayence's opening of the original Stanley Hotel, Abraham L. Block. Refurbished several times over the years, The New Stanley Hotel stands today as a modern deluxe edifice on Kenyatta Avenue, and it is still in the Block family.

Although the New Stanley Hotel was purchased by Abraham Block in 1947, the beginning of his hotel empire started shortly after his transaction with Mayence Bent. Block continued to speculate with what little money and material possessions he had. A couple of years after the mattress episode, Block again gained some fortuitous knowledge of another commercial dilemma. He heard of a land deal that had soured. Some individuals had tried to purchase an undeveloped plot of land in Nairobi. Upon inquiring, Block learned that this plot might have strong commercial potential if Nairobi's commerce developed in the future. So Block pawned his gold watch and chain, obtained the money and purchased the piece of denuded wasteland.

I don't think that Block realized that his land deal, albeit on a slightly smaller scale, had characteristics of a purchase similarly made when the pilgrims bought Manhattan Island; commercially the results eventually turned out to be the same but he was not the recipient of the vast profits. Today this roughly seven square block plot fronts on the north along what is one of the most economically active thoroughfares in Nairobi, Kenyatta Avenue. The land Block bought is between the New Stanley Hotel and the Post Office, and extends south to the city square and the governmental complex. Block did not realize any profit from his purchase for about twenty-three years, and in 1927 he traded the property and £500 in cash for the Norfolk Hotel.

The Norfolk Hotel was already an established, well-known hotel that catered to the rich and famous. Designed and built by a couple of local hoteliers, Major C. G. R. Ringer and R. Aylmer Winearls, the Norfolk opened on Christmas Day in 1904. Early in 1905 the owners commissioned an advertisement that established the hotel's reputation as a resort in the Highlands of Nairobi. They were successful. In its early years Norfolk had the ambiance of an upscale resort hotel. Built of stone with a tile roof similar in shape and style to a manor house surrounded by a white picket fence, the Norfolk had thirty-four well-furnished bedrooms and a couple of cottages for married couples. After their marriage in Mombasa and arrival in Nairobi, Karen Blixen and Baron Bror von Blixen stayed in one of these cottages before venturing on to their farm in the Ngong Hills.

Located in the hilly section of Nairobi along a northern stretch of Government Road (today Harry Thuku Road), the Norfolk Hotel was indeed situated in park-like surroundings. (Although the usual city development has occurred in Nairobi, as in any modern city, today Norfolk's location appears much like a prosperous residential area in a university town. The hotel is just up the street from the main entrance to the University of Nairobi.)

Before the Second World War, Norfolk's services included hot and cold baths, French cuisine, ricksha and carriage service to and from the railroad station, luggage service that included long-term baggage storage, a barbershop, billiard room, and a banquet hall that could seat over 100 guests. Where the New Stanley Hotel satisfied the needs of the bourgeoisie, Norfolk indulged the aristocracy.

In its heyday Norfolk attracted the elite of Europe, Asia and British East Africa. It serviced royalty, celebrities, and affluent vacationers. It was the jumping-off point for extended hunting safaris into the bush. Such notable white hunters as William (Billy) C. Judd who escorted Theodore Roosevelt into the bush; Alan Black, a distinguished captain of a clipper ship who coined the term "white hunter" and was employed as a guide by Lord Delamere; Jack Riddell who lead Winston Churchill's safari; Denys Finch Hatton, Bror von Blixen, and others might have been observed on the street in front of the Norfolk readying for their expeditions. Finch Hatton and Bror von Blixen guided the Prince of Wales who, shortly after he bagged a lion, heard that his father King George V was near death, returned to England to be crown King Edward VII. Aristocrats usually lodged at the Norfolk Hotel to await organization of their safaris.

When safaris finally were organized and about to depart, the area around the hotel became extremely active. Food, tents, bedding, water, and other commodities were collected and loaded onto pack animals by their grooms. Porters, gun-bearers, *askaris* (security guards), and cooks took charge of their stores, stocks and supplies. Amid chants, grunts, and shouts they all assembled procession-style along the street outside the hotel grounds. These were gigantic endeavors that required, depending on the degree of a client's sense of comfort and luxury, hundreds of porters and other support personnel, and sufficient resources for a four-month venture into the bush. Teddy Roosevelt's hunting trip involved nearly a thousand individuals.

Although the days of the great hunting safaris have passed into history, the Norfolk Hotel, albeit modernized, remains much as it did in the days of early Nairobi. It is still steeped in an air of adventure. The Norfolk continues to provide lodging and luxury with the colonial aura of the past. The prominent war correspondent, columnist, and novelist Robert C. Ruark immortalized the Norfolk in some of his novels.

I can understand how, knowing the history of these hotels, staying at either the Norfolk or New Stanley would arouse romantic emotions and inspirations, the necessary ingredients to create best-selling adventure stories, the room costs at both were unfortunately well beyond my means at the time.

* * *

Because of my late arrival into Nairobi, I had needed the assurance that I would have a bed available and a temporary base from which I could search for lodging within my means. Otherwise it would have been very difficult upon arriving in Nairobi during the night, tired and strung-out, and try to find a secure place to sleep. My pre-arranged reservations at the Ambassador Hotel served this purpose very well. I could have spent my entire visit there, but I would have had to scrimp on some of the other things I wanted to do while in Kenya. Because of the Ambassador's location in the middle of the city, it was becoming stressful and I was developing a sense of claustrophobia. Therefore, my plan for my fourth day in Nairobi was to find a comfortable, quiet hotel.

Travel guides, read before I left the United States, listed an assortment of inexpensive hotels on the blocks behind the Ambassador Hotel. Since they were just a short walk away, I checked them out. These were less than inexpensive. If I had only the change that I once had in my piggy bank, I could have afforded a room in one of these hotels for at least a two-week stay. Room rates ran from about one to ten dollars a night, with breakfast included for any room over three dollars. The slightly higher priced hotels were clean and run by very nice people. Most had communal bathrooms and bathtubs rather than showers, but so do many European bed and breakfast inns.

Many of the small, locally owned hotels are located on Tom Mboya Street, River Road, and the streets in between. Most are clean and well maintained, but others are the types that rent a room by the hour.

A major problem is the area in which these hotels are located. They are in the heart of the oldest part of the city, surrounded by dirty, disintegrating and abandoned buildings where squatters and the city's derelicts reside. During the day the narrow streets are filled with vendors, adventuresome young travelers trying to visit Africa for less than a dollar a day, and a sweaty, ragged-shirt crowd, all mixed with pickpockets and petty thieves. In the evening, after the day darkens, the sun sets and breezes calm, sleazy bars and other hangouts that attract the local go-home foot traffic open and street humanity increases with drunks, gangs of ruffians, and muggers - some of which can wield a machete-sized panga with the talent of a butcher. Add, to this melee the prostitutes who are always around. But in the evening they are more aggressive and strongly resist to taking "No" for an answer. Even the presence of a wife hanging on her husband's arm will not deter them. This is the seedy side of the city where, if the breeze is right, the sewer-like stench of the Nairobi River - a river composed of shallow puddles and pools of coal black water in which only mosquitoes can live - competes with the fetor of stale beer, urine, and curry. A hotel in this area of Nairobi would definitely play havoc with my stress level.

An attractive agent at the Tourist Information Office located on a park-like island off Moi Avenue across from the Nairobi Hilton set me up with an excellent room at the Milimani Hotel. When I told her what I was looking for, she, with great confidence, assured me that she could secure a room for me in a very desirable location that would meet all my needs.

"Should I try to reserve you a room?"

Her personality, enthusiasm and self-assurance were so magnetic that I felt a complete trust in her. I nodded.

She called the concierge-manager of the Milimani Hotel. "Mrs. Sawyer will see you this afternoon. She will hold a room for you." The agent smiled and hung up the telephone. "Is there anything else . . . or can I lock the door and go to lunch?"

"Thank you very much. You've been very helpful. No there's nothing else . . . except, what's your name?"

"Sela."

"Well, Sela, could I take you to lunch? I know I haven't seen the hotel or my room yet, but I trust your knowledge and I'd like to show my appreciation."

"I only have a little time, but that would be very nice."

"Yesterday some fellows introduced me to the Thorn Tree Café at The New Stanley Hotel. It's only a short walk."

"The Thorn Tree is OK."

Lunch with Sela was pleasant and refreshing. Although our conversation covered the wonders of Nairobi, Kenya, and going on safari, I did learn that some young Nairobians actually had career goals that might take them into the professional world rather than into the procession that coursed the streets. This shouldn't have been such a moving revelation. But after my street experiences during the past couple of days, I had asked myself where this country was going if everyone was looking for a handout or trying to rip off their neighbors

* * *

Sela's position as a city Tourist Information Agent was temporary. She was waiting for a flight attendant's position to open with Kenya Airlines. She had made the top of the airline's list of prospects, but it would be a couple of months before such a position would be available.

During our conversation, I asked Sela if she would consider having dinner with me some evening and tell me more about this city. She said she would, but she also said that she didn't want to be seen too often with me because she wanted to maintain her reputation. Sela qualified her statement by explaining that when a young black Nairobian female is seen too often with a white American or

European male, she would be viewed as the gentleman's concubine. Even if this were not true, it could affect her professionally.

I respected her concern, although it seemed common for women in Nairobi, at least on Kenyatta and Moi Avenues, to be quite forward. I told Sela that her statement pleased me, because in the last few days I had been approached several times by young women; many of whom only wanted a pack of cigarettes.

After lunch Sela returned to her office, and I hiked up Kenyatta Avenue in search of the Milimani Hotel. I never saw her again, although I did return to the Tourist Information Office about two weeks later. The new agent said that the position Sela vied for finally became available. He thought that Kenya Airlines had sent her to Bombay, India. If I ever get to Bombay, I'll have to look her up.

* * *

"A tropical hideaway just minutes from the city center," is how the Milimani Hotel described itself on the cover of its brochure. It surely was all the brochure portrayed. Sela had found the perfect location from which to explore and ponder my Kenyan discoveries and experiences. Located a comfortable forty minute hike, about 2.6 km from the Ambassador Hotel, I could venture west on Kenyatta Avenue, across the busy intersection where Kenyatta Avenue crosses Uhuru Highway, the major thoroughfare between Mombasa and Uganda, past Nairobi's two major parks, Uhuru and Central, into some rolling hills where Kenyatta Avenue splits into Milimani Road and Valley Road. The Milimani Hotel stands near the intersection of Ralph Bunche Road and Milimani Road. From the road most of the Milimani Hotel is hidden by trees.

I met the hotel's co-manager, Hananna, a Dutch woman with South African heritage, outside her office just off the lobby across from the registration desk. She explained that the hotel was part of a chain run by African Tours and Hotels, and that the Milimani Hotel rarely had American visitors because of the lack of advertising in the States. Their guests came primarily from Africa, with an occasional visitor from Europe.

This quality I found to be very attractive, because I wanted to be in a place where I could experience an essentially undiluted African culture. American tourists have a definite influence on the ambiance of places they visit.

Hananna continued to highlight the amenities that staying at the Milimani would provide. The hotel had large, modern rooms with balconies that overlooked the swimming pool. There were two fine restaurants, one in the garden that specialized in African barbecue dishes and an indoor restaurant where breakfast and lunch were served as well as continental dishes for dinner. The latter, she boasted, had an excellent selection of French and South African wines. And, of course, all rooms had daily maid service, complete security, and room service. The local watering hole was off the lobby decorated in an African motif. Hananna's sales pitch ended with a deal I couldn't refuse. I could have all, including the daily breakfast, for the next five and a half weeks at $26.00 per day. It didn't seem to take long to walk back to the Ambassador, repack my belongings, turn around and hike back, with a suitcase in my hand and backpack on my back, to the Milimani Hotel.

I had two twin-sized beds, a separate bathroom, a long desk with two desk chairs and bookshelves along the wall opposite the beds, a cushioned chair and a small table with a lamp next to each bed. One of the tables had an alarm radio. A balcony across the width of the room opened through a pair of sliding French doors. The balcony had two plastic lounge chairs and a small table. This was the best part of the room. Although I couldn't see the sunset because the balcony faced east, I could watch the sunrise and enjoy the cool morning breezes if I got up early enough. But no matter what time of day it was, the balcony served as a great place to kick off my hiking boots, put my feet up and write up my observations and adventures while having a cup of tea or something stronger.

DINNER

I spent the day exploring the neighborhoods around the University of Nairobi and visiting the campus. The day was exceptionally hot, dry, and dusty. And it seemed that at every street corner I came to, beggars confronted me. Three young men even challenged me with an offer, ". . . I could hardly turn down." So to perk myself up, I stopped for a beer, just across the street from the University of Nairobi, at the classic Norfolk Hotel and found a table on the veranda. But this exercise only added to my weariness, since my day's activities and a liter of Tusker Ale left me in a state of lethargy. I walked back to my hotel disinterested in the lengthening shadows and increased go-home traffic along Kenyatta Boulevard.

"A soothing dip in the pool, few winks on the chaise, a shower, a quiet dinner, will bring this day to a proper close," I mumbled as I exited the elevator at my floor.

Several hours later my plans to relax accomplished, I entered the hotel's open-air restaurant and approached the maitre d'.

"A table for one, please," I said, "somewhere out of the way."

Without looking up from the guest list the maitre d' pointed, somewhere behind himself, toward the grill. "Secluded tables are along that path," he said in a pleasant, efficient tone. "Find yourself one and I'll send a waiter."

I went in the direction the maitre d's finger pointed, along a path where individual tables were enclosed on three sides in trellised cubicles. Flowering bougainvilleas climbed upward along the trellises, then arched over at the top to form a tangled, viny roof. Bushes of hibiscus and lemon flowers marked the entrance to these exclusive sanctuaries.

Subtle aromas of bath oils, colognes, perfumes emanating from vegetation-surrounded patrons mingled with the fragrance of nearby frangipani trees and scented the evening air. Exotic, but it'll probably make me sneeze, I thought. I entered a cubicle down the path where the air seemed fresher, moved around the table and sat facing the entrance. I glanced around. Low interior lighting and the arborescent walls separating the individual cubicles made it difficult for me to decide whether or not any of the vegetated chambers near me were occupied. Occasional movement within, especially when it interrupted the glimmer of candlelight penetrating the foliage, suggested that a couple were occupied.

"Comfortable evening, Sir?" The waiter asked. His red waistcoat, white shirt and black slacks, although muted by darkness, simulated elegance. He presented a menu.

"Yes, fine for relaxing and enjoying a delicious meal." My stolid, insecure face smiled. I tried to relax, opened and examined the menu. The three candles centered on the table barely illuminated the printed list of entrées, but the savory aroma emanating from the grill furnished stronger gastronomic stimulation. "I'll order whatever's on the grill."

"Very good, Sir. Hartebeest is grilling tonight. A steak? They're large, or chops?"

I inhaled deeply. Woody smoke, roasting muscle, exotic flowers spiced the air. "Make it a steak, medium-rare."

"Sir would care for a bottle of wine?"

"No. I'll order by the glass when dinner is served. But for now, please bring me a double brandy. I'd like to kick back and enjoy the ambiance of the evening."

"Begging your pardon, Sir?"

"Never mind. Just bring me a brandy, please."

"Very good, Sir," the waiter said. He started to walk away, hesitated, slowly turned back. "It's cool tonight. Sir needs a *warm* companion. After dinner will be more delightful." He winked.

"No! Don't do that." My rejection flew through the entrance, uninhibited. The thought of his suggesting a prostitute amplified my uneasiness.

A soft draft wafted over the table. I stared at the flickering candle flames. "Nah. He wouldn't do that," I mumbled. "That's just what I don't need, a warm companion. They're more an annoyance than enjoyment."

I tapped my fingers on the table for a moment regretting the decision to eat in the hotel's outdoor restaurant. I had forgotten that the roaming prostitutes were allowed to work this area of the hotel since it was not only open to guests, but also to the public. Access was from the street and the lobby. Even though they were allowed in the lobby and access to the bar, the interior restaurant was off limits unless these women were in the company of a gentleman. A gentleman could quickly be provided because most maitre d's, waiters, security guards, desk clerks, and other hotel employees acted as prostitutes' agents: brokers for intimacy. Pimping, although carried out somewhat discretely, is acceptable in the cities of Kenya and appears not to have the stigma and criminal element that it does in North American cities. Not only does pimping produce extra money, but it also seems to have more status than waiting on tables.

The dancing candle flames fluttered.

"What! Who are you?"

"Mary! Manley said you were alone and would enjoy some company for dinner."

"Manley? Is that his name? You just go back and tell Manley that I am not interested. I am not buying anyone, other than myself, anything for dinner. Do you hear that?" I caught my breath. "Manley huh? Well you just go back and tell Manley what I said."

The intensity of my response surprised and startled her as much as her appearance in the cubicle surprised me. Also she didn't understand why a man didn't want to have her. It's humiliating to be rejected. Dejection replaced her smile.

"I can comfort you," she said. "Make you feel better. You're tired and I can be your companion. You'll see, it will all be good."

Mary had slipped into the chair next to mine. Her brown satin skin exposed by a subdued, low cut, flowered blouse blended with the shadows of the cubicle. Nervously, she ran her hand inside her blouse, attempting to emphasize her breasts.

"You bought me a drink last night," she said. "Don't you like me tonight? You buy me a drink . . . we will talk. I can be warm. And you will then like me and buy me dinner."

I studied Mary's face, her smooth cheeks, her deep, dark, naive eyes. There were three young women in the hotel bar last night, I remembered. I had had dinner with one of the curators from the Nairobi Natural History Museum and, when he brought me back to the hotel, we decided to have a nightcap. This had turned into a flirtation with three young women in the bar. We bought each of them drinks, smoked cigarettes and talked. They were all interesting and young . . . too young, like college girls. I never even learned their names, but I did remember something about them.

"One of your girl friends had a scar on her cheek. A Kukuyu traditional scar she told us. She lived in Limuru. Your other friend didn't talk much, only smoked a lot. And you are Mary. Well Mary, I'm glad to know your name. I remember last night, but not very much of our discussion. I wasn't planning to meet any of you again."

Mary's demeanor suggested she was a native of Nairobi, and a regular in this part of the city. I remembered the corn-braided hair, high cheek bones, and deep, rich brown almond-shaped eyes.

"It's not that I don't like your company. You are a very attractive girl, but I'm tired, had a long day, and want to be alone tonight."

Mary pushed back away from the table. She rotated her body toward mine, crossed her legs. Her skirt stopped just above her knees, exposing slender but shapely legs. "I have to go downtown," she said while slowly rubbing her toe against my shin. "I need new shoes. You can buy me nice shoes and then we have dinner. I know a nice club where we can relax. I'll show you a good time."

"It's late. I don't like shopping. And muggers are out in force."

"We can take a taxi."

Her activity with me began to weaken my composure. Fatigue from the day's activities, enhanced by brandy and the sensuality of the moment, lowered my resistance.

The waiter, carrying a plate that contained a hartebeest fillet and the other components that comprised the entrée, appeared between the hibiscus bushes. "Bon appétit, Sir." He laid the plate in front of me. His appearance shook me from my reverie. Quickly I snapped back to reality.

With considerable conviction, I told Mary that I had no plans to be with her tonight "You can go downtown by yourself," I said. "You can go downtown yourself. Please leave. *Now!*"

Mary looked at me in disbelief. That a healthy man would not want a woman who had offered herself to him so openly, without reservations, was foreign to her. "What is wrong with you Americans? You do not like women?"

"You should go. Find yourself someone else to buy you dinner, and shoes. Maybe, if you are lucky, he'll even buy you a dress." I could see her disappointment with my command.

She uncrossed her legs, put her hand into her blouse and, again, nervously fondled her breasts. "I'll need to take a taxi," she said with a petulant expression. "It'll cost thirty shillings. Do you have thirty shillings for me?"

I smiled. "Your companionship is costly."

From my pocket I removed a fifty shilling note and gave it to her. "Have a good evening," I said.

She rose from the chair and looked at me. "You could have had a better evening," she said as she turned and walked past the hibiscus.

My fillet cooled and the waiter forgot the wine. What a hell of an evening. Perhaps tomorrow will be better.

FLOWERS, FISHES, PREHISTORIC MEN AND TAXIS

Thrilling feeling and a sense of wonder engulfed me as I stood in front of the small rectangular crypt - actually a glass display case - in the middle of the dimly lighted Gallery of Paleoanthropology. The crypt contained a skeleton, albeit not of recent origin, but of a 1.6 million-year-old human. The fossilized remains of a twelve-year-old *Homo erectus* boy, one of the most complete pre-human skeletons in existence, lay exposed in his tomb exemplifying an ancestor of *Homo sapiens,* the humans of today.

As a grammar school child in the late 1940s I had an inkling that humans existed farther back in time than history recorded. In my portal to the world, The Lincoln Library of Essential Information that I ravenously read each evening after finishing my homework, there were several short paragraphs written on Cro-Magnon and other prehistoric human civilizations. My mother, in her attempt to aid the education of her sons, bought this single-volume encyclopedia for us to read. The two thousand, one hundred and seventy-four pages between its covers generated fodder for my childhood fantasies and adventures.

* * *

At the time that I attended elementary school, very little public information was available on prehistoric human beings. It wasn't until the 1960s when articles by and about Louis Leaky's discoveries appeared in print that human evolution merged with my avid interest in Africa.

While standing in front of the skeletal remains of *Homo erectus,* goose bumps progressed across my arms and back. I believe I experienced a thrill like my anthropology professor must have felt the day he found fragments of hominid jaws and other bones while working with the Leakys at Olduvai Gorge in Tanzania. My professor showed us these bones as he taught the course in Human

Evolution that I took during my undergraduate days at the University of Wisconsin. I even remembered what he said in his excitement, "Darwin started this, you know. He theorized that animals evolve through time . . . so isn't it magnificent that we now have evidence to show that humans also have a rich evolutionary history!"

Wow! What a rush I felt, standing there in the Gallery of Paleoanthropology; a gallery established by Louis Leaky at the National Museum of Kenya (Nairobi Museum of Natural History). Leaky became the first curator and director of this museum. His presence, and that of his wife Mary and son Richard, is very apparent. Many artifacts found by the Leakys, as well as other anthropologists, are displayed for public view in this gallery. Also on display were several casts of *Australopithecus afarensis* skulls found by Louis and Mary Leaky at the Olduvai Gorge site. Casts of a trail of hominid footprints discovered in hardened volcanic ash deposits at Laetoli in Tanzania were also displayed. These footprints confirmed that upright bipedal locomotion existed 3.75 million years ago. Several dioramas and wall-displays showed what life was like a couple of million years ago.

Although not on public display, the almost complete skull of *Homo habilis* discovered by Richard Leaky at his Koobi Fora site near the shore of Lake Turkana was housed in the museum's research collection. When the discovery of this skull was made public, it created quite a stir among paleoanthropologists, because it made the genus *Homo*, the lineage of modern humans, contemporary with hominids in the genus *Australopithecus*. This discovery disrupted the original evolutionary tree devised for humans, which hypothesized that the ancestor of *Homo* was *Australopithecus*. Richard's *H. habilis* skull dated initially to 2.9 million years, which placed its age a million years older than the *H. habilis* specimens Louis Leaky had found at Olduvai Gorge. This suggested that relatively modern humans were running across the East African plains simultaneously with less developed bipedal hominids. The age of the Koobi Fora skull was later adjusted to 1.8 million years, which quelled the controversy. Thus, Richard Leaky's find was about the same age as *Homo* skulls discovered farther to the south at Olduvai Gorge. But because of the skill's completeness and the fact that it could house a brain of about 200 cc, Richard Leaky's find was still of considerable anthropological importance. This was larger that any previously found *H. Habilis* skull. The larger brain case supported the removal of the *Australopithecus* ancestor from the human evolutionary tree. This revision showed that the genus *Homo* evolved independently of *Australopithecus*. The latter eventually went extinct, while *Homo* evolved in Africa along a line that started with *H. erectus* and moved through *H. habilis* to *H. sapiens*.

The characteristic that separated *Australopithecus* from *Homo* was tool making. Such prehistoric technology is displayed at the museum. Interestingly, the implements devised by early humans were made primarily to support their survival. While I viewed these tools, I wondered which of our modern tools were absolutely necessary for survival. I would estimate that 99 percent of today's technology is useful only to improve life, but not necessary for its survival. In fact, much of our modern technology may prove, in the long-term, to be a detriment to human life.

Most of the hominid fossils come from sites located in the East African Rift Valley. The Rift Valley extends roughly in a north-south direction, slightly above sea level, from the Ethiopian coast of the Red Sea, through Kenya and Tanzania. Because of the richness and diversity of hominid fossils found there, anthropologists call this region the "Cradle of Human Evolution." Along with the hominid fossils found at the dig sites are the remains of many different extinct mammals, reptiles, and birds that once roamed the African terrain along with the prehistoric humans. This material is also on display at the Gallery of Paleoanthropology, as are replicas of cave painting by more recent Stone Age and Early Iron Age humans.

Louis Leaky was also involved in the development and administration of the Coryndon Museum in Nairobi. When the Coryndon became the National Museum of Kenya, Louis became the curator of the paleoanthropologic collections. Consequently Richard and his brother Jonathan had much opportunity to play and learn in an environment that stimulated their imagination to an extent available to few children. They were fascinated by, and involved in, many of their parents' activities at the museum and in the field. Early on in his life Richard became interested in the museum's collections. His earliest contributions, however, were not in paleoanthropology, but in ichthyology, the study of fishes. He and Jonathan learned the museum technique that allowed them to make plaster of Paris casts of fishes, well enough and with sufficient detail that their models could be displayed in the museum. Many of the fishes that hang in the Fish and Reptile Gallery are those made by Richard and Jonathan Leaky as young boys.

Being an aquatic and marine biologist, I was especially interested in the fishes displayed in the Fish and Reptile Gallery. In fact, I discuss the biology of lungfishes in one of the lectures in the Ichthyology course I teach at my university. Lungfishes are highly specialized members of the order Dipteriformes. There are only three extant species of lungfishes in the world and one species, the African lungfish, lives in Lake Turkana in northwestern Kenya. The museum had one on display. This was the only authentic lungfish I had ever seen. In addition to many of the common species of Indian Ocean fishes found off Kenya's coast, the museum also has a large collection of freshwater fish in the family Cichlidae. These are small to medium-sized, highly colored fishes. Many cichlids are prized as aquarium fish, and one in particular has been brought to the United States and aquacultured as a food fish. Cichlid fillets can be found at almost all fish markets under its genus name *Tilapia.*

Over many millennia the cichlids have evolved into an innumerable diversity of species that inhabit the freshwater Rift Valley lakes, e.g., Lake Tanganyika and Lake Victoria. Unfortunately, adaptation and behavior in the Cichlidae has become specialized. Evolutionarily they are so highly developed that they are not able to compete with exotic fish species - fish species not endemic in cichlid habitats. Ichthyologists estimate that Lakes Victoria and Tanganyika once contained between 300 and 600 cichlid species. One hundred and twenty-five members of the Cichlidae from Lake Tanganyika are displayed in the Fish and Reptile Gallery of the National Museum of Kenya. Most of these have gone extinct within the last 50 years because of the introduction of a single exotic fish, the Nile perch.

The Nile perch is endemic to Lake Turkana, because the water from this lake once emptied into the upper reaches of the Nile River. The Nile perch grows to 300 lbs., and it has lured sport fishermen to this desolate lake. Although the Nile perch is of limited commercial interest, its desirability as a food is of major economic importance. It is easily caught by using basic fishing techniques, e.g., long-lining and gill netting; however, the remote and inhospitable location of Lake Turkana discourages development of a commercial Nile perch fishery. Many communities along the shores of Lake Victoria, on the other hand, have the necessary development to support the processing and distribution of a fishery's products. Therefore, the Nile perch was introduced into Lake Victoria in 1952 and into other freshwater Rift Valley lakes in the years following. The results were a commercial windfall, but an ecological disaster. The Nile perch is a non-selective predator. In this short time it decimated the cichlid populations.

Since Nile perch is served in many of Nairobi's restaurants and throughout Kenya, I wanted to taste this special fish that essentially ate most of Lake Victoria's endemic fishes. So I stopped at the Nairobi Hilton Hotel's restaurant and ordered a Nile perch lunch. It definitely didn't taste like, nor have the texture of my favorite fish, salmon. In fact, it tasted fishy, somewhat like mackerel, and it had a soft texture. I have since tasted its flavor in fast-food fish dishes and frozen fish sticks. Although not of great economic importance in the United States, Nile perch does turn up in the commercial market as the "mystery" component of various processed fish products. Many people like its taste and properties. Most of the Nile perch catch is consumed locally or exported to Europe and Asia.

Since mammals are a major resource of Kenya and other sub-Saharan African countries, the National Museum of Kenya has many educational displays that depict the ecology of elephants, rhinos, lions, various antelopes, and other commonly observed animals. One of the most exciting is a life-sized model, constructed of fiberglass, of an elephant named Ahmed. Ahemd is an open air display in the museum's courtyard. He once roamed Marsabit National Park, the park located in north central Kenya east of Lake Turkana. In an attempt to preserve a threatened species the President of Kenya mandated that Ahmed receive twenty-four hour protection because of his extremely long tusks. His tusks were so long they cut furrows in the soil when he dipped his head. Each weighed about

120 lbs. Ahmed became the symbol of Kenya's conservation effort. He died of natural causes and his skeleton is displayed, completely articulated, in the New Hall along with several fully articulated skeletons of other large African mammals.

In the Botanical Paintings Gallery of Kenya's National Museum hang some magnificent watercolors of common plants and flowers that enhance the scenery of the Kenyan bush country. Prior to actually seeing these originals, I had noticed reproductions of many of these paintings in books on African flora. The fascinating thing about these works of art is that some were painted by none other than Joy Adamson, Elsa the Lioness' protector.

The artistic talents of Joy Adamson and her descriptive contributions of African floral paintings are not well publicized. Joy is best known for her talents as a writer because her three volumes about Elsa the Lion became best sellers. The trilogy recounts how Joy and her husband, the famous white hunter and British game warden, George Adamson, raised and cared for lion cubs and later returned them to the wild. The books titled, *Born Free: A Lioness of Two Worlds; Living Free: The Story of Elsa* and *Her Cubs;* and *Forever Free: Elsa's Pride* were published in the early 1960s. These books also formed the basis of the film series *Born Free.* Joy wrote several other books on the natural history of African wildlife. Because both she and her husband were staunch conservationist, they were instrumental in the organization of conservation groups and the development of educational projects. Unfortunately, both of the Adamson's lives ended tragically. Joy was murdered in her bed by a disgruntled servant, while animal poachers brought George's life to an end.

Just outside of the main museum complex, but part of the National Museum of Kenya, is the Snake House. This building houses many of the common snakes and lizards found in Kenya. It also contains several endangered species. One, the Gaboon viper, is the largest and rarest viper species. It primarily inhabits the equatorial forests of West Africa and has only a splinter population in western Kenya. The Gaboon viper is of particular interest because it is one of the deadliest snakes in Africa. The toxin it produces works in two stages: first poisoning the blood, then the nervous system.

One of the functions of the Snake House poisonous snake collection is to provide the venom used to produce antibodies to counteract the fatal effects of the toxins. Consequently, the Snake House employs snake handlers adept at working with very poisonous snakes. The snake handlers are trained by Jonathan Leakey on his snake farm in the town of Baringo. Interestingly, the Leakeys are involved in all aspects of the National Museum of Kenya.

The National Museum is on the western side of Nairobi in a district of rolling hills called the Parklands. It was actually built on a rather historic location. One of Kenya's first pioneers, John Ainsworth, built his house on what is now museum ground. At the time, the site was uphill from the swampy area that eventually became the foundation of downtown Nairobi. When Ainsworth settled in Nairobi around 1899, he was head of the Imperial British East Africa Company (IBEA). The IBEA essentially managed East Africa before the British government took it over in the late 1800s when it became known as British East Africa. The IBEA Company also attempted to build a narrow gauge railroad, called the Central African Railroad, from Mombasa to the interior. The attempt met with defeat several miles west of Mombasa because of the lack of accurate survey maps.

Ainsworth had a penchant for gardening and horticulture. He surrounded his residence with beautiful gardens filled with exotic flowers, shrubs and trees. Many of these still adorn the landscape around the National Museum. Ainsworth eventually became the Secretary of the Agricultural Society of Kenya and went on to experiment with several agricultural crops, primarily cotton and sisal, to determine if these could be successfully grown in British East Africa.

I visited the National Museum twice during my stay in Kenya. Since I had, by my second visit, seen and encountered firsthand many of Kenya's animals, plants, vistas and habitats, and had become comfortable with its culture and people, the second trip was more meaningful. As a scientist, it was easier for me to interpret the museum displays after having had an opportunity to make some direct observations in the field.

However, the actual interval during which I was transported to and from the museum on my second visit turned into quite an adventure. As I walked toward downtown Nairobi after breakfast, trying to decide what to do with the day, it started raining about the time I reached the intersection of Kenyatta Avenue and Uhuru Highway. This was a major rotary interchange with traffic speeding around it. Located almost next to this intersection was a field where cars parked and taxis congregated. Because of the rain, I decided to hire a taxi to transport me to the museum, which was approximately a kilometer away, and an uphill trip. Since most of the museum was indoors, I could spend the day roaming about inside and remain dry. By the time I managed to cross to the parking lot, it had muddied, so I wasn't too particular about selecting a taxi. I commissioned the taxi of an old man whose vehicle was parked nearest the curb. He caught my attention by waving and asking in a loud but gentle voice, as I passed nearby, if I needed a taxi. I thought that if I chose him I wouldn't have to walk through the parking lot and get my boots muddy. Perhaps I should have been more selective, cautious, and taken notice of where the old man parked relative to the other taxis in the field. From his location he would not have been considered one of the "in taxis," but instead, a renegade. He did have a kindly face, though, and his gestures were not threatening. Besides, he appeared to be wanting, and I had no desire to get wet. So I opened the back door, slid into the backseat and said, "Take me to the National Museum please."

"Yes, Sir," he answered, as he pressed the accelerator, bounced over the curb and drove onto the highway. The engine, which sounded like a lawnmower trying to blast free of its mounting bolts, brought us to speed.

The rain increased but Pep - he introduced himself after I settled in his vehicle - didn't close his window. Instead he stuck his left arm outside and took hold of a wire attached somewhere near the front of the windshield frame and began to pull it to the side, out, away from the door and then push it back. Although he was being deluged, he could see ahead because with each motion of his arm the windshield wipers moved to and fro. When I slid to the far right to avoid being wetted, I noticed that the door handles on each of the back doors were missing. There's no way I could get out of the wreck if we should crash - a strong likelihood given the traffic and my driver's distraction while handling a moving vehicle.

The rain subsided as we turned into the parking lot of the museum. Pep turned toward me after he stopped and said he'd have to open the door from the outside to let me exit, since the inside doorknobs had broken off sometime ago.

"So I noticed," I said.

"On your return trip you should sit in the front."

"Yes, good thought," I answered as I stepped onto the asphalt. "How much do I owe you?"

"Ten shillings." He put out his soaked hand. "I will wait to return you."

"No, you go ahead. I plan to be here for several hours. And, I plan to walk back now that it's no longer raining." I turned and headed for the entrance to the museum, but turned back to look at the vehicle. It was a wreck, a well-worn Trabant, newly painted, by hand, with a brush, so it appeared to be dressed in a thick crust of white paint trimmed in blue. I wondered how this car, designed and built behind the Iron Curtain in East Germany, had found its way to East Africa.

I looked back once more as I entered the museum, Pep had the Trabant's hood up and vapors issued from the engine compartment. He appeared to be trying to force a rag into something or rubbing hard to clean some surface. Whatever. I entered the museum with no regrets for refusing his offer to wait and take me back the city-center. Initially I felt sorry for the fellow because he was trying to make an honest living, but he had little with which to compete against Mercedes, Ford, Fiat, and Nisson taxis. It was natural for him to be a bit aggressive in his approach to getting a passenger.

Pep did not disappear from my life. I am surely glad I didn't tell him where I was staying, because, like peanut butter stuck to the roof of your mouth, I was stuck with him for the rest of my day. When I left the museum, there was Pep in the parking lot surrounded by a couple of policemen.

Too late! He spotted me before I had time to duck away.

"There's the gentleman who commissioned me to wait. He will correct the problem," Pep told the policemen.

Pep had parked the Trabant in a no-parking zone, refused to move or "shell-out" any shillings to pay a fine. The police were about to take him off to jail and impound his taxi when I appeared.

"They want 200 shillings, Sir."

"Why did you stay? I told you I wanted to walk."

"I cannot pay. I do not have Ksh 200. The only money I have, are the ten shillings you paid me." He fidgeted. "If I go to jail there will be no money to buy food. My wife will be angry because her lazy son might have to find work. They will leave me and go live with her parents. She likes to be cared for."

"Why did you stay? Is the car broken?"

The police were getting restless and Pep became increasingly anxious. To me it appeared that Pep tried to exaggerate his plight because, when I came on the scene, his whining increased. The police were rather nonchalant about his concerns and, I think, would have left had Pep not made such a scene of self-pity. It's possible that he may have been in cahoots with the cops. Together they probably had an ongoing scheme to extort insignificant amounts of money from unsuspecting tourists. In Western economics these practices amount to no more than an aggravation, but in Third World countries the minions make their keep. Whatever, two hundred shillings amounted to a little less than $15.00. Besides, if I paid Pep's fine, for the moment I'd be viewed as his emancipator. I'd also have a good story. I handed the policeman two one-hundred shilling notes. They seemed happy and departed.

"Thank you Sir. I will take you wherever you want to go at no charge." Pep walked to the right of the Trabant and pulled open the passenger-side door.

"Parking seems to be a major crime," I said. "Do you get many parking tickets?"

"Oh no, Sir. This is the first time. Please sit in the front seat so you can exit when you like."

Pep held the door open. I shrugged my shoulders, ran my hand through my hair, scratched my neck, and got in, unconvinced.

Since the sun was shining and the air was hot and moist, he had all the windows rolled down. I noticed that a mossy green velure-like material covered the dashboard, framed the inner edges of the windshield, and covered the roof. Across the upper edge of the windshield dangled a row of ball-shaped tassels. Gentle breezes caused them to flitter metronomically. Only two instruments filled the empty spaces on the dash, the gasoline gauge and speedometer. The steering wheel was completely wrapped, I hoped to thicken or adorn rather than support, in white surgical tape and black electrical tape. My door did not catch or close completely, when I attempted to pull it shut. I would either have to hold it closed or wrap the wire around the center post where Pep had tied it originally.

Again the lawnmower under the hood screamed and we took off. On the trip over, I didn't remember seeing Pep shift through the gears. Now I found out why. The shifting lever and post were completely missing, so Pep had to use a tire iron to move the linkages on the transmission, which as I suspected, was totally exposed. He seemed quite adapt at doing this with ease, although he would have had to release the steering wheel, because on the trip to the museum his left hand was occupied moving the windshield wipers. I didn't notice this because I was too busy trying to keep dry. What had I gotten myself into, I wondered?

Pep literally wheeled the Trabant into the traffic on Uhuru Highway - Kenya's version of Interstate-75 where it passes through Atlanta. With the accelerator pressed to the floor, a trail of black exhaust jetted back toward the museum and the Nairobi Casino. I tried to stay in the seat and keep the door from flying open - Trabants don't have seat belts. This speedy exit was necessary to enter the flow of traffic. Vehicles on Uhuru Highway cruised around 60-90 mph, top speed of a new Trabant is about 40 mph, and I was in an ancient model. We, at least, had one advantage; we trailed a cloud of noxious black exhaust, which might slow approaching vehicles and certainly made us visible from behind.

Pep, at top speed, zipped in and out of the right lane as he passed trucks moving slightly slower than the Trabant. I death-gripped the side of my seat trying to keep myself from being tossed onto the highway in case the door that I attempted to hold closed, should happen to swing open. The intersection with Kenyatta Avenue was only a short distance so I'd be on the sidewalk shortly, if this trip didn't end suddenly under the bed of a truck or the side of some other vehicle.

My nose filled with the scent of burned motor oil as we approached the intersection. I now understood what Pep had tried to do with the rag I had seen him with earlier. Either he was attempting to wipe up the crankcase oil that the engine regurgitated onto the motor block or plug the oil-fill tube. It was time to get out of this vehicle! "I'll get out at Kenyatta Avenue," I yelled. I assumed Pep would have to negotiate the rotary at the intersection before he could come to a stop by the muddy parking lot and let me out. Wrong. He shot through the intersection and came to a halt just past it on the sidewalk along Uhuru Park. Luckily, there were no pedestrians. Only a cacophony of horns blared behind us. None of the trucks rear-ended the Trabant, although they probably wanted to in the worst way because of the sudden, unexpected maneuver off a major thoroughfare.

* * *

"Perhaps the Sir would allow me to drive him through Nairobi National Park later?" Pep yelled from the driver's seat as I exited.

"Perhaps not." Though he said that there would be no charge, with a smile of relief I handed him a ten-shilling note for bringing me back alive and struck out across the manicured lawn of Uhuru Park. I knew he couldn't follow me there.

CONTRIBUTIONS OF A PRESUMED FAILURE

East Africa, the land, wildlife, its native peoples and their cultures challenged and invigorated Karen Blixen, author of the world famous memoir *Out of Africa.* She considered her years spent in Kenya as the best part of her life. Though her marriage to Baron Bror von Blixen-Finecke ended in divorce, it did provide her the aristocratic status she most earnestly sought as well as the coffee plantation she developed, managed and eventually owned. Unfortunately, the coffee plantation went into insolvency and was liquidated and the long love affair she had with the noncommittal Denys Finch Hatton ended with his untimely accidental death in a plane crash in Tsavo. In addition to these disappointments, syphilis, contracted from her husband just a year after their marriage, left her with a humiliation and psychosis that tormented her until her death in 1962. It would seem that Karen's life in British East Africa was a monumental failure, yet she loved her life there.

Karen Blixen's time in, and love affair with, Africa is aptly described in *Out of Africa.* She wrote this memoir (published in 1937) after returning to Denmark knowing that she would never again visit the farm she had left behind. The nostalgic opening sentence, "I had a farm in Africa, at the foot of Ngong Hills," suggested the loss she felt for having to forsake the place to which she devoted so much of her energy. Her desolation was reinforced, as described in her writing, when she stepped from the train as it stopped for water at Samburu Station, to catch a final glimpse from that distance of her beloved African farm. Karen ended her memoir with a description of what she saw. Her last sentence summarized her forlorn sentiment: "The outline of the mountain [Ngong Hills] was slowly smoothed and leveled out by the hand of distance."

Karen hated Europe. She found life in her homeland boring, stifling, and ". . . a world in which nothing is ever happening." Biographers described her environment in Denmark as complacent, respectable, moral, and claustrophobic. Some authors portrayed Karen Blixen as a controversial, eccentric woman, full of life and immense strength to influence people and fate. But she had to continuously swim upstream to realize her power. Denmark thwarted her abilities. Karen's behavior and desires were, in a sense, those that have only recently been recognized as acceptable in women. She was entrepreneurial, inquisitive and assertive, qualities suffocated in European women of Karen's time. Psychologically, her survival required the challenges provided by Africa and the problems of coffee plantation ownership. The morés of Western Europe were less a part of the dynamic, developing African frontier culture. Native Africans and immigrant bourgeoisie respected Karen's abilities and instincts and, to a limited extent, the local British gentry tolerated these qualities.

The disappointing marriage and romance, perceived humiliation from her bout with syphilis, and her tenacious attempt to maintain the failing coffee plantation resulted in the undoing of her life in Africa. Because of these circumstances, she was forced to return to the pedestrian culture of Denmark.

After visiting the Blixen estate I can almost understand Karen's reluctance to leave what she had created in Africa. The manor and grounds are beautiful. The vision of the Ngong Hills from the terrace doors instills peace and serenity. European aristocratic prestige radiates from the place and adventure lies just beyond its boundaries. But if, today, East Africa is a land of severe contrasts and difficulties, how much greater these qualities must have been in the early nineteen-hundreds when Karen lived there. The difficulties must have been magnified hundreds of times. Karen Blixen, at least, overcame and established a foothold, a pioneer's grasp, in this country and made significant contributions to its history. It is not easy to give up one's advances especially if the endeavor is at great personal expense and uses a third of one's lifetime energies. It's like a fence post, once it's in place it is difficult to extract. But such decisions must enter everyone's life at some level. Most of us live with the consequences, move on, and become richer after the experience. Because of the tenaciousness of Karen's personality, the problems and the setbacks that she encountered sapped much of her vitality. She had difficulty resolving her status after Africa.

Knowing the political, medical and cultural challenges she faced, I'm surprised that she succeeded as long as she did.

When I toured the interior of the house, I found that it was sparsely furnished. Most of the furnishings were items assembled for the movie *Out of Africa;* few pieces were authentic. At the time I was there, museum personnel were negotiating with residents in the area to buy back some of Karen's original possessions. The gramophone that she and Finch Hatten listened to during the final days of their relationship caught my attention as it did the other visitors. It was displayed on a wooden box located on the patio near the two chairs in which Streep and Redford sat as they portrayed Karen and Denys. The phonograph is authentic. When I looked at this instrument, strains of *If I Know A Song of Africa* softly floated through my mind and I felt sorry for Karen and her plight.

LICKED BY A GIRAFFE

I felt the blast of warm breath expelled from the giraffe's nostrils envelop my lower arm just before its viscid tongue encircled my wrist. The tongue tightened, then slid outward to my hand and sucked away the food cube I held. These long-necked, long-legged, docile animals enchant visitors with bright, ping-pong-ball-sized eyes and lengthy eyelashes. But it's the long, prehensile tongue, which they use to wrap around branches of acacia trees to strip away leaves, that will lay upon you a proper kiss.

One afternoon I visited the Giraffe Center on the outskirts of Nairobi. This center provided me with a unique experience, definitely an incomparable encounter. It furnished an opportunity to create a friendship with an unusual animal, the Rothschild giraffe. From a balcony on the Center's second floor, I came eye to eye with several resident giraffes. The balcony rail was high enough to allow these fifteen-foot tall mammals to rest their head and be petted, scratched and fed by visitors. After receiving a morsel from a tourist, they seemed to flutter their eyelashes in thanks as they slurped a juicy kiss on the visitor's arm. Where else in the world can a human become so familiar with a giraffe?

Three species of giraffes once freely roamed the grasslands and deserts of East Africa: the reticulated, Masai, and Rothschild giraffes. The Rothschild giraffe (*Giraffa camelopardalis rothschildi*), a subspecies of the Masai, has always been less abundant. Its color is paler than that of the Masai giraffe and the spots cover the legs only above the knees. The margins of the Rothschild's spots are also smoother than those of the Masai giraffe, which are jagged and irregular. The most distinctive feature of this subspecies is the number, and position, of horns on the top its head. Rothschilds have three to five horns, two lateral just in front of the ears, one frontal in the middle of the head and one or two behind that. The Masai giraffe has two lateral horns and occasionally one in the mid-front of its head.

The Rothschild Giraffe was named to commemorate the zoological contributions of Lionel Walter Rothschild, a noted British naturalist from the early 1900s. Rather than follow the footsteps of his father, the first Lord Rothschild, a banker and financier, into the world of finance and banking, Lord Lionel Walter Rothschild devoted his life to natural history. In addition to his responsibilities as an aristocrat, Walter published many scientific papers, established The Walter Rothschild Zoological Museum (now part of the Natural History Museum, in London), and authored a seminal volume on zoology titled *Noviates Zoologicae.*

By 1980, the Rothschild giraffe was on the verge of extinction. Poaching and predation had reduced its population to only 139 individuals.

Through the efforts of Mr. Jock Leslie-Melville, the grandson of a Scottish Earl, and his wife Betty, an author of children's books, the extinction of the Rothschild giraffe was averted. The Leslie-Melvilles, in the late 1970s, founded the African Fund for Endangered Wildlife in Kenya and extended their fund raising efforts to the United States. Their efforts garnered sufficient funding to purchased a 120-acre ranch on the outskirts of Nairobi. With the aid of Kenya's Wildlife Department, they developed a program to translocate breeding pairs of Rothschild giraffes to several refuge locations. Five giraffes were placed on the Leslie-Melville ranch. The program was successful. Since its founding, the population of Rothschild giraffes has increased to over five hundred individuals.

Early on, the Leslie-Melvilles realized that many of modern Kenya's urban children had never seen a live giraffe, nor, for that matter, any of the other animals unique to the African experience, a disheartening fact that they believed needed to be corrected. Consequently, they converted their property into an education center and named it the Giraffe Center. Not only did the center provide a refuge for the Rothschild giraffe, but it also created an opportunity for the children to be in contact with these unusual animals and learn about their country's unique resource and how to protect it.

On the property of the Giraffe Center is the house once owned by the Leslie-Melvilles. Now known as the Giraffe Manor, its architecture resembles the great manor houses of England. The house is easily seen from the Center's balcony.

The Giraffe Manor is a hotel for the rich and famous. I heard that one of the perks available to guests, besides solitude, is being awakened in the morning by a nudge from a giraffe's nose. Resident giraffes poke heads through open windows to satisfy their curiosity. And, because giraffes freely roam about the property, guests can share meals with them on the veranda. Accommodations are pricey, but the experience would be unforgettable. Maybe someday I'll give the place a try. For now, I'll settle with taking my turn at getting a few licks from a grateful giraffe.

MALACHITE LION

A couple of days after I took residence at the Milimani Hotel I decided to stroll into downtown Nairobi, about a twenty-minute hike down Milimani Road to Kenyatta Avenue and along the avenue into town. My route passed through an affluent residential district, between Central Park and Uhuru Park, and across the major north-south Uhuru Highway before it entered the city's center of commerce. I encountered few pedestrians along this comfortable, pleasant walk until I came into the commercial district. But on the outskirts of town, I passed within a few feet of a smiling beggar, a total invalid. He seemed to extend his hand as I approached. But being true to my conviction of avoiding such confrontation, I approached, avoided eye contact, did not acknowledge, walked on by. As soon as my back was to him, he uttered, ". . . thank you for your thoughts. Have a nice day."

He probably said this to passersby that do not give him a couple of coins. But his words did as they were intended; they laid a guilt-trip on me and on any other insensitive, obdurate person that passed him. His words would, unless of course, one is totally heartless.

Now, I do not pretend to be one of those hardened souls. I do feel compassion for the down-and-out and those that have-not. As much as I would like, I cannot support all the disabled and destitute persons that put out their hands. My travel budget was certainly limited, so I preferred to dodge the confrontation. But in this case, I had a more fretful reason. One of my greatest irritations is that handouts, once given, become expected, especially when the contributor and receiver meet regularly. This would be the situation with this beggar as long as I stayed at the Milimani Hotel. Experience had taught me that panhandlers rarely change locations.

Nevertheless, his words haunted me. I knew I would be confronted by him every time I walked into town. But a Kenyan Shilling is only worth about six cents, I concluded. And the coinage, less than a shilling, was only worth a mere pittance. So on my return trip, which would occur later that afternoon, I decided that I would give him the change in my pockets, but he was not at his location.

* * *

The next day there he sat in his area, the manicured grassy strip between the curb along Kenyatta Avenue and the sidewalk. Two large trees shaded the verdant section in cool shadows. He was sitting on a small oriental rug, a basket in one hand and a book in the other, his puny, atrophied legs folded in front of him. I approached, looked down at him and stopped. Like the last several times I had seen him, his face was bright, even cheerful, but he did not extend his hand, just looked at me.

This beggar was different. Unlike the typical panhandlers cloaked in dusty, tattered clothing that I had seen in doorways and alleys off Kenyatta Avenue, he appeared clean and well appointed. He was wearing a checked sport shirt, camel-colored slacks, and leather sandals that hung loosely about his frail feet. His satiny, brown skin, and his deeply colored eyes reflected keen intelligence. If it were not for the slightly wasted torso and atrophied, ineffectual legs, he was a handsome man probably in his early thirties.

"I'm sorry I ignored you when I've passed by those other days," I said. "But, I didn't have any change . . . and, you weren't here in the afternoons when I returned."

Using his hands, he repositioned his legs to allow him to sit more upright. "Do not feel concern. I am accustomed to the reactions of non-Africans when they see beggars. My malady disturbs them . . . no doubt it did you. Most do not encounter poverty and disease on the streets where they live. So when they see me, they are disturbed. Some may feel pity, but few want to become involved. So they go by trying not to notice."

"You're absolutely correct. I'm sorry."

"You needn't be. I have an affliction, but I have to survive. It is very hard to get work when your body is destroyed by polio, so sometimes I use the remorse of the healthy to my advantage. Good fortune and affluence kindle guilt." His intent gaze softened into a welcome smile. "I am James," he said. "We should be friends." He extended his hand toward me and I accepted.

"Yes. I'm Richard, an American visiting Kenya." We shook hands.

"I meet very few Americans," James said.

"I'm not surprised. Most stay in the Hilton and don't venture much beyond the city center. I'm staying just up the road at the Milimani Hotel and I like to walk into the city."

James sensed my restlessness. "You should go to your destination. Perhaps you will have time to talk when we meet again. I can tell you of our ways."

I handed him the coins I had saved. "Maybe this can buy you lunch."

"Thank you. I will eat maize." James pointed down the avenue toward a copse of trees where several men milled about. One stood next to a blackened, smoking fifty-five gallon drum grilling sausages and ears of corn. "They are my friends and will provide me with food."

"I passed them yesterday and their cooking smells very good."

"We should have lunch then."

"Yes."

James waved and I proceeded downtown.

* * *

Most of the days that I walked into town, I saw James in his usual location. From his response, when he saw me, I believed that my arrival brightened his day. Actually, I had a similar feeling about our encounters. Our meetings made this normally routine hike special and interesting. Although polio incapacitated his body and relegated him to a meager existence, his attitude had an uplifting effect.

I learned that James was a well-read, educated man. He had almost received a degree in art history from the University of Nairobi, but because he contracted polio, he had to drop out near the end of his third year. Had the university the facilities to support the handicapped, as most do in the United States and Western Europe, he could have completed his education. But, as he said, in Kenya, support for the physically disabled is nonexistent unless the person is an aristocrat, has a benefactor, or has a special talent. He said that he did have work, so I assumed he had a *special talent* of some sort. I had asked him what he did, but he always managed to evade the question.

The closest residential areas near the site where James sat were several blocks away. Except for a few small office complexes, Kenyatta Avenue along this stretch was park-like, so it was obvious to me that James did not live anywhere near. Also, because of the sparse pedestrian traffic, this piece of the avenue certainly would not be a panhandler's road to riches. So early on, I asked him why he chose this site to seek charity.

"Air is cooler, dustless, under the trees," he said. "The grass softer than a sidewalk or a store front. People that walk by are friendly and, like you, they know me, want to talk. And, I do not beg. I do not have to beg. But all my friends are kind and generous. I think helping me makes them feel good. And, whether they do or not, I always wish them a good day." He looked toward the forested hill about a block away. "Those men over there are my caretakers. They protect me, bring me food . . . and, carry me here whenever I want to enjoy being out-of-doors. This is a nice, comfortable place to sit and watch life. I need that in my work."

I looked toward the fellows hanging around the fifty-five-gallon grill. "I'm curious. What do you do for work?" He looked away, as if lost in thought, and never answered so I went on toward downtown, without saying goodbye.

Actually, James never did ask me for anything. It was my guilt that led me to give him my change, and by doing so, I believed that I established a kinship with him. As our acquaintanceship progressed my initial impression was confirmed. I found him to be a dignified young man who did not bemoan his affliction but instead he embraced his world.

During the six weeks I was in Kenya, I went on several trips outside of Nairobi, but returned to spend two or three nights at the Milimani Hotel. As was my custom, I walked downtown past James's post and stopped to visit with him. Our discussions were always fun and enlightening. We talked about life in Africa and the United States, philosophy, science, politics, and a host of other subjects. A particular topic he brought up proved my belief that the Kenyan economy and that of other similar countries was based on some degree of corruption at all levels of authority. I learned early in my trip that if I wanted anything special, those who could provide it expected something beyond the normal compensation. James mentioned that such transactions are usual and have been a part of human culture since the beginning of time. As an example, he provided the scenario of a man who tried to gain assurance that the woman destined to become his wife was hardworking and faithful. To secure such surety, he had to provide livestock and gifts, not only to the prospective father-in-law but also to his future brothers-in-law, their close male friends, and sometimes, the tribal chief. So, James said that if you want something special, or want it done efficiently and promptly, you will need to provide a bribe. To eliminate such blatant transactions, Americans and Europeans have integrated their "extra" costs into the price of the service. We have not done so here he told me. I agreed, but I mentioned that in some countries this practice is abused especially by governmental officials. James nodded.

On my trek to Amboseli, my travelers' checks were stolen and upon my return to Nairobi, I went to the American Express office to replace them. During my return to the hotel on the afternoon I obtained the replacement checks, I found James still watching the traffic on Kenyatta Avenue. His presence, and the fact that American Express replaced the checks, made me happy. Yet, I really needed to express my feeling about the whole situation to someone. James, I thought, would make a good listening post, one who would reply and provide a sympathetic ear. So I told him my interpretation of the theft. His nonchalant response surprised me. He actually believed no one really suffered any indignities in the transaction. In fact, he said, the maid, who probably stole and then resold the checks, received enough money to buy food for her children. The buyer was compensated when he passed the checks onto his contact. And the contact, got his due when he passed them on to his contact. And so on, as the checks progressed along the commercial chain. "The only irritation is that you had to spend an hour of your time to make a claim at the American Express office. But, your checks were replaced," he said. "You really lost nothing but a moment in your life."

James' answer to my perceived problem was the same as that of the bank teller, so I did not receive the sympathy I expected. I was in Kenya and, here, this is the way life revolves. Problems involving someone's money is of little concern, since most do not have any.

"So you visited Amboseli?" James changed the subject.

"I went there for the weekend."

"I was born near that park. My family had a small farm near Namanga. I spent my early childhood there and left when I was about twelve years of age. Mostly I knew my mother. My father, an educated man, was a Kikuyu tribal leader, so I never really got to know him. He was always in Nairobi supporting the African National Union as a member of the Mau Mau. He wanted to be part of Jomo Kenyatta's forces, but those forces killed him not long after he arrived in Nairobi. My mother said that a group of Mau Mau guerrillas assigned to assassinate a British leader, a major somebody, mistook my father and his band of rebels for British sympathizers. Apparently my father's squad was on this major's farm near Mount Kenya trying to confiscate his cattle for the cause, but the other Mau Mau squad did not know this. They thought my father and his men were instead working for the major and were trying to hide his livestock, so they shot them without asking any questions. A sad end for my father, but that was the primary danger that faced these guerrillas. There were many Mau Mau splinter groups, so most times the right hand did not know what the left hand was doing. Jomo Kenyatta finally pulled everything together and in 1963 Kenya became an independent country."

"That is quite a story," I said. "But how did you come to Nairobi?"

"Two years after Kenya's independence, my mother traveled to Nairobi to try to find my father. She brought me with her. When she found out that my father was killed some years before and she was not notified, she became very disturbed and despondent. The few shillings she had to support us were spent and we had to beg on the street. After about a week of begging, she met a missionary priest and told him of my talent. She convinced him that I would have a better life if he found work for me at the mission. 'Perhaps you could put him into a school,' she had said. The priest knew that my talent would be a benefit to his church, so he agreed and gave her a few shillings. She passed my hand into his, waved and walked away. Both of us were in tears. I never saw her again."

"Interesting," I said and thought for a moment. "You mentioned that your mother told the priest of your talent. You have never told me what you do. What is your talent?"

"Yes. Several weeks ago you did ask about my talent, what my trade is. I should tell you. You have seen the wooden animals that tourists buy; I carve such figures. I also sculpt figurines from many different kinds of minerals found around East Africa. That is my talent and the priest wanted to develop it so that my carvings and statues would bring money into the church. The priest kept me confined in a small apartment near the church. He called it a studio. He did not allow me to go away; said I had to pay back the money he gave my mother. I was his prisoner and did as he directed, made many carvings. He sold them to craft shops, the craft center, gift shops, hotels, and the street markets. Never gave me any money from the sales; said it cost him much to support me. When I asked how much he received for my carvings, all he said was that my carvings were too mediocre to be of any value. After about two years I escaped, found some men that knew my father, and they hid me away in a room off Tom Mboya Street. The priest would not look there because it was not safe for him, too many thugs, terrorists, and criminals live there; many rooms in this area housed renegade Mau Mau rebels, and they were armed with pangas. They'd kill a man just for his shoes. Even priests were not safe."

"This place was good for me." He nodded toward the men around the fifty-five-gallon grill. "And my father's friends helped and protected me. I kept carving animal statues. But now *I* sold them to the shops, boutiques and markets *myself.* My sales brought me many shillings, enough to help my friends and allow me to enroll at the University of Nairobi to study art history and sculpture. This is where I learned to carve minerals. But, before I could complete my studies, I contracted polio and had to leave the university."

"How unfortunate," I said. "You were coming along so well after your difficult beginning. And then this dreaded, debilitating disease ruined your life, your work."

"No, it was for the best . . . not the disease, but that I had to leave the university. My studies did not allow me much time for carving. I was not earning enough money to live while I was at the university, so I had to borrow from my friends. This was not good since most did not have work and had families to support. But they always said they wanted to help their artist. I owe them much."

"You are lucky to have found such loyal friends," I said. "But what do you do now? I see you here some mornings and very rarely in the afternoon."

"I carve and sculpt when I am not here. Polio did not stop me from doing what I enjoy. After many months my friends convinced me that I could go on, be famous, although I am a cripple. So I continue. Now my wooden animals and my stone animals are much in demand. I do not make many so my work can stay in demand. I spend more time perfecting my craft."

"I'd like to see some of your work," I said.

"Go to the Nairobi Museum in June. They plan to show my work. You will see my best."

"I will not be here. I leave for the United States in a week, Sunday evening to be exact. Is it possible to see your work at a craft store?"

"Then we must meet Thursday morning." He smiled. "I will bring a piece . . . one of my finest and most difficult."

During the next two days I did not see James, although I passed his site on my way downtown. Before I returned to the U. S. I wanted one of James' carvings so I visited the city market, the Kenya Craft Center, and other shops. There were so many pieces from which to choose, but none had an artist's signature. When I asked, the proprietors told me that most of the carvers are obscure individuals. Most of the stores bought their supply from dealers. However, at one store - a dank place near Tom Mboya Street - the owner mentioned that he had several pieces that he had bought from a priest. He showed them to me: a giraffe with painted spots, four ebony wood figures, a twenty-four inch tall waterbuck cow nursing a calf, and an elephant with authentic ivory tusks.

The waterbuck carving showed the greatest craftsmanship, precision and authenticity. Although unsigned, from James' descriptions, I believed that he had carved this piece. After a few minutes of haggling, I purchased the figure for about forty dollars. I planned to show this to James, and if he were the artist, I would have him sign it.

A radiant smile came over James' face when I approached Thursday morning. The day was perfect, crisp and bright, not a cloud in the sky. As I walked toward him, I held up the paper bag that I carried. "Some treats for us to enjoy this beautiful day," I said. The hotel had given me some extra rolls and strawberries for breakfast so I brought them along to share. A cloth bag in my left hand held the carving of the waterbuck.

"Although it is good to see you, your arrival comes with sadness," James said. "This will be our last discussion for some time."

"Let's not make this a solemn affair. I brought some snacks so we can have a picnic and talk about your work. Let's enjoy ourselves, and celebrate that we got to know each other."

James' smile returned when he saw the strawberries. "They are most delicious," he said while biting into a plump berry. "These are not something I am normally able to eat since these berries are rarely grown in Kenya. They must be imported from Europe."

"Enjoy."

"What do you have in the other bag?"

I removed the waterbuck carving. "This I bought yesterday at a craft store on Tom Mboya Street because I thought you might have carved it."

"It is a very beautiful piece, but it is not one I carved." James examined the piece. Thought for a moment. Held it up and seemed to trace the intaglio texture on the base with his fingers. "This was carved by Peto Mbugua, a very good artist. I met him once, when I was at the university. He did not make many carvings before he died of AIDS a few years ago. He was still a young man."

"It's indeed attractive work, but I am disappointed it is not one you carved. At least I bought a rare waterbuck carving, one that cannot be duplicated. So that makes me happy, but I still don't know what your work looks like."

James fidgeted about on his rug. "Richard sit, and enjoy the strawberries with me and I will show you." He grabbed his right knee with one hand, lifted it and removed a small wrapped package from under his leg.

"This is what I do." He slowly removed the paper from the object.

"You unwrap packages?" I teased.

From the last bits of paper he removed a four-inch long figurine of a lion, its head transposed to one side, jaws open, canines bared, as if caught in the moment of a roar. James handed it to me. It was carved from some opaque mineral that contained many fine black reticulated veins that gracefully divided its satiny emerald-green surface into irregular sized units. A diffused white band that integrated into the emerald-green encircled the statue's body. The lion's mane, dynamically textured, swept leftward, billowed, as the head rotated. Every minute detail from the nares, eyes, toes to the flare at the tip of the tail was done with precision. The craftsmanship of this sculpture was exceptional.

"James, this is beautiful. It's certainly a work of art. I've seen many figurines in the stores, but nothing of this quality. What is this green material?"

"It is malachite. I have made only three carvings with this mineral, because large sculptures are difficult to make from malachite. Malachite is a soft, brittle mineral composed of copper and limestone and it chips, and powders, easily. Craftsmen can work small pieces because they usually do not have any fracture lines. However, pieces larger than about three cubic centimeters may have fracture lines, sometimes many, which are mostly invisible, so when the artist carves near the line the rock will crack into two or more fragments. Then work is destroyed. This is why most malachite objects are small, like chess pieces, jewelry, and other miniature art objects."

"I first learned about malachite when I was a boy," James continued. "My father, uncle and I traveled to Tsavo. En route, while crossing a dry riverbed, I found three green-colored rocks. When I showed them to the adults, they became excited and my uncle yelled, "This is malachite . . . valuable stones that are mined near here." He told me to put them in my bag and take them home."

James then told me that, when he attended the university, he was taught that malachite and other semiprecious stones could be carved. After learning of the qualities of malachite, he said that he very carefully tried his skill at carving the stones he had collected when he was a child. Two broke into smaller pieces, so he carved them into smaller objects. By the time he worked on the third piece, he had gained the care and skill needed to work malachite. Maybe that particular stone did not have a cleavage line. Whatever the reason, it did not fracture and James had successfully carved the beautiful malachite lion that he placed in my hand.

"After my first success, I purchased more malachite and was able to carve two other statues. These I sold. They brought a good price. Maybe sometime I will carve more."

I fondled and rotated the malachite lion about in my hands. It felt cool, smooth - slippery, but after what James told me, I began to feel nervous holding it. "This is indeed a beautiful piece of work, but I think you should take it back," I said. "I might drop it. And, if I did, I could never pay you what it's worth. It's invaluable art. It should be in a museum."

"No Richard, it should be in your hand. I want you to have a piece of art that I made so you can remember James, the crippled artist you met in Nairobi."

"I just couldn't accept such a gift." Overwhelmed with gratitude, I held the malachite lion tighter, until my hands got sweaty. I wanted this object, but I knew it was more than I deserved. "I have nothing to give you," I pleaded.

"You gave me your friendship. The malachite lion will become your treasure, a memento of our discussions. It will remind you of your time in Kenya when someday you write your book." He held up his arm in a halting gesture. "You must go, because my men have come to take me home. Please remember James. And maybe, when you return, we will again meet and talk."

Three men that came up from the forested knoll down Kenyatta Avenue lifted James into a chair-like contraption. These were James' protectors; the guys from whom I bought roasted ears of corn when James and I had lunch. They nodded a greeting to me and started to carry James toward the avenue. James waved. *"Bon voyage," I heard him say.*

* * *

My trip to Kenya occurred in 1987, over ten years ago, but whenever I look on the shelf above my computer monitor, the malachite lion brings back many fond memories. I wonder if James is still carving.

SAFARI

One of the greatest thrills of visiting Kenya or any country in East Africa is going on a safari (safari is actually a Swahili word for travel). In the early twentieth century the excitement of a safari motivated many adventure seeking European aristocrats and affluent Americans to visit Africa. It gave them opportunities to hunt for trophy game, observe the unusual, and experience the raw, primitive nature of this continent. Though somewhat modernized, this attraction still holds true.

After arriving in Nairobi one of the things I quickly became aware of was that almost every male in this city wants to be hired as a safari guide. Regrettably, less than ten percent know where they're going, less about how to get there, or what to do once they lose sight of the skyscrapers. There are as many safari agencies in Nairobi as there are saloons in Milwaukee and churches in Birmingham. Although they come with various facades and prices, many are less then bona fided. Since a safari adventure topped my agenda, I had to do some research so as not to be taken for just a *ride.*

I learned that if time were of the essence any local taxi could be hired for about twenty-five to forty dollars for a drive through Nairobi National Park. Going this route, the client gets a thirty-minute to one hour trip within the boundaries of the one hundred and seventeen-square mile park. The only observations made from the taxi, besides seeing dust trails, are the insects that imprint on the windshield. Wildebeests, gazelles, giraffes all disappear in a blink as the taxis, driven at NASCAR speeds, "bebop" over the corrugated and potholed access roads that crisscrossed the park.

Now, Nairobi National Park is a magnificent safari experience, but a comfortable visit requires spending at least a day. It is about eight kilometers from the center of the city - well within reach of most "ol' clunkers" - and contains, except for elephants, most of the game animals and birds that are identified with the African experience. Large mammals such as lions, hippos, and a diversity of antelope-types are in abundance and roam freely across the park's vast fields and valleys. Nairobi National Park is also a rhino preserve, so the potential for a glimpse of this rare treasure is very good.

I found it best to sign on with one of the day trips offered by reputable travel agencies. These are very affordable with well-planned itineraries that usually include side trips to such local sites as the manor house once occupied by Karen Blixen, an orphanage for animals, the Bomas of Kenya (a cultural center), Giraffe Manor where the endangered Rothchild's Giraffes are maintained and protected, and before returning to Nairobi, lunch at the Carnivore Restaurant.

For the extended safari that I had planned I shopped around. My choices for adventure at various degrees of comfort were many. I could go to a lodge (a hotel-type experience) or stay in a manicured permanent tent camp. In the latter the guests were housed in walled tents, with plenty of headroom, built on a concrete floor. The shower and toilet were found in a three sided cottage-like shelter connected to the sleeping tent. Guests feel the excitement of living in a tent, but have the luxury of a private, though rustic, bath. In some of these tent-lodges the inside is very much like a hotel room because they contain beds draped in mosquito netting, small side tables, chairs, and a washstand with a pitcher of water and a washbowl. On my weekend in Amboseli National Park I found these camps to be extremely comfortable and very secure against any attacks from wild beasts, but little protection from the very conscientious lodge staff.

What I really wanted was a trekking safari; I wanted to hike paths, follow game trails, and bushwhack through the scrub like the great white hunters used to do. But for a variety of rational reasons, the most important being, the security of the traveler, hiking is not allowed in Kenya's national parks. So the closest I could come to what I wanted was really a camping safari where the guest can pitch a pup-tent at a campsite and sleep inside in a sleeping bag. There are such trips.

When I asked around, one of the recommended agencies that allowed such close-to-the-earth adventures was Gametrackers Limited of Kenya. This agency scheduled camping trips to all the national parks and many other remote locations in East Africa. It provided transportation, guides, cooks, pup tents and even rented sleeping bags. The tents had ground cloths that were sewn in and door flaps that laced, so once inside the tent, zipped into a rugged sleeping bag, the camper was comfy, protected, and isolated from the elements. And since the price of a safari to the Rift Valley and Masai Mara National Park fit my budget (about $180 for six days), it didn't take much convincing for me to book passage on this a great adventure.

* * *

On the day my safari adventure began I hiked down Kenyatta Avenue toward Uhuru Highway to the muddy field at the intersection where cars parked, taxis stopped to await a fare, and buses and trucks assembled before being loaded with cargo. This was the place where a week earlier I had met Pep, the resolute old entrepreneur who, for a few hours a day, turned his dilapidated, hand-painted, East German-made Trabant into a taxi. A gut-level feeling warned me that I should beware of running into this persistent ol' coot, so reflexly I tightened the shoulder straps of my backpack, pulled the brim of my hat lower, and entered the field between a bunch of parked cars. Unconsciously I looked back at the collection of taxis. He wasn't around; maybe the "Trabi" had died. Relieved, I made my way toward a small group of Caucasians standing near some massive trucks that reminded me of the transports Rommel used to ferry troops and supplies around the Sahara. On the doors of these "landrovers" were the "Gametrackers Limited" logos.

Gametrackers used these giant lorries to convey their clients to the rugged desert regions around Lake Turkana. Because the rainy season had begun in the north, the trucks now sat idly. The vehicle designated to haul me around on this Rift Valley/Masai Mara Safari was hidden by these monsters. Allocated to my safari was a three-quarter ton, four-wheel drive modification built by Mitsubishi. A wooden, roofed, open-air compartment that contained cargo space and seating for about sixteen passengers was built onto the truck bed. Roll-down canvas curtains protected passengers from inclement weather. Tents and sleeping bags for the number of persons the vehicle carried, and personal luggage, food and all necessary utensils, drinking water, and fuel for a week's trip were stored under the seats, below the bed, and on top and across the back of the passengers' compartment. This was a succinct vehicle, a rugged safari truck. Although it would have been much more romantic to have a hundred or more chanting pack-bearers, as in the old days, filing behind us carrying our supplies, the notion of taking a safari in Africa, even in this truck, excited me.

The safari left Nairobi with eight curious and excited trekkers about ten o'clock in the morning and progressed northwest along Uhuru Highway toward Naivasha. On the outskirts of Nairobi vast tracts of land were divided into farm fields. A group of fields surrounded a small aggregate of rondavels, the typical cylindrical dwellings with pointed thatched roofs that house the members of an extended Kikuyu family who owns and work the farm. As the safari truck continued on, we gradually ascended into the highlands. Forests of coniferous trees began to appear and the air cooled considerably. The fertile soil, comfortable climate, and proximity of these highlands to Nairobi, caused this region to quickly become colonized by English and European settlers. Today, as in the days of the African pioneers, this is some of Kenya's most coveted farmland.

About thirty miles west of Nairobi we stopped at a complex of kiosks situated beside a lookout near the village of Longonot. The scenic overlook, situated about 7,500 feet above sea level, was located near the edge of the Great Rift Valley's eastern escarpment. The overlook was about a quarter mile from where the edge dropped vertically almost 6,000 feet to the valley floor. From where I stood, I could look westward approximately thirty miles across the expanse of the valley to its western escarpment. Roughly midway across this canyon rose Mount Longonot, an extinct volcano. Its barren conical peak, which topped at near 9,000 feet, obscured part of the view to the south.

Magnificent colors and textures radiated from this vista, a geological spectacle surpassed by very few places on this earth. Nature's grandeur, its artistic masterpiece, the scene contained verdant pastoral fields and forests atop the escarpment. Far below beige-gray dust devils wisped across a desolate desert floor and up the burnt magenta slopes of the volcano. A shimmering horizon, where the misty purple western escarpment merged with the pale blue sky, focused the scope of this wonderful scene. High above the valley large black birds, their identity masked by distance, surfed on the rising thermals.

The area atop the rift escarpment near the overlook was a place of contradiction. The surroundings resembled a countryside in northern Michigan or Wisconsin with wooded lots of pines, small fields of potatoes, greens and corn, and several grazing herds of sheep and cattle, a cold temperate environment fifty miles south of the equator. Merchants in the kiosks even sold fleecy Cossack hats and sheepskin vests; natives wore these.

About thirty miles from Longonot the highway reached the crest of the escarpment and began its descent into the Rift Valley. The many tight switchbacks made downward progress slow, but exciting. On the right of the safari truck the unbarricaded precipice fell away almost vertically. The cliff wall, with its orange-brown slabs, ledges, boulders, and slipping gravel, rose on the left. Some scrawny vegetation grew within the crevices. Families of baboons lived between these outcropping ledges and in the caves. These animals slowed the trip even more than the hairpin turns, but their comical antics made their presence enjoyable. The baboon children chased each other on the roadbed. Primate families leisurely strolled along the median as if they were on their way to the market or grandmother's house, or they just sat in one of the lanes and chided us as we tried to pass. If disturbed they would scream and bark, and bare their teeth, but quickly moved aside when our driver tapped the horn a few times. He said that the baboons have pretty much taken over these precipices. Since baboons are somewhat territorial, a human walking alone might be attacked. In about twenty minutes the truck reached the bottom of the cliff and the roadway stretched to the horizon across the flat, hot, dusty terrain. Our driver sped the truck forward toward Naivasha and lunch.

After lunch we continued northwest across the dusty, xeric landscape toward Lake Bogoria. In the middle of nowhere, a four by six-foot sign appeared by the side of the road. A map of Africa with a prominent blue line painted across its center divided the continent in half. On this line, but slightly off the center, was a dark blue circle. It was as if Africa had a belt around its waist with the belt buckle skewed to the right. A faded blue line was painted across the highway at this site as well. Our driver stopped the safari truck over this line and shouted, "You are all on the Equator." The sign stood next to the highway, strategically located, to inform tourists of their position on the earth and that they were about to cross from the southern hemisphere into the northern. The only things missing on the sign were the words, "You are here," and an arrow pointing to the circle. What a thrill to stand on the world's most well known geographic boundary. As typical of tourists everywhere, we all photographed each other standing next to the sign.

A short distance after crossing into the northern hemisphere, our driver turned onto a gravel road. This road descended gradually into a trough and approached Lake Bogoria along its western side. However, unlike the barren landscape on which we had traveled most of the day, this region contained growths of fig, acacia, and baobab trees, a few tall palms and field shrubs, broad–leaved plants and thick clumps of grasses. As if someone had burst a can of red paint over the canopy, flowers of flame trees mixed within this forest and added brilliant red streaks and spots to the green-gray panorama. From the eastern side of the lake, the Laikipia Escarpment rose in an almost thousand-foot sheer wall. This was indeed a scenic oasis at the bottom of the Rift Valley.

Our driver pulled into a clearing that served as a parking area for the campground next to a lake. When the vehicle came to a stop, the breeze generated by its forward motion stilled. This is when we all realized the air in this area was about forty degrees hotter than on top of the escarpment. Not only that, but the air in this depression was also heavy with water. I felt as if I had entered a Turkish steam bath - a notion that was not so far fetched. All around the parking area were small geysers, boiling pools and hot springs. With whooshes and roars, the geothermal heated water jetted from deep in the earth and coursed toward the lake in a network of streams. Several of these little streams passed lakeward beside the parked safari truck.

Being an aquatic biologist and having read about the fauna that reside in the cooler sections of these mineral-laden steams, my desire to explore was overwhelming. But the warm, oozing mud between the streams and along their banks made it evident that I could not venture beyond the solid ground where we were to camp. With one step off the gravel knoll, onto what appeared to be substantial black soil, my foot sank to a depth above my ankle before I quickly jerked myself free. My boot, sock, and lower pant leg appeared as if they had been painted black. Not only that, but my step released a strong vaporous blast of sulfurous gas. Since this muddy floc extended from the camping area to the edge of the lake, I could not get to the shore. This was a disappointment because I wanted to collect, or at least see, the little critters that inhabit this African soda lake.

Frustrated, I collected my gear from the safari truck and pitched my tent. Because it would be cooler in the shade and a few hundred feet from the hydrothermal activity, I set the tent in a coppice of acacia trees. Besides that, some white-browed sparrow weaver birds entertained me while I worked. These nondescript brown and white birds picked up pieces of dried grass and carried them to nests hung from branches of acacia trees like fragile baskets. Amid constant chirping from members of the flock, they worked diligently to intertwine the grassy threads into their abode.

The campsite at Lake Bogoria reminded me of some I visited in the American southwest. Yet surrounded by paradisiacal beauty a few miles north of the equator, this place made me a bit apprehensive. When I walked around, my legs felt tense and uncertain. It was as if I were walking on thin ice. In a long stretch of my imagination, I was. The geothermal activity and being in one of the lowest spots in the African Rift Valley, was enough to impress upon me the geological instability of this place. This was one of those sites where the crust of the earth is the thinnest. Although not as thin as newly formed ice on a pond in early winter, here the earth's crust or lithosphere is only a few miles thick. In other parts of Africa, such as the land adjacent to the rift valley, and on other continents, the crust extends down about thirty to forty miles. This thinning of the earth's crust is caused by huge bubbles formed by the upwelling of molten magma that cools before the bubbles break. Occasionally the lava reaches the surface and forms a volcano. When the upwelling first began about ten million years ago, it created a hot spot that caused the crustal material to bulge, much like the bubbles that form on the surface of cooking oatmeal. But unlike the bubbles of hot oatmeal that are about a centimeter in diameter and pop because of weak surface tension, the diameter of the earth's lump is measured in miles and its crust is rigid, so when it swells, tensional forces cause the bulge to crack. These gigantic cracks are what form the rift valleys.

The tectonics in the African Rift Valley are still very active. In fact, the floor of the valley floats on molten magma and the escarpments are gliding apart. The African Rift Valley is the only place located on a continent where continental plates are actively separating. The African Plate (the western escarpment) is slipping away from the Arabian Plate (the eastern escarpment) at a rate of about a half centimeter per year. At one time Arabia was part of Africa.

On the earth the best known of these continental drift regions is the mid-Atlantic ridge, which extends almost from the North Pole to the South Pole. Along this ridge the North American and South American plates have been separating from the continental plates of Europe and Africa for the past one hundred and forty million years. Although the width of the actual rift valley along the Mid-Atlantic Ridge is small compared to the distance the continents have separated from each other, the chasm created by the movement of the plates is on the order of thousands of miles. As we all know, the separation between the continents on the east and west of the Mid-Atlantic Ridge is filled with a great volume of water, the Atlantic Ocean.

A similar geological fate is predicted for the African Rift Valley. Water from the Indian Ocean has already spilled into the northern portion of this gigantic crack to create the Red Sea. The geological forecast is that eventually, in a million years or so, the East African horn will break away from Africa and form a new continent. The Indian Ocean will then flood this new basin to create a new ocean between West Africa and East Africa.

So when I crawled into my tent that evening, my sleep was plagued with ambivalence. Would I awake in the morning to a crashing, swirling deluge, or as a vassal to the fire goddess Pele? Or, would tomorrow bring another beautiful sunny day?

* * *

By eight o'clock in the morning the oppressive heat and humidity returned. "Saunatized" was how I felt after dismantling my Lake Borogia campsite. Although the beautiful scenery abounded and the geothermal vents were spectacular, the wildlife in this desert paradise was limited to a flock of flamingos feeding just offshore. I wanted to see them fly, see their reddish ballet of flapping wings against the brilliant blue sky. But no matter how much I shouted, I couldn't frighten them into flight; no matter what I did, they knew they were protected by a wide moat of black, stinky, juicy mud. So I contented myself with watching as the weaver birds built their nests and Hildebrant's starlings chased insects through the grass. I got a real surprise by seeing a Kori bustard and three crowned cranes cross the road about a hundred feet from the safari truck. Mammals were not evident, even though the Lake Borogia area was supposed to be the haunt of the greater kudu. I didn't see one.

Our somewhat sweltering, languid demeanor when we departed Lake Borogia was rejuvenated by the breeze created from the movement of the safari truck. As soon as we cleared the Lake Borogia trough and rose to higher ground, the air around my body seemed to cool. Even though the temperature hovered about one hundred degrees Fahrenheit, the desert air was dryer. My perspiration soaked shirt became a comforting evaporator, but this was short lived due to the heat and lack of humidity.

Lake Baringo, the next stop on the itinerary, is only an hour's drive from Lake Borogia. This lake is not in one of the national parks, but a weekend resort, a get-a-way, where middle class Nairobians can escape their weekly drudgeries. A community of small cottages and shacks, similar to what can be seen around some lakes in northern Michigan or Wisconsin, are nestled randomly along the gradual slope toward the lake's western shore. On the southern edge of this haphazardly arranged hamlet, where the dusty main road enters, is the burg's center of activity, a strip mall. The dilapidated rectangular clay block structure, its dull white makeup streaked by seasons of heat, dust, spatter and rust, housed a general store supplied with only the bare necessities: a handcraft-souvenir boutique, a bait shop and boat rental whose interior was strewn with boxes and crates; and a café that doubled as the local saloon. All the cubicles had windows with open shutters, but no glass, and entryways with no apparent doors. Their interiors, minimally supplied with electricity, were dark and dingy.

When our safari troop arrived, we parked by the saloon-café and went inside for an opportunity to experience some local cuisine. Inside, the room had several table and chair setups. Each arrangement stood on a sheet of plywood laid on the dirt floor. A bar, with about four stools, was placed facing the window so that the bartender could also serve, through the open window, the clientele that hung about outside. Along the back wall, perpendicular to the bar, was a horizontal refrigerator where bottles of beer and soft drinks were stored. On the wall above the cooler hung a portrait of President Moi next to a poster advertising the movie *Out of Africa* featuring Robert Redford and Meryl Streep; a rusting Coke-a-Cola sign and a darkened Tusker Ale neon. To the right, just inside the door and next to a sink, hung a bench upon which sat a hot plate, several loaves of bread, containers of lettuce and vegetables, and a row of bottles containing various condiments.

I ordered the daily special, a sandwich of mystery meat generously covered with barbecue sauce, a bundle of sautéed carrots, and French fries. The meal arrived at the table from some hidden area; a clean kitchen, I hoped. I never found out from where the meal came, maybe through the door I had initially overlooked because my eyes hadn't totally accommodated to the interior darkness. When I finished eating, I requested directions to the restroom. The bartender pointed to a door located in a back corner of the saloon opposite the bar and beer cooler. It opened into a hallway. He directed me through the door and told me to follow the hallway. At its end I would find the *restroom.* On my trip down this lightless passage I thought I might pass the kitchen. I never did. But at the end of the hall, I came to another door that opened into an outside enclosure that contained a pit-type latrine.

The food that arrived from some unknown source, which I had eaten heartily, made my stomach momentarily, queasy. I did polish off two bottles of Tusker's Ale. This beer, I figured, would kill any parasites and pathogens I may have ingested with the meal. It must have, because I never became ill during the whole time I spent in Africa.

Except for the portion hidden behind Gibraltar Island, most of Lake Baringo could be seen from the level of the strip mall. The panorama was more open than at Lake Borogia. Set in a valley that sloped gradually toward a craggy cliff, the lake made a rather serene view, but its murky waters only hinted at the blueness of the sky. A dry idyllic vista stretched northward along the western shore beyond the community of cottages. The southern vista was dominated by a heavily vegetated marsh. Just beyond the marsh, mounds of what appeared to be ruddy-colored boulders dotted the scene. Gibraltar Island, a sparsely forested, rocky island about a half mile off the western shore, contained a camp ground for those who enjoy primitive living conditions, and the Goliath Heron sanctuary. Several motorized canoes scratched the surface, while a lone day-sailor slid across the wakes between the island and mainland.

I had just finished the last of the Tusker Beer that I ordered for lunch when a couple of local men I shared the table with asked if I cared to take a cruise around Gibraltar Island. They told me that they had access to a dugout canoe equipped with an outboard motor and for a few shillings they'd be happy to run me around the island to view the birds and photograph hippopotamuses and crocodiles. Their offer would, very definitely, provide me an opportunity to get some close-up pictures of the hippos. Such a rare chance I could not pass up, especially one that would get me nearer to the hippos, so I agreed.

Within a matter of minutes, I was seated in the motorized dugout, rough–hewn from a very large tree trunk, and ferried onto open water toward Gibraltar Island's rocky shoreline. We approached it from the west, swung around its northern point, and cruised parallel with its eastern shore. About half way down the island, standing vigilantly, were three Goliath herons. These are the largest heron species in the world, standing five feet tall from their toes to the top of their skull. The Goliath heron closely resembles the great-blue heron in its stature and behavior, but differs by having chestnut colored feathers on its chest, neck and head, and charcoal-colored ones covering the rest of its body. Just a short distance away an African fish eagle sat atop a dead tree trunk. Because of the white feathers on its head and anterior body, during flight it somewhat resembles the bald eagle. The African fish eagle was perched strategically near herons, so that if it had a chance, it could steal the heron's catch, a common behavior of the fish eagle.

After slowing to allow me to take several photographs, the driver continued along the island, turned after we passed the southern tip, and began to skirt about the turbid shallows near the marshlands. This was exciting because this was the area where I saw the brownish-colored boulders earlier from the landing at the saloon. Now I saw there were fewer, and they weren't boulders, but the gigantic heads of hippopotamuses. Slowly the driver approached one, told me to ready my camera, be prepared to take photographs, because as we come near the hippo will raise its head, gape its maw and release a terrifying bellow. Jokingly, he said, "If the jaws don't get ya, the bad breath will."

Hippopotamuses are purported to be the most dangerous animals in sub-Saharan Africa. They weigh over a ton and appear to be slow, placid and clumsy, but their ponderous bulk is deceptive. Hippos can readily walk underwater along the bottom of a lake and run rapidly on land. They are unpredictable, territorial, very protective of their offspring, and both the males and females are aggressive toward human beings. They defend themselves, or attack, open mouthed with their large canines exposed. When disturbed a hippo will rise-up rapidly from underwater and, if it happens to be under a small boat, it will overturn it. Most reports are of humans being bitten to death after they are dumped into the water. If the hippopotamus doesn't get the struggler, crocodiles will.

I didn't know how dangerous hippopotamuses were, nor did I even think about it when I hired the guys to take me on Lake Baringo to photograph these beasts. When we were getting underway, the boat operator even assured me that the crocodiles and hippopotamuses in this lake were docile and didn't bother tourists. "They see humans all the time," he said, "so they're familiar with their antics in the lake." Even though hippos weigh over a ton, I felt secure with what he said and never gave it much thought. Until, to provide me with more photographic opportunities, the driver slowed the dugout or brought it to a complete stop and revved the outboard motor several times. The noise from this activity is loud on the surface but greatly amplified underwater especially when the sound waves reverberate off the hippo's large body. This must make them madder'n hell, because every time the driver made a series of revs the surface of the lake around or near the boat would mound and explode in froth and flying spume. A large, disturbed brownish mass mushroomed forth near the dugout, water pouring from a glistening mauve-colored entrance to a cavern armed with a pair of eight-inch long scuzzy, cream-colored canines. I had to cover my camera several times to keep it from getting splashed. The bottom of the lake must have been covered with hippos, because these creatures were popping up all around the canoe. To make matters worse this disturbance fired the curiosity of the large crocodiles lazying along the reeds. They began slipping into the lake and gliding toward us. I was in the midst of playing Russian roulette with Mother Nature's Goliaths. Any moment our canoe could be slung skyward. Momentarily, I visualized myself thrashing about, gulping lake water, while trying to fend off a behemoth or a set of leather trimmed jaws. Even so, in those few minutes, I took many exciting pictures, but my confidence began to waver and my anxiety surged. I quickly let my companions know that I had taken a sufficient number of pictures and wanted to return to shore. They happily obliged.

* * *

The next stop on the itinerary was Lake Nakuru, a spectacular soda lake located near the western escarpment of the African Rift Valley. This is the lake where millions of greater and lesser flamingos feed in the shallows and where filmmakers photograph gigantic flocks of flying flamingos. In fact, the scene in the movie Out of

Africa, in which Robert Redford attempts to show Meryl Streep the wonders of flight by flying over some magnificent sights and above several flocks of flying flamingos, was shot at Lake Nakuru. The flamingos, and their protection, are why Kenya, early on, made Lake Nakuru a National Park.

We arrived late in the day and had only about an hour of sunlight in which to pitch our tents. The campsite, located in a darkened forest of large trees, had an ambience that differed from that I had experienced in the past two days. Although it had not rained recently, the air was cool and humid and scented with a subtle, musty, earthy odor. The soil in this forest, black, damp and soft, was also unlike any I had previously encountered on this trip. It was as if I were bedding down in a waterless swamp.

I quickly set up my tent, placed my gear inside, and laced the door flaps closed before gathering with the group around the campfire for dinner. Earlier our driver had warned us not to leave any shining objects exposed and to secure the entrances to the tents. He explained at dinner that the campsite was infested with hordes of black-faced vervet monkeys. These are curious creatures that will rummage through backpacks, suitcases, and other human belongings and take whatever is edible or attractive. They are not usually active after dark, he told us, but it is best to keep our possessions contained and secured. When I crawled into my tent, I had an eerie feeling that hundreds of eyes were peering at me from the surrounding darkness.

Screams and shrieks mixed with the calls of birds awoke me about six o'clock the next the morning. When I parted the tent flaps to see and identify the commotion, I was greeted by a riot of monkeys running helter-skelter around the campsite, chasing each other, and being chased by the driver and cook. There were monkeys everywhere, a few somewhat staid adults, but mostly little hellions of various sizes. It was apparent the latter had successfully entered the safari truck and penetrated the food supply, because they were running about carrying eggs, bottles of ketchup, bananas, bread loaves, spoons, knives and forks, the cook's ladle, and a red handkerchief. As soon as one had an opportunity to stop, he attempted to eat whatever he carried. But the periods of rest could be measured in micro-seconds, because if the driver or cook got near enough, the monkey would get whacked with a broom; but most often the thieves encountered their own kind, who were determined, amid a tangle of screeches and growls, to wrestle the prize from its possessor. If their prize was not edible, they dashed up a tree to flaunt their booty, hide it, or throw it at a rival or a human. When thwarted and treed by one of the humans, the monkeys quickly wreaked vengeance by defecating into one of their hands and hurling the fecal grenade at their attacker. This behavior and the sheer numbers of monkeys in the area explained the prominent stench that permeated the campground.

I quickly found myself involved when a couple of primate hoodlums approached my tent. Seems they were interested in my tube of toothpaste. Immediately I scrambled out of the tent and laid a stomping, hollering, arm-flailing chase in an attempt to discourage them. I realized that my strategy failed because, although they initially ran, the little pests turned toward me, shrieking, brandishing their teeth, menacingly swinging their arms, and began to approach. These little devils can inflict nasty bites and scratches, and are possible harbingers of the dreaded AIDS virus. They also knew I didn't have a weapon. But their strategy wasn't to attack or inflict pain, but to seize and hold my attention so their buddies could rally a flank assault and ransack my tent. This almost worked, but the cook foiled their attempts with the broom. The troop then quickly lost interest in my possessions when they were attracted by noise and activity that erupted near the campfire.

Several campers stood near the driver while he threw opened, partially empty ketchup bottles toward the monkeys. The vervets grabbed them and tried to extract the remaining ketchup from inside by running an index finger through the narrow opening. But the possessors were constantly under attack by those without, so there was little time to consider an effective strategy to extract the delectable contents that taunted them by sticking the tip of a finger into the bottle. In an attempt at expediency, they'd drive in several fingers simultaneously only to get them stuck. Now they ran about shrieking, screaming, and waving the bottle in the air as if attempting to rid themselves of some clinging parasite. And during this melee, they were, of course, being chased by the hordes that also wanted the secret stuff in the bottle. After a few laps around the campground, the one stuck with the bottle would do a couple of somersaults and start to hammer the bottle against the ground in an attempt to free his fingers. It's amazing how strong a glass ketchup bottle is, because none broke during the violent pounding. When the possessor stopped to rid himself of the bottle, he'd immediately be fallen upon by the pursuers. The encounter created a momentary fur flying, spinning, twisting, churning skirmish. Miraculously, from this rumpus emerged a winner brandishing the ketchup bottle by its neck and waving it like a victorious club while he scurried up a tree.

The tree branches provide a bit more peace, so a vervet with a bottle had time to try all sorts of tricks to access the remaining ketchup, which by this time was stuck to the inner sides of the bottle. I even saw one monkey attempt to insert his toe through the opening, but to no avail. There was no way a monkey could retrieve the remaining dregs from a near empty bottle. Frustrated, one of the monkeys heaved a bottle toward the campers.

Because of the monkey madness at the campsite, we decided to delay breakfast until after a short game drive. We broke camp and loaded the safari truck while the monkeys were distracted by the park rangers. We drove out of the forest and into a large verdant meadow where herds of waterbucks and topis grazed. Eventually, the road ran parallel to Lake Nakuru. I could see the multitudes of the lesser and greater flamingos that made this park so notable feeding along the shoreline. Overhead flew flocks of white pelicans and pink-backed pelicans, and occasionally I'd see an African darter, the African relative of American anhingas, perched on a shrub branch drying its wings.

I wondered about the presence of these fish-eating birds around Lake Nakuru, since soda lakes are not usually inhabited by fish populations large enough to support birds. The driver clarified my question. He mentioned that some year ago a tilapia fish species was introduced into the lake to control algal growth. This fish quickly became established. Its high rate of fecundity produced massive numbers of juveniles to attract and maintain these birds.

The road terminated at an overlook atop a high precipice called Baboon Cliff. Here we had our breakfast and the only creatures that came to visit were the docile but curious rock hyraxes. These inquisitive rodent-like mammals about the size of a rabbit are, because of the shape of their teeth and the skeletal structure of their feet, allegedly related to elephants rather than rodents. While I sat on a boulder at the cliff's edge eating toast and drinking tea, several emerged from surrounding crevices and just sat there and watched my every move. When I offered a bit of toast, they turned and wandered off.

Baboon Cliff is several hundred meters above Lake Nakuru and part of the western escarpment of the African Rift Valley. One can almost see the entire lake from the summit and get an idea of the immense numbers of flamingos using it as a refuge. The perspective from top of Baboon Cliff appears as if the lake's entire shoreline were highlighted in strawberry foam. The view is indeed the capstone of this national park. My only regret is that I never had the good fortune to see a large flock of flamingos in flight.

CAMPING IN THE MASAI MARA

As if someone slowly lowered a dimmer switch, the orangish brightness across the Masai Mara National Park darkened to red when the sun descended below a far-off rise. I watched the plains relax, cool. A lone acacia tree on the distant ridge, lost during daytime in the golden intensity of the expansive shimmering grassland, appeared amplified. Its emaciated mushroom shape silhouetted against the fiery horizon. On the Mara, night closes fast as it does everywhere near the equator. The glow along the horizon quickly extinguishes. Now only the campfire, around which Sammy manipulated a couple of skillets and pots with a coal shovel, illuminated the area.

Sammy was our cook, employed by Gametrackers Limited, the tour agency with whom I booked this adventure. He was a handsome Kikuyu man in his thirties, about six feet tall, well built, with soft facial features and a very friendly, happy personality. He interacted little with the tourists, but a greeting or an attempt to involve him in a discussion or a question asked of him resulted in a nod and a shy smile. Even though he seemed to understand English, he was not able to communicate in the language. Occasionally he did attempt to utter some simple English words, but he spoke mainly Kiswahili. Sammy's inability with my tongue gave me a perfect opportunity to refine my conversational skill in Kiswahili. Therefore, I developed a friendly rapport with him. By the end of the trip, between a mix of his bad English and my bastardized Kiswahili, we were able to understand each other. However, it took Ben, our safari driver and guide, to translate the more complex messages to and from Sammy.

In contrast to Sammy, Ben, in his forties was short, about five and a half feet tall, with a slight build and an aloof, in charge, business-like personality. Although he didn't mix with the group, he was cooperative and in tune with our needs and desires. His skill was off-road driving across the unmarked range of grass and scrub, over potholes, furrows, hummocks, and down stream beds at speeds sometimes reaching fifty miles per hour. His driving was impressive, but, bouncing over the many obstacles, I found that the little pads protecting our buttocks from the solid parts of the seat were too thin.

Ben also had a special knack for spotting game. His sense of reading natural clues that animals leave when they pass through or occupy an area was fantastic. It provided us special opportunities to view not only the common animals, but also rare ones. On one game drive he alerted us to the potential nearness of a rhinoceros. Before any of us could react, Ben spotted the rhino's horn moving through the grass about one hundred yards away. Hemingway, in *Green Hills of Africa,* wrote that his guides also had this uncanny knack of finding and tracking game. Ben seemed to be a chip from that block of guides, game trackers, hunters, and businessmen. His personality matched all traits. He also spoke fluent English, French, German and Kiswahili.

Besides Sammy and Ben, eight of us started the safari in Nairobi. Two days later in the town of Narok along the road to the Masai Mara National Park, two others joined the trip. The majority of these tourists were actually living in East Africa and on holiday exploring the countryside. Allison, a young woman in her mid-twenties who taught in a private school in Nairobi, was on the trip with her parents Stan and Muriel. They were from Yorkshire, England. Anne, another teacher, but in Nairobi's public school system, shared the safari experience with her brother Michael, an upper crust sort of fellow who spoke like the Roger Moore version of James Bond. He had recently graduated from The University of London and was attempting to tour the world before settling down to work for the rest of his life. He had stopped off in Nairobi to live a short time with his sister. A couple of twenty-some-year-olds, spirited teachers from Somalia traveling together, supplied the trip with jollity. Wendy, a rugged, cargo pant-combat boot outdoorsy-type who looked as if she'd be a threat to Paul Bunyan, and Ilene, a bright-eyed, cute scullery maiden who spoke with a strong cockney brogue, entertained us with complex word games and comical, bawdy English jokes and stories. Their quest on this visit to Kenya was to live as inexpensively as possible. The couple who joined the safari on the third day were American Peace Corps volunteers. Joan and Steve worked somewhere in the Mt. Kenya area. Joan was a tall, quiet, lithe woman who enjoyed photography. Sammy found her vegetarianism troublesome because of the scarcity of vegetables. Joan survived on potatoes, rice, cauliflower and squash during the four days she was with us. Steve, on the other hand, ate everything, and in abundance. His inconsideration and lack of social graces aggravated the entire group. His excuse for being on this safari, and literally for being in Kenya, was Joan. The two were an item. So Muriel, Stan, Michael and I were the only nonresidents in this motley, but very interesting and congenial crew.

After a day of traveling across the bush chasing game, eating dust and burning in the heat, the campfire atmosphere was very welcome and relaxing. Since attempting to update my journal in this subdued light was difficult, I took the time before dinner to kick back, listen to the crackle of burning wood, and daydream. But from somewhere out in the dark emerged the specter of grass being rhythmically crushed. This, of course, throttled any euphoric musings. "Not to worry," I told myself, because also standing near the campfire were three tall, very lean Masai men wearing red togas and nylon warmup jackets; on one I recognized a Chicago Cubs logo. In this century the jackets replaced the lion skins that were once thrown over the shoulders to shield against a night's chill.

These Masai warriors were hired to guard our camp against the attack of wild beasts. Each held a spear with a very sharp metal head in one hand and brandished a menacing-looking club in the other. Though these weapons appeared crude and prehistoric, they were deadly. I tested the sharpness of one of the spearheads, and there's no doubt that I could have shaved with it. The clubs had a knob on one end that could pulverize a brain. And, of course, Sammy had his shovel. I felt confident that the invisible creatures roaming near our camp recognized the same guards that have for centuries repelled predatory efforts on their cattle and knew not to reckon with these men. So I returned to enjoying the campfire and disregarded the unknowns that lurked in the dark.

I wonder if Hemingway was ever bothered by night sounds and unseen events occurring around his camp. Probably not! I'm sure he had within easy reach his Springfield and Mannlicher rifles designed to bring down elephants, rhinos and buffaloes at several hundred yards. The Nikon that lay next to me would stop a charging beast-of-the-jungle, but only virtually.

An interesting characteristic of our Masai guards was their ears. Their earlobes, which had been elongated and contained a large hole, formed a fleshy ring that hung below their ear, and on some, midway down their neck. To achieve this curious deformation, the Masai puncture the earlobes of a child early in its life. As the child grows, the lobes are continually stretched and the hole is enlarged, by placing larger and larger objects into the opening. The fellows guarding us explained this traditional disfigurement and demonstrated one of its practicalities. When Masai encountered a dust storm during a trek across a desert, they fold the earlobes over the upper half of the ears, secure them behind the ears' upper margin effectively closing off the auditory canals to keep out the dust. I watched the tallest of the three flip and unflip his earlobe over the top of his ear as if it were a rubber band - how fascinating, yet how unnatural.

Both the Masai and some Kikuyu enlarge their earlobes mainly for ornamental purposes. Early European settlers in East Africa found this to be a disgusting practice, but in some instances it was handy. Some occasionally tied their native workers to a horse by passing a length of rope through the hole in the worker's earlobe, and then tying it to a ring on the saddle as a punishment for shirking responsibilities or not doing their jobs properly. The settler would mount the horse and canter about the range with the poor worker running behind to keep his ear from being wrenched from his head. In other situations slavers used to tie their captives together, in order to transport them, by passing a rope through their earlobe holes and tying the ends to staffs held by guards. This insured that the slaves, their hands tied behind their backs, marched together in a line. Arrogant, superior-minded humans, in self-righteous situations, always find a way to use abnormality, difference, and frailty as tools to justify savagery.

One of our group asked why the Coleman lanterns placed on the camp tables couldn't be ignited while Sammy was cooking. Sammy quickly became animated, turned toward us and chattered a response in his native tongue. Although it appeared that Sammy understood what was asked, we had no idea what he said until Ben translated his message. According to Ben, what Sammy tried to tell us was that "unlike the glow from a campfire, the light from the lanterns attracted mosquitoes." I think Ben agreed with Sammy's response, because he did not want the lamps lighted. So we continued to sit in the flickering ring between the light and the dark while Ben expounded on the behavioral activity of the Masai Mara mosquito population. He tried to convince us that mosquitoes most actively search for their prey during the early evening and for several hours after dark.

"At this time the mosquitoes are in greatest abundance" he said. "And the intense white light from the lanterns attracts them."

Although Ben was a good guide and game spotter, he was not a biologist. Scientifically, his rationale for keeping the Coleman lanterns dark doesn't hold water. Mosquitoes are not attracted to light, but to body odors, sweat and carbon dioxide. With the small amount of water available to us, no one had taken a shower in the last four days. So our troupe was a prime target for mosquitoes. Our distinctive *bouquet d'homme* should have enticed swarms of these pesky hummers, but didn't. This was one of the benefits of going on a safari during the dry season. Mosquitoes are sparse during this time of the year in the Masai Mara.

Coleman lanterns were definitely a distraction. They were not really a part of the ambiance of a safari camp like campfires and kerosene lanterns. A Coleman lantern's continued hissing while the fuel vaporizes into the mantel, and the stark, blinding white light it emits, produced anxiety rather than tranquility. I'm sure that somewhere during their training to become safari leaders, Sammy and Ben received instructions to minimize the use of artificial illumination. They were probably told to give tenderfoot safari-tourists a chance to experience the raw atmosphere of night on the African veldt illuminated in the serenity of glowing, flickering embers.

I enjoyed sitting in front of the fire, its heat warming my face and the night cooling my back. A perfect milieu before dinner in which to reflect, ponder, and meditate on the intensities I experienced during the day. And never once, was I bitten by a mosquito.

Perhaps Sammy enjoyed cooking by the light of the campfire. He may have needed a warm, calm atmosphere to prepare his evening's *chef d'oeuvre.* He was extremely skilled at cooking on an open fire. Using the coal shovel, he divided the margin of the campfire into several pyres. The brightness of the embers suggested the degree of heat contained in each pile. Upon little mounds of hot coals he placed the pots, pans, and skillets that contained the fixings for the evening meal. During the process of cooking Sammy shifted, exchanged, added to, and stirred the various mixtures with his paddle. Periodically he removed one of the pots from a pyre and exchanged the embers for hotter ones from the campfire. Or, he surrounded the pot containing water for tea or instant coffee with more hot coals; he, in fact, almost buried it. He mentioned to me that these maneuvers maintain the food at proper cooking or heating temperature. In between his activities around the campfire, he made salads, chopped additional vegetables, or kneaded and arranged bread dough on a board.

Sammy also baked in the field. He had a camp oven: a metal box of about two cubic feet with the interior divided into two chambers, an upper and lower. Into these chambers he placed the dough, closed the oven door, passed a metal rod through the ring on the top of the oven and - with someone's help, like mine on several occasions - lifted and placed the oven in the center of the campfire to bake what it contained. To remove the oven from the campfire the same procedure was followed, but in reverse. Timing the bake interval appeared crucial, because Sammy had no idea of the temperature within the oven, nor did he have a means to measure it. He baked often. The oven seemed to always be in the middle of the campfire. His ability to time the baking process seemed intuitive because the breads were always properly done. The crusts were never burned nor were the centers doughy. We always had bread, although it may have been a day or two old. Biscuits were usually available for breakfast as were sandwich buns for lunch.

Our dinners were simple, mostly stews and casseroles, fresh or steamed vegetables, and occasionally some sort of meat supplied protein to the concoctions. Near the end of the trip our dinners included grilled goat or pork chops. Potatoes, brown rice, couscous, lentils and English peas were staples. Early in the trip lunches of green salads laced with carrots, tomatoes, and cauliflower were standard fare, but in the heat of the Rift Valley fresh vegetables deteriorated rapidly. Eggs, fried ham, cereals and papaw slices (African Papaya), constituted a breakfast. Hot water for tea or instant coffee was always available.

When Sammy completed cooking in the evening and arranged the food on a camp table, Ben lighted the Coleman lanterns. This was our signal to partake of the buffet-style repast.

After dinner, with more intense illumination from the Coleman lantern, I was able to record the day's events in my journal. We all told stories or Wendy and Ilene involved the group in word games.

One such word game required the participants, given a bunch of supposed unrelated clues, to determine what the individual in question desired. For instance, given a young lady from Mississippi who chose meetings but not gatherings, strawberries but not grapes, carrots but not celery, cottages but not houses, the player would be asked to describe what the lady liked. Comparing the lady's likes and dislikes, one can determine that she liked anything that had double letters in its name.

Sometimes Stan told us about his work as a joiner. In America he'd be called a carpenter. Mike described the kinds of birds and wildlife that he saw while sipping tea in the backyard of Anne's house. Her house was a rental in the Karen section of Nairobi. She mentioned that her house was near Nairobi National Park. In fact, she said that the park boundary was about one hundred yards away, across an open field of scrub. Since there wasn't much of a fence, animals wandered into the field, and sometimes directly into her back yard. So her back porch was a great place to watch birds and game animals. From their discussions I surmised that Mike was enjoying his visit with Anne. I never did learn how long he'd been in Nairobi or how long he planned to stay.

Satiated Steve and emaciated Joan usually retired to their tent shortly after dinner. Within an hour or so, we all were laced into our sleeping bags. The first game drive of the day started about six o'clock in the morning. I'm sure everyone was tired, and not just from the strenuousness of the trip, but from not getting good nights of rest. During the entire trip, I never heard anyone say they enjoyed sleeping on the ground. I know I didn't.

When I tried to sleep in the wilds of Kenya, completely enclosed in the tenuous safety of a tent, I was plagued with anxiety and excitement as well. There are unknown things that snoop about just beyond the tent's walls. The cacophony of sounds, snorting, sniffing, grunting, yelping, roaring, scratching that goes on throughout the night is not conducive to restful sleep.

Lions are known to approach quite near the campsite. They prowl among the low shrubby trees that grow about two hundred feet from our circle of tents. Thoughts of their probable nearness plagued my mind throughout the night. My apprehension was reinforced by periodic roars. Add to these bawls the hyenas' flighty laughter as they sneaked about sniffing around the tents, my anxieties approached urgency. So I rolled deeper into the sleeping bag only to feel some strange little creature crawling beneath the tent floor and under the area where I lay. This was especially disconcerting when I realized its length felt several times longer than its width. I closed my eyes and resorted to counting sheep, trying to delude myself into thinking that if lions could perceive my thoughts, they might chase the sheep. Eventually, I fell into an apprehensive slumber only to have discomposing dreams harass my psyche.

Mornings are more euphonious. They start before the sky brightens. A symphony of quiet, melodious chirps begins around four o'clock; those of the crickets and other vocal nocturnal insects have ended. Just before dawn, the distant moans of lions become softer, more rhythmic. The strange "yok, yok, yok" of a red-billed hornbill determines the cadence of the dawning melody. I unlaced the flaps of the tent, looked in the direction of the campfire and saw three tall, thin legged, spear wielding silhouettes standing next to a pile of glowing embers. I'm sure they had remained alert all night, because nothing appeared to be disturbed. As the daylight poured from the crack along the horizon, a crescendo of bird songs, antelope bellows, baboon chatter, and the distant trumpeting of elephants filled the emerging day.

At this time of day the air is cool, a slight amount of humidity enhances the "uriny" odor that rises from the great herds roaming the distant grasslands. I crawled out of the tent, then stood, stretched and watched the dynamic birth of a new day. The sky brightened from a stark blue-black. It passed through pastel hues of reds and blues which became diluted by shades of bronze, beige, and gold as day's onset progressed. Thin white clouds on the horizon fractured the embellished sky into beams that radiated upward from the horizon, then outward until the heavens saturated into intense blues of the day as the sun cleared the horizon.

I sighed, yawned and wished for a cup of warm tea, but there was not enough time. Our first game drive would leave in ten minutes and I had to prepare myself for the day through a series of repetitious morning behaviors. This was not easy, since there was no clean toilet in which to relieve myself, nor water for a shower and very little for brushing teeth.

One of the difficulties of a camping safari in Kenya is dealing with the primitiveness of the camp's "facilities." bathroom, lavatory, water closet, or whatever one may call it. Ground troops called theirs a latrine, but ours wasn't a trench like the ones used by the military. Instead, it was more or less a circular meter-sized hole in the ground placed about fifty feet away from the camp in a stand of scrub bushes. In an attempt to provide some privacy, the hole was surrounded by a dilapidated bamboo fence. Both males and females use the same facility, except that the females usually asked one of the Masai guards to escort them to the facility and stand guard outside. Since the latrine was hidden from the campground and situated in the brush, there existed a definite potential for encountering wild beasts.

After returning from the latrine, I poured a cup of water from the tank hanging from the game truck, pushed a dab of toothpaste onto the brush, brushed it over my teeth, and tried to completely rinse my mouth with one gulp. This didn't work very well. My mouth remained mint flavored until after breakfast. I poured the rest of the water from the cup into my hands, rubbed it onto my face and into my hair. My main objective was to arrange my chaotic collection of cowlicks into a less electrified appearing coiffure.

Perhaps I've given the impression that water doesn't exist near the campground. It did, however. A stream, where the Masai's cattle and some wild beasts go to drink, flowed along one edge of the campsite. If one disregards the possibility of encountering snakes, crocodiles, angry hippopotamuses, or a lone lion, the stream could be used to wash the hands. But, freshwater streams and ponds almost everywhere in Africa contain even more dangerous, less apparent critters. Many are infested with the larvae of schistosome parasites. These microscopic larvae of flatworms, upon contact with a host's skin, quickly burrow in and move into the circulatory system where they take up residence, mature to adults and feed on many of the blood's savory products, stuff the host needs to survive. These flatworms cause the very debilitating disease known as schistosomiasis or bilharzia. And they are not the only pathogens found in fresh waters of Africa. There are others, so washing or bathing in a stream is never recommended.

* * *

Ben started the engine on the safari truck. Sammy rejuvenated last night's campfire. Binoculars and camera were strung around my neck. With a game identification book, a personal journal, and some telephoto lenses stuffed into my photographer's vest, I climbed into the passengers' seat next to Ben. Seat selection on the truck was on a first come basis. Four bench-like seats were arranged across the truck's bed and there were two seats in the cab. The best positions for viewing were the seats along the sides of the bed and the passenger seat. The latter offered the least visual restriction and was thickly cushioned, making it also the most comfortable seat. The passenger seat, normally occupied by Sammy, had an almost 360 degree field of view and for photography; it was the best seat in the vehicle. Other members of the safari didn't object to my choice of seating, when I explained that I had more than just a passing fancy to photograph the wildlife. Also they may have taken pity on me because I was the only solitary member on this tour. I didn't always take the best seat in the house, however; on the Masai Mara portion of the trip, there were three game drives scheduled per day. This allowed plenty of opportunity to exchange seating arrangements; however, for the most part, the others wanted to sit with their partners. Those who were not particularly interested in taking in the sights - only along for the ride - took the seats in the middle. As it turned out, all the seats in the safari truck were acceptable for observing the animals.

With all aboard, Ben slipped the shift lever into drive and we bounced out of the circle of tents and onto the dirt road that lead into Masai Mara National Park. At the entrance, a couple of park rangers dressed in spiffy military green uniforms, each with a World War I vintage Enfield rifle slung over his shoulder, issued Ben a one day visitor's pass. After Ben pressed several shillings into the palm of the closest guard, they greeted us warmly and waved us on.

* * *

Travel brochures claim that the Masai Mara National Park is Kenya's best. Its abundant wildlife, ranging over the rolling fields of grass, thickets, and groves of trees, is accessible for easy viewing by visitors. The park is located along Kenya's border with Tanzania and comprises the northern expanse of the Serengeti Plain. Therefore, it's not a surprise that the Masai Mara contains the greatest diversity of free living herbivorous animals, and their associated predators, in the world. And it's all within less than 0.3 percent of Kenya's total landmass, an area of six hundred and seventy square miles. Since the animals don't recognize political borders, they can freely roam, unimpeded over roughly eight thousand square miles of grassland composed of the Masai Mara, Serengeti, and Lolita Hills, a geographic region about the size of the State of Massachusetts.

The grasslands of the Masai Mara are the focus of one of the most prominent large animal migrations. Vivid films of the great wildebeest migration have been produced by such well known documenting agencies as The National Geographic Society, Discovery Channel, National Wildlife Society, and the British Broadcasting Company to inform the world of this spectacular natural event. I was recently thrilled by the event when I viewed the IMAX film titled, *Africa, The Serengeti.*

I did not see the wildebeest migrate during my visit to the Masai Mara. I was there in April. The wildebeests migrate in June.

Nevertheless these animals were where they were supposed to be. Their presence dominated the Masai Mara landscape.

When the migration begins, the hundreds of thousands grazing on the vegetation in the Masai Mara coalesce and begin their trek toward the lush grasses of the southern Serengeti, a trip of about 600 miles. This southern migration is very difficult because the females are carrying calves and en route they will encounter the Mara River, their most severe obstacle.

This river flows southwestward toward Lake Victoria and essentially cuts across the Masai Mara and Serengeti Plains. During the rainy season, which, in the northern Serengeti (the grasslands of Masai Mara and Loita Hills) occurs in May-June, the river rises to flood stage.

The wildebeests need to cross the Mara River to get to their destination. During the crossing they will encounter deep, fast flowing, tumultuous waters, the possibility of being ambushed by crocodiles, and a ten to fourteen-foot climb up a sheer mud-slippery cliff that forms the southern bank of the Mara River. When thousands of anxious individuals swim en masse across this raging river and funnel into stampeding files at the few points of egress, many slip and fall become overwhelmed and get trampled or drowned if they first do not get mauled by crocodiles. Loss of life at this first barrier is tremendous. Roughly twenty percent of the migrating population does not clear this first hurdle.

Once the wildebeests reach the southern Serengeti they give birth to their calves. There are more than enough offspring to replace those lost at the Mara River obstacle. The animals feed on the grasses and the young grow. When the grass supply diminishes around November, the herds again migrate north, back to the Masai Mara and Lolita Hills. Again they cross the Mara River, but this time the crossing is made during low water levels and not totally en masse. Once they reach the northern range, the herds disperse and individuals cross the river at a more leisurely pace.

Standing on the north bank of the Mara River at one of the crossing sites I felt empathy for the wildebeests' instinct-driven plight and sorrow for the many that would never make it to the calving grounds. When I scanned across the river during my visit in April, the flow was barely noticeable and disturbed only by the activity of a couple of hippopotamuses. Several crocodiles lay sunning on exposed sandbars and downstream, in the vegetation along the shoreline. The north shore declined gradually to the water's edge, while across from me rose a vertical cliff breached in several places by erosional forces and the hooves of millions of wildebeests from past migrations. In about a month eager and excited wildebeests will again be trying to climb these eroded crevices to clear their first obstacle. If I were to climb the twelve to fourteen feet through one of these clefts to reach the top of the bank, I would need the assistance of a rope because the angle of the climb is nearly vertical. And, I'm viewing the problem during the dry season! When the rains come and the wildebeests need to climb, the mud will make these rifts so slippery that even a rope, to aid the climb, would be of little value.

* * *

Ben slowed the safari truck as it passed over the rise about a half-mile from the preserve entrance. In front and to the right a vast dale opened. It seemed to extend for miles. He continued to follow the road along the slope, as it progressed parallel to the valley, about a half-mile above a dry streambed. This vantage provided an unlimited vista of massive herds of wildebeests, zebras, little Thompson's gazelles, impalas and African buffalos. He stopped the vehicle, switched it into four-wheel drive, and then, at slow speed, turned off the road and continued through the grass obliquely down the slope toward the streambed. In a short distance we came upon a small herd of Thompson's gazelles. The natives call these cute little antelopes - they're only about thirty inches high at the shoulder - "Tommies." I could almost pack one into my backpack and take it home as a pet. First I'd have to chase and catch it. This would be impossible, since they are so swift. For their survival they have to be able to outrun a pursuing cheetah or leopard.

We passed within about twenty feet of the Tommies. They didn't seem to be frightened, but they did stop feeding to look us over. Not so for a herd of about twenty impalas. As the truck approached, the herd broke into a synchronous series of vaults that rapidly took them about one hundred yards away from us. Their ballet-like leaps seemed to keep them airborne for several seconds at a height of almost ten feet. The span they covered in a single leap was nominal by impala standards, but would set a world record for a broad jump that a human could never break. They stopped and stared back at us. These are very sleek, streamlined antelopes, with the males wearing a pair of striking ebony-colored horns that are widely spaced and lyre-shaped.

On all sides were enormous herds of mixed antelopes. Drab gray-colored wildebeests grunted unconcerned and continued to feed when we passed. With so many thousands around, their murmur filled the valley. Interspersed among the wildebeests were small groups of zebras. These black and white striped horse- or mule-like animals seemed to always be in linear groups of four or five individuals standing side by side and arranged fore-and-aft to each other so they could be vigilant in both directions. I found that two species live in the Masai Mara. The common zebra, which has few, wide black and white stripes, and Grevy's zebra, with many narrow sets of stripes. Ben told me that Grevy's zebras also have larger ears. That, in fact, made it easier to distinguish the two zebra species that commonly associate with each other.

Four other fawn- to roan-colored antelopes added more diversity to the immense herds. The roan-colored Jackson's hartebeest is larger than its related fawn-colored subspecies, Coke's Hartebeest. Both are uniformly colored. Coke's is also called a "kongoni," a name I associate with the hunting trips Hemingway described in *Green Hills of Africa*. He or his crew normally shot a kongoni for dinner. When the animal was dressed, Hemingway had the kidneys set aside so they could be fried for his breakfast the following morning. (I tried both kongoni steaks and kidneys at the Carnivore Restaurant in Nairobi. The steaks are tender and fantastic, but I didn't acquire a taste for kidney.)

* * *

I also observed one other hartebeest, Hunter's hartebeest. This is a species distinctly different from the other two. It is slightly smaller than the kongoni, fawn-colored, but with a white chevron across its forehead. This species is the more uncommon hartebeest. The easiest to single-out in the herd are the topis. These are medium sized, copper-colored hartebeest-like antelopes with blackish patches down the upper parts of their limbs and along the nasal portion of the face just below the eyes. Topis are gregarious so tend to occur in large numbers. On one of the game runs I was able to photograph an eland, the largest of the African antelopes. The eland is robust, a faded roan-color, has spiral horns, and a distinct dewlap that hangs under the neck. Elands are solitary and not routinely seen.

We came to the bottom of the valley, crossed the dry stream bed and went up the opposite slope. Ben rounded an edge of a copse of tangled leafless shrubs, vines and acacia trees. In a cove of this thicket, hidden from the stream, stood a herd of African buffalo. These massive black bovine critters have a pair of imposing horns that begin in the middle of the forehead as robust bases that spread sideways to the edges of the skull, then extend outward, tapering into a wide upward curve to terminate in a pointed apex. The entire group of these formidable creatures stopped feeding to stare when we slowed to photograph them. "Males are very protective of their harem," Ben said.

"And, they've been known to overturn a van if their charge is successful." He pointed to an individual, slightly hidden by the brush, that appeared to be a head taller than the others. "The male. He's becoming agitated." We proceeded up the slope away from him.

In amongst the grasses and in between the legs of the buffalos frolicked a flock of cattle egrets. These are the same whitish, heron-like birds that are seen all over the world in warm climates feeding on insects disturbed from their lairs by the movement of large herbivorous animals. Up to this time I didn't realize the ubiquitous distribution of this bird. It's as common in the fields of south Alabama as it is here on the plains of Kenya.

One of the perks while driving across the open range is the opportunity to see African birds. For an ardent birdwatcher like myself, the Masai Mara is a paradise of species about which most ornithologists only read. As we drove through the grass, we flushed many of the species typical of the African grasslands. Most spectacular was the male long-tailed widow bird. Their luxuriant tails were often more than two feet long. Because of these long curling tail feathers, the males had difficulty flying. As we proceeded across the plain, we observed the long-tailed males, from fifty to a hundred yards in front of the truck, as they flew straight up about six to ten feet above the ground and dropped back into the grass.

Four species of widow birds inhabit the Masai Mara, the long-tailed, the red-collared, Jackson's, and the white-winged. Except for the latter, whose tail is only slightly longer than that of other species of birds inhabiting the grasslands, identification of the different widow bird species can be made by comparing the lengths of the tail feathers of the males. I have yet to see a white-winged widow bird.

I used my binoculars to identify tawny and long-crested eagles perched high in the branches of dead trees. The game truck flushed guinea fowl, secretary birds, sand grouse, and several other species of ground-living birds that rarely fly, from their grass cover. We had a clear view of them as they ran onto the road or into clearings.

Ostriches, the largest of the flightless birds, were easy to see, but difficult to photograph without a high-powered telephoto lens. They were extremely wary and ran as soon as the truck came into view.

The most brightly colored birds I observed were the barbets, red-crested cuckoos, and lilac-breasted rollers. In one clearing a mixed flock of blue-eared starlings and superb starlings were feeding. I am sure that if any of these species of starlings had been accidentally introduced into North America, we'd probably have accorded them more worth than their inelegant relative that found its way across the Atlantic Ocean. The African starlings are splendid, colorful birds.

Two reticulated giraffes stripped leaves from a lone acacia tree growing on the slope. These stately animals are at least seventeen to eighteen feet in height. There appeared to be room enough to drive the safari truck beneath them without touching their belly. They were docile and curious, so we were able to drive rather close to them. In spite of their long legs they were quite agile, but appeared ungainly when they lumbered off at a gallop. Giraffes are widespread in the Masai Mara National Park and are seen in most open areas away from cities and towns. We observed them to occur as solitary individuals or in groups of two to five. We did get a rare and spectacular glimpse of a line of sixteen giraffes galloping across a range in the Rift Valley.

On some of our game drives we came upon several solitary elephants feeding. But most impressive was a herd of twelve that included a single male with a very long pair of tusks, six females and five youngsters. The youngest, a juvenile about three feet in height, played among the females: walking under them, pulling their tails, slapping its trunk against their legs, and even stealing some of the grass they collected. Ben said that this calf was less than a year old. The large elephants were gentle with the youngster and seemed to enjoy its attention. The larger juveniles spent their time feeding or butting each other.

When Ben drove slowly toward this elephant herd, the male separated from the group and stood facing the approaching truck, flaring his ears, and rolling and swinging his trunk. He was twice the height of the truck. "He might charge if we get too close," Ben said. "He'll let us know with a loud trump and snort. Then we'll stop."

We were able to approach within fifty feet of the herd. Ben assured us that all was well as long as the youngster did not get separated from the females and move behind the truck. All of us were able to take some excellent photographs.

Our stomachs growling, we reached the road across the valley and Ben turned our heading back toward camp. Although we had been out for about four hours, we had not covered much distance so the drive back was quick. Sammy had a pot of scrambled eggs, a tray of toast, a bowl of what looked like grits, a plate of papaw slices and plenty of hot water for tea and coffee awaiting our return; definitely a breakfast to quell complaining stomachs and relax the spirit.

* * *

With so many antelopes available, lions were a distinct feature in the Masai Mara. Lone, mature males were easy to notice because they lounged in the grass just off the roadways. They usually reclined in a head-up, vigilant position, a perfect pose for taking a close-up portrait that allowed the luxurious, burnt gold-black mane to complement and enhance the facial features. Periodically they yawned, exposing their formidable teeth. Since the lions acted oblivious to the safari truck, Ben could approach to within fifteen to twenty feet of them. A yawning male lion photographed, from such a short distance with the aid of a short-range telephoto lens, definitely provides pictures that show the potential ferocity of these felines. Later, when viewing the pictures, seeing the teeth guarding the gaping maw, one can almost sense the roar and feel the breath.

Sometimes sleeping lions reclined in comical positions. One lay on his back with all four legs stretched skyward. Another folded his forelegs across his chest in a funeral-like display with his hind legs extended out behind him and his tail along the center of his abdomen. Occasionally one of the females stalked nearby or slept under the shade of a tree.

We watched one pair of lions become intimately involved. The female initiated the entire process. She woke the male with a few jabs, kicks and what appeared to be love bites. In an intoxicated, sleep-arrested, half-slumber he voiced several feeble protests, mounted her and completed coitus with “wham-bam, thank you, Mam” speed. He then rolled off, reclined and recaptured his sleep. Her response to all his lethargic carnality was a swift swat across his face. He quickly reared, bellowed a deep throaty roar and, vocally and physically harangued her until she backed her ears, kowtowed, and hobbled away. After licking a couple surface scratches, or maybe ridding himself of a flea, he resumed his snooze. Within about twenty minutes her coquettishness returned and their lusty dalliance restarted.

The result of these intimate couplings is the production of delightful, boisterous lion cubs. I had an opportunity to see a trio playfully following their mother during a later game drive. They were no more than a week or two old. As the safari truck came abreast of them, the tawny-colored cubs scuttled behind the female. She stopped, quietly growled and stared across the range away from the road. In a moment, her three loveable, stuffed toy-like tots appeared from beneath her belly, their faces pointed inquisitively in our direction. From my associates sitting behind me I heard a multitude of "Ohs" and "Ahs . . . aren't they darling? I'd love to take one home." The camera shutters clicked. Soon the moppets lost interest and began playfully skirmishing, chasing and biting each other's tails. When one of them bit the mother's tail, she gently swatted it and headed into the grass. The cubs followed.

Later we spotted a pride of five older juveniles lying atop a knoll. The manes of the males were just beginning to show. It appeared as if they were wearing brush collars. They formed a handsome group, lying confident and serene, their heads all facing in the same direction, vigilantly watching the activity across the plain.

Ben's radio blared a message that some lions had made a kill about a half mile from where we were. "This you'll have to see," he said and turned the truck onto the meadow, accelerated across causing birds to fly and antelope to stampede. The kill wasn't hard to locate because, as we were approaching, four Nissan safari vans were circling into position. Ben pulled in about twenty feet from the carnage. The lions had killed a topi, and except for the head, had consumed most of the animal, including muscle and entrails. The primary males, already sated, were lolling a few feet behind the feeding frenzy, licking blood from their paws and off their faces. They were oblivious to the tourist vehicles and the excitement around the skeletonizing carcass as bloody muscle was being stripped from the skeleton by females and the variously aged juveniles, the second tier of eaters. With the fur around their faces and paws full of crimson gore, and in between barbarous stares and growls, they stripped and tore meat from the carcass, and sometimes from the clutches of their neighbor. This frenzied combat was only intensified by suicidal jackals, darting and yelping between the lions, trying to garb a tidbit only to be repulsed by a fierce feline snarl or swat. Hysterical hyenas scampered around the periphery of the melee, while vultures and marabou storks waited patiently in open spaces between safari vans, taxis, and our truck.

I have seen this gory spectacle many times on various natural history television programs, so seeing it first-hand, and at close range, was not very distressing, but it was impressive. The only differences between the TV versions and the real-life scene being played in front of me were the gawking tourists hanging out of the eight safari vans that eventually encircled the dining lions. All the usual actors were in their places, but in the modern version of this scenario the audience was included.

After the lions were satiated, the carrion feeders moved in and went on to reduce the topi to a blanched skeleton surrounded by piles of amorphous detritus. We departed for a short drive to the Fig Tree Lodge, one of the upscale resorts in the Masai Mara, to take a much needed shower and shave. For a small fee, the hotel allowed us the use of their facilities. I would have paid a larger fee for this convenience, because after four hot, dusty days my skin and hair felt like they had accumulated half of the Masai Mara. Besides, after cleaning up we had an opportunity to relax on the lodge veranda and have a cocktail before returning to camp for dinner.

On the drive to the Fig Tree Lodge we flushed a serval. This is a small cheetah-colored feline predator with large ears and a short banded tail. It was stalking a small herd of Thomson's gazelles, but when we drove by it dashed into the grass.

* * *

On one afternoon we returned from a game drive to find Sammy and the Masai guards using makeshift bows and arrows that they had constructed from sticks of a nearby bush to shoot the juvenile baboons scampering through the branches of the two large trees next to the stream. Although the baboons' behavior was comical, these bold little waifs had harassed us from the first day we made camp. They dashed in and stole anything that was sparkling or tasty. They made off with Stan's red baseball cap, which he left on a table while he was setting up his tent. We watched three of the critters chase the thief through the trees trying to capture ownership of the prize. The cap was never seen again.

These baboon children are curious and fascinated by eggs, apples, toothpaste, flashy objects, and anything else they perceive as food or a potential toy. They have been known to enter an open tent and go through a camper's pack. And if challenged in their quest, they bear their teeth and pretend to chase the one who is attempting to thwart them until they see a clear path that allows them to escape to the nearest tree. They then break off the fleeing attempts, dash up the trunk, relax on a branch and taunt their pursuer with screams and handfuls of excrement. Their behavior was reminiscent of our earlier encounter with the vervet monkeys.

After several days everyone had tired of baboon antics. It was time for revenge, so the guards tried their best to discourage the little beasts from entering the camp. Although the guards knew that their efforts were futile and short lived, they seemed to enjoy the fracas they created. Blunted arrows continued to fly into the tree. Occasionally one would sting a youngster's haunches and cause it to scurry, squealing higher into the branches. Others followed screaming and bearing their teeth. At the base of the trees the females were also chaotically running around, yelling, barking, jeering and charging the guards, rolling in the dust, and throwing dirt and stones into the air over their heads.

During this commotion Ben told us to remain in the vehicle for our own protection. While the others hung out of the windows cheering the guards and hooting the attackers, I sat crossing my legs and biting my lip. After a couple of hours of bouncing over the fields, during which I also drank the contents of my canteen, I was in dire need of a rest stop. When the pandemonium finally subsided, I jumped from the truck and headed down the path to the latrine. But directly in the middle of the path, a short distance beyond and out of sight of the camp, arms crossed over his chest grinning at me with tooth and vengeance, sat the largest patriarch of the campsite baboon population. Now these guys are big, sixty or so pounds of muscle, able to make hamburger out of my fragile body. His presence definitely plugged my plan to pee, but my imminent need was extremely strong and strengthened in this fearful situation. I thought as I concentrated on the eyes of the baboon, this big guy would probably not enjoy watching me urinate near his favorite sitting place. The act of micturition in his presence might not communicate the proper message, so I stifled the urge. I continued to agonize and pondered the notion of reasoning with him since he was supposed to be the head baboon, the all-knowing seer. I am sure he realized his kids were stealing from, and harassing, the camp and that they got caught and received due punishment, so retribution had been paid and we should all be friends again. How ridiculous he should think such thoughts, but I really had to pee - badly. So with a show of deference I proceeded to go around him. He nodded slightly and shifted. I passed and didn't look back.

* * *

On the last afternoon in the Masai Mara National Park we stopped to visit the *boma* where our Masai camp guards lived. A Masai *boma* is an enclosed compound fenced with tightly packed and intertwined branches of the Acacia tree. Acacia branches are covered along their entire length with three-inch spines. The fence effectively bars lions, hyenas and other large predators from the interior of the compound. Within the *boma* were several *manyattas*, the loaf-like, windowless houses whose walls are constructed of mud and cattle dung and covered by a gradually slanting, gabled thatched roof. The grounds within the compound were clean, well trampled and absent of vegetation. They contained several corrals to house cattle, sheep, and goats.

The *boma* where our guards lived covered an area of about ten thousand square feet. It had four *manyattas* and about two empty corrals, since during our visit their herds were feeding on the open range adjacent to the *boma*.

Upon our arrival – it was as if we were expected – we were quickly inundated with chattering, giggling, smiling women, baldheaded girls (a bald head is the sign of an unmarried female) and young children as soon as we stepped from the safari truck. There were about twenty persons loosely robed in red, red and blue plaid, and a mix of bright yellow and red, toga-like wraps. As soon as I exited the truck, three young, bald girls surrounded me, literally attached themselves to my arms, touched my hair and my beard, and began trying to sell me beaded bracelets, necklaces, belts, and other handmade baubles. These were pretty young women with soft, satiny brown skin and winsome personalities, but innocent and naive. Their sales approach involved handing an item to a potential buyer and not taking it back, and sometimes boldly putting the item in the position where it is to be worn, such as a bracelet put on the wrist or a necklace hung around the neck, and not allowing the bearer to remove it. I had to aggressively and physically remove and forcefully return any bauble I did not want to purchase. Attempts to haggle resulted in transacting, instead of money, material goods such as T-shirts, large red railroad-styled handkerchiefs (they didn't like the blue ones), or my wristwatch, items with which I did not want to part. It was like dealing with someone from ancient times. The experience was invigorating, but exhausting. I must say, however, I did enjoy their primitiveness and insouciant manner.

When I eventually purchased a couple of items, the young Masai women happily showed me through a *manyatta*. Inside, these houses are very dark because there are very few openings to the outside and the walls are blackened with soot accumulated from cooking over open fires within the *manyatta*. I had once heard of an American engineer who tried to educate the Masai in the use of chimneys, only to be rebuffed by the native knowledge that the smoke repels pesky little critters such as mosquitoes. I was momentarily sightless when I crawled from the bright sunlight through the low primary opening to the interior. Once inside I was able to stand to full height. One of the young women held onto my arm to aid my balance until my eyes adjusted to the very low light. Eventually, I saw that the interior had a dirt floor and it was walled into several cubicles: a bedroom for the male who usually sleeps by himself or with one of his several wives and a room for each wife and her children. Wives' rooms also doubled for storage of goods and animals. A central area was used for cooking, eating and socializing.

I was very surprised that, except for the smokey scent, the *manyatta* had no malodor and the interior was very clean. Likewise, the people themselves were very clean. And I didn't see any individuals who were sick nor any who showed signs of parasitic maladies - such individuals may have been hidden. Although the Masai have the historic reputation of hardy warriors, I found the people to be charming, kind, considerate and warmhearted, but inquisitive and persistent. Visiting their village was like going back to a simpler time when humanity lived in tune with the natural environment.

After the visit to the Masai *boma,* Ben again drove to the Fig Tree Lodge. Only this time the plan was not only to shower and shave, but to have an end-of-safari party. We enjoyed a few cocktails and dinner in the restaurant. Afterwards we retired to the veranda to tell stories and reminisce about our trip. While we sat and enjoyed the evening, the sky darkened and wild sounds rose from the grassland.

The last bit of excitement was an impromptu game drive after dark. On our way back to the campsite, Ben, instead of staying on the road, decided to shift into four-wheeled drive and take off across the mara. His excuse was that the trip would be shorter. In the beam of the headlights, and with a mind-set dampened by alcohol, the monotony of grass falling rapidly in front of the vehicle as we cruised held me spellbound. My trance broke whenever the truck bounced over a ditch or when pairs of icy blue eyes began to scatter through clearings and disappear in the darkness. At one point two hyenas ran at top speed ahead of the truck just at the point where the headlight beams rolled over the ground. They ran, yelping, back and forth from one side to the other within the shafts of light, crisscrossing each other's path, forming a frenzied, braided trail through the grass in front of the truck. I saw their eyes blaze blue in the light when they periodically flipped their heads back to check the truck's position. Several jackals entered the race and quickly out competed the hyenas in speed and sound. Just before we reached camp, and after the scurrying animals broke off to the side, a frightened warthog squealed and ran into the grass.

* * *

The next morning on the way back to Nairobi I pondered the dilemma of the animals I saw on this trip. The game drives provided an awe-inspiring, magnificent experience, but they left me a bit sad. It was not because the safari had come to an end, but because the future of the animals that range across the grasslands looks bleak. Already many of those I observed are endangered and a few, the rhinoceros for example, are on the threshold of extinction.

Theoretically, within the confines of national parks and game preserves, the animals are protected. Although attempts are being made to manage these preserves and parks for the benefit of the animals, the animals do not recognize park boundaries so they freely roam beyond the confines of the protection. They can move uninhibited beyond park boundaries where they encounter poachers or come into opposition with human desires and developments. In either case, the animals will lose. Even in the parks their lives are in jeopardy because they often meet the same violations they would face on the outside. No matter how conscientious a country's policies are for animal preservation, financial and political constraints limit abilities to manage and protect these wonderful game parks. This is especially evident in the Third World countries such as those that comprise East Africa.

KILIMANJARO, ELEPHANTS AND THIEVES

I feel exhilarated. Mount Kilimanjaro is in front of me. From where I sit on the veranda of the Kilimanjaro Safari Lodge, the mountain encompasses the entire vista - a world famous mountain rising into the clouds about thirty or forty kilometers away. This grand spectacle has graced the stories of many famous authors and has been part of the mythology of many native African cultures. I wonder if the frozen leopard carcass really exists near Kilimanjaro's summit? Near here they supposedly filmed Hemingway's famous story of Africa, *The Snows of Kilimanjaro.*

From my vantage I survey the slope toward the mountain. I see many vultures, but about one kilometer away there is a scraggy skeleton of a tree where several rest on its branches. Maybe that is where the injured and paranoid character, Harry, played by Gregory Peck, lay upon a cot babbling irrationally at the foreboding figures while Ava Gardner stood next to him, comforted him. She also tried to convince him that he had nothing to fear from the scavengers, because help was on the way.

A long time has passed since I've seen the movie, *The Snows of Kilimanjaro,* but the scene I'm looking at appears correct. I have the book lying in front of me. After I quench my thirst and wash the dust from my throat, I plan to spend the rest of the day reading. I roll the bottle of Tusker beer back to my lips, drink, and thrill at the thought of relaxing and reading Hemingway's classic in the shadow of the majestic mountain. I am sure others have felt this excitement.

The week before on a flight from Malindi to Nairobi my seat-partner, a Kenyan businessman, pointed out Mount Kilimanjaro. We passed to the north, but its summit was partially visible above the clouds. He mentioned that it's rarely completely visible during the day because of the winds around the mountain. During the night they blow from inland. They're very dry and produce no clouds. But during the day, the winds come from the east and bring in moist oceanic air. The water vapor condenses to form a massive cloud bank when it contacts the ice fields atop the mountain. He regarded the mountain with a sense of pride and told me that if I wanted to see it in its entirety I could do so during the first hours after sunrise.

Mount Kilimanjaro is so spectacular because it stands alone on a desert-like plain. It's a solitary mountain, an extinct volcano, and is not part of a chain or range of mountains. From where I sit the ground gradually slopes into a valley, then rises in a parabolic curve to Kilimanjaro's 5895-meter summit, Africa's highest mountain. Except for a low wire fence that surrounds the lodge, I have an unobstructed view across this entire panorama to the bank of clouds that hide the mountain's icy cap. Although the terrain appears xeric, with short dried grasses, shrubs, and swirling dust-devils, there are permanently wet low-lying areas that contain pools, marshes and streams. Melting of the snow cap atop Kilimanjaro provides a continuous supply of water.

Somewhere toward Kilimanjaro runs the border between Kenya and Tanzania, probably down in the valley. When the border between the two countries is open, visitors can go on a safari to the mountain. Some disagreement caused its closure several months ago. Someday, when the border is open, I would like to visit Tanzania, ascend Kilimanjaro and descend Tanzania's other mystical place, the volcanic crater called Ngorongoro Crater. But for now, I'll just relax until dinner and read Hemingway.

* * *

I had come to Amboseli because I wanted to taste and enjoy the amenities of a more affluent tourist experience in Kenya before returning to the United States. I wanted to know what comforts a stay at a safari lodge in a national park would offer. I had presented my request to an agent at the Nilestar Safaricentre in Nairobi and he arranged an overnight stay in Amboseli National Park that fell within my means. Nilestar provided transportation in a Nissan van-like safari vehicle, a driver who drove to, from, and around the park, and lodging and meals at the Kilimanjaro Safari Lodge, all for about eighty dollars. The safari left Nairobi Friday morning and would return to Nairobi late Saturday afternoon. "Sounds great!" I said and booked the tour. But, I fantasized the conveniences and perks that go with the aura of wealth that I imagined for myself.

"Would there be any others sharing *my van?"* I asked.

"Of course," came a very positive reply, "You did not purchase a private trip." The agent quoted the prices of private tours booked by such individuals as newspaper reporters, diplomats, movie stars, and others of influence and affluence. *"C'est la vie,"* I'm only a professor. To allow myself such extravagance I'd have to survive on hotdogs and beans for the rest of my trip. So much for my attempt to emulate the rich and famous.

As it turned out, I had only to share the van with two others, a German fellow who didn't speak any English and a fidgety Japanese lady who didn't say much. But she wanted a bit of air and asked the driver how to open the side window on the van. She quickly muted into a sulk early in the trip, after she heard his glib remark to her request. "Since this van was made in Japan, you should know how to open the window," he answered. She took offense. Although I think he tried to joke with her, his nonchalance lacked diplomacy. When we eventually reached the lodge, she commissioned another van to take her back to Nairobi.

By midmorning we reached Namanga, a town on Kenya's southern border with Tanzania. Just beyond the turnoff to a dusty dirt road, Namanga's main street, the paved Kenyan highway A104 from Nairobi, enters Tanzania. Well-armed Tanzanian border guards sauntered about behind racks of spikes that were guaranteed to shred the tires off any vehicle that tried to cross without inspection and permission.

We turned into Namanga, drove past several weathered wooden storage buildings, and pulled into the parking area of the Masai Service Station. Well seasoned by the sun, wind and sand, the station resembled a 1940 vintage truck stop. It had gasoline and diesel pumps under an awning, a repair garage, a café and a souvenir shop. Apparently business on Saturday morning was light, since I saw no vehicles anywhere. The entire town resembled a movie set of a ghost town.

Inside the Masai Service Station I met Mr. Joseph Musau, the proprietor, a handsome, charismatic, savvy businessman in his early thirties. He was dressed in a plaid sport shirt, Levi jeans, and what appeared to be brand-new sports sneakers. While serving us the coffee we ordered, he quickly pointed out the various woodcarvings, necklaces, spears, shields and other trinkets displayed about the café. In the adjoining room, the tourist shop, there were hundreds of carved giraffes – some six feet tall – lions, various antelopes, buffaloes and many other examples of the African fauna. Especially impressive were the carvings of common olive baboons – they were so lifelike. These sculptures were covered with what appeared to be the skin of a real baboon. All the carvings were very well crafted and they exhibited the minute details peculiar to the specific species. They were the best carvings I had seen during my stay in Kenya. Joseph said that they were all produced by local artists and craftsmen and that sale of these crafts provided the locals with their only chance to make a meager income.

As Joseph continued his sales pitch, his demeanor became more focused toward making a sale. "The Masai are a poor people," he said, "but very hard working. Their children wear ragged clothing and are always in need of medicine. So if you buy a small item, your purchase will provide fever pills, . . . maybe a shirt for a little boy, . . . or food for the table. Who knows? A dollar, mark or yen will bring much happiness and survival."

By this time, coffees in hand, our small troop of weekend explorers was now "ohing" and "ahing" at the items displayed in the tourist shop. The quality of the sculptures did not require any strongly guilt laden salesmanship. They sold themselves.

On the pretense of giving the tourists an opportunity to buy a coffee or soda, the real reason for the safari tour agency's scheduled stops is to provide local entrepreneurs and retailers with customers. Tourists are most sought after and catered to at these kiosks. Remote enterprises depend heavily on the tourist network, and the Kenyans have developed an exceptionally intricate network. A driver will always stop, whether the clients wish to or not, at a kiosk or service area where it seems he is part of the family. I never did find out if the driver or the safari agency received a cut from the sales. The rest stops were entertaining, and we didn't have to purchase anything except a drink, if we so wanted.

In the case of the Masai Service Station, I could not pass up such quality workmanship. The carvings were indeed works of art. For about twenty dollars I purchased an eighteen-inch tall sculpture of a hartebeest female nursing its calf. But this was not before Joseph and I discussed the wealth one accumulates as a college professor.

When Joseph learned that I taught biology, he became more amiable. He asked if I had ever heard of Stuart and Jeanne Altmann? I told him I had and that, if possible, I wanted to meet them. The Altmanns supervised a long-term study on baboon behavior and their research camp was located in Amboseli National Park. Joseph told me that the Altmanns had returned to the University of Chicago about a year ago, but that their research camp still in Amboseli was being run by some of their graduate students.

Joseph continued to tell me about the animals in the area, but, since he lived in Namanga, I asked him if a film I had recently seen had any truth. The movie depicted an assault on the town of Namanga by an army of starving baboons. Since, according to the film script, the incident took place in 1984, only three years earlier, it should be fresh in the minds of all residents of Namanga.

"Yes." Joseph said. "But only partially true. Many remote settlements in Kenya experience attacks by baboons during drought and famine. The apes know that there is food and water in the houses and in gardens, so they go on desperate, ravaging rampages to get what they need. They smash windows to gain access into houses and barns. Then they ransack, pillage and plunder. If humans get in the way or try to defend their property they are attacked. We had to fight them with clubs, shovels, pitchforks, axes and pangas. Many people were injured and several were killed. But the attacks by baboons are not any different from a horde of humans that come to plunder towns and villages. At least the apes had reason. Humans don't always have a reason. When all is well, humans and animals live in harmony."

"Many baboons must have perished?"

"Yes." Joseph pointed toward the baboon display. "That is where the skins to cover those sculptures came from. You seem to appreciate fine wood carvings. Come." Joseph led me to a rear door.

"Let me show you my warehouse. Maybe you will find something you will like. I'll make you a good price."

We went out the door and into a large windowless building. Inside there were hundreds of magnificent pieces. "I supply many dealers in Nairobi and I ship anywhere in the world," he said.

I fondled the head of a six-foot giraffe.

"I will trade the giraffe for those Banana Republic cargo pants you are wearing," he said. "And, I will ship the piece to the U.S.A. for you."

"How did you recognize the manufacturer of these pants?" That my pants could become an article of barter, surprised me. But why not, Joseph dealt with the world. Why should he not be aware of the clothing, or anything else of value, produced in other countries?

"Catalogs," he said, "but I cannot buy anything because the duty and tariffs are too high. Even if I could, the merchandise I ordered would be stolen when it reached Nairobi. If you include your Gortex hiking boots and those red bandanas, you can select any other carving in my warehouse and I will also ship it to the States."

"Joseph, your offer is really tempting. But, the only problem is that if I pay you with my pants, I won't have anything to wear. And, I need my boots to hike about in Amboseli. It would be a little hard to walk barefooted. I'll have to decline your offer even though I may never again have such an opportunity."

"When you return to Nairobi, you can buy pants and boots. Then hire a taxi and bring me the Banana Republic pants and the Goretex boots. Our trade arrangements will remain the same." He looked at me. "But you still have two red bandanas? I will trade for those."

I had brought with me to Kenya four large handkerchiefs, two red and two blue similar to the ones that were once popular with railroad engineers, to keep the sweat from trickling down my neck. The blue ones I could not give away, but the red ones were prized by the Masai because of the color. Red is their culture's primary color. I had two red handkerchiefs, and I could part with them. We could deal.

"Is this shield authentic?"

"It is made of goat skin and edged with goat fur. The design is painted in red ochre. Because it is small, it is the shield a Masai carries when he runs across the country. It is not used in warfare. You can have it for the red bandanas."

We made the trade.

Later I learned that the shield really was authentic. In fact, so authentic that after it hung in my university office for about six months, I noticed a little mound of frass beneath it near the file cabinet, and realized that the goat fur along the margin had thinned. A closer inspection of the fur showed an infestation of some sort of dermestid-like beetles gnawing away the fur trim. To save my prize shield I resorted to drastic eradication measures. I enclosed the shield in an airtight box that contained cyanide crystals used in insect killing jars, for a week. This worked. I still have the Masai traveling shield decorating my office wall, but it's slightly bald.

Joseph and I returned to the café. I could see my driver and the other two travelers impatiently waiting to continue our journey. So I told Joseph I would try to return next weekend for another round of haggling. We shook hands. I joined the others in the van and we drove off. Sadly, the opportunity to return to Namanga never materialized.

For about forty kilometers we sped along the dusty, potholed, corrugated road toward Amboseli National Park and the Kilimanjaro Safari Lodge. A few kilometers into the park the road paralleled the bone-dry bed of Lake Amboseli. This dry lake bed formed a flat expanse of stark white sand that stretched to the horizon. Even more striking than the contrast between the vivid blue sky and the white lake bed was a wildebeest running across the scene. The animal gave life to this tableau. Its highspeed gallop threw a dusty contrail that defined the animal's direction. From a distance of a couple of kilometers, the beast appeared to run in place. The entire prospect appeared two-dimensional, as if the sharp and distinct jet-black wildebeest, moving along the shimmering horizon, was unzipping the connection between the glaring plain and azure background.

We arrived at the Kilimanjaro Safari Lodge at about half past two o'clock. Check in was straightforward. After I completed the task, the desk clerk assigned a young woman to show me to my cabin. She picked up my bag without any form of acknowledgment and marched out the door. I followed, but thought her behavior to be unusual. All the other bellhop-types, male or female, I had met at least had said hello. Many were inquisitive and freely participated in small talk while they guided me to the room. Usually I have found that the women who carry luggage and even the maids try to make extra money by being amicable. If a client pays any attention, he is presented with all sorts of propositions and services she is willing to provide.

Physically this girl did not differ from the others I had met in Kenya. I assumed she was of Kikuyu descent, medium built with pleasant features, but none really outstanding. As we walked the path toward my cabin I asked about the weather, the dinner schedule, the location of the dining room, whether the mosquitoes were bad, where I could get a beer, but she remained silent. In fact, she maintained an air of aloofness that bordered on arrogance.

She opened the door to the cabin, walked in and dropped my bag onto the floor next to the bed. I heard the thud when I entered and became concerned. "My camera equipment is in the bottom of that bag. Please be careful," I said.

She smirked. Pushed open the door to the bathroom. "You can wash-up in here." She then sauntered toward the bed. "Mosquitoes. There are many. And they like white tourists. Keep the fan turning so they cannot land on you." She then jumped onto the middle of the bed and released the mosquito netting that hung above. It dropped onto her. Mechanically she demonstrated how to arrange the netting around the bed from inside the net then she pulled the drawstrings that closed the bottom around the mattress. "Make sure you sleep inside the net." She then rehung the whole business and rolled off the bed. "Dinner . . . at seven-thirty. The desk clerk will tell you where. I only carry bags and clean rooms. Don't give out information."

She started to leave, but turned toward me when she heard me unzip my backpack and remove my bag containing toiletries. From my pants pocket I took out several shillings, gave them to her and thanked her. She grunted disparagingly. She mumbled something. Stuck the shillings into her bodice, stiffened herself erectly and squared her shoulders, an action that tightened the blouse and protruded her breasts. "I arrange the netting. Make your bed before you return from dinner. And, clean room while you are at breakfast, but I will not come to you tonight, Tourist!" With an insolent shrug she marched out.

"I don't remember asking you," I mumbled. A friendly cuss, I thought . . . guess she didn't like the tip.

I unpacked my bag and arranged my belongings, but became concerned about the potential loss of my traveler's checks. In Nairobi I had kept the checks and other valuables locked in the hotel safe. But, since I planned to be here only one night, I thought I wouldn't need strong security. I had six, one hundred dollar checks stashed in my pack, so I became a little anxious. Besides, I thought, Miss Hospitality had access to my room and would actually be in my room several times in the next twelve hours. Her attitude did not make me feel secure. I decided to hide the checks behind the lining of my toiletry-kit. Even if someone looked into the kit, the checks would not be obvious. They disappeared behind the cloth very nicely. I felt a bit more comfortable and zipped the kit closed and placed it on the shelf in the bathroom. I brushed my hair, changed pants, picked up my copy of *The Snows of Kilimanjaro* and went to look for the lounge which turned out to be a patio-type covered extension on the east side of the dining room.

* * *

Mosquitoes became quite invasive. The maid was right. The little devils were abundant. I scratched my arm with the binding of the Hemingway novella, finished off the remains of a Tusker beer, put the book and the bottle on the table. The light was getting too dim to read anyway, so I decided to finish the story later in bed.

I stared at the mountain. Kilimanjaro's slopes and its cloudy crown had a reddish glow, at least what I could see of it. It was more exposed now than it had been all afternoon. The little nub on its eastern slope became visible. All of Kilimanjaro will probably be uncovered tonight, but it'll be too dark to see anything, I thought. Tomorrow I will arise early to watch and photograph the color of the mountain change as the sunlight moves up its slopes, but now it's time for dinner.

Suspended below the dozen or so ceiling fans, all rotating almost in phase, were lighted soccer ball-sized globes. The light they emitted, mixed with nearly bare, mustard-beige walls, gave the dining room a soft, but bright, luminescence. A dark stone fireplace seemed to rise up the far wall and pass through the room's high ceiling. On the wall behind me hung a large portrait of President Moi. These were the only wall decorations. Since the tables, arranged in neat rows, were round and the chairs, wooden folding types like the one I sat upon outside in the lounge, I surmised that this was a multipurpose room. The furniture could be quickly folded, rearranged or removed.

As I entered, the drone of many voices mixed with the clinking din of silverware hitting dishes. The room's acoustics favored noise. Only table cloths and napkins could mute this racket.

Each table had eight chairs around it. Several tables away, I spied an empty chair. I joined the group seated at this table. They spoke only French, but I learned that they were from Paris. *"Je parle peu Français,"* I said in an attempt to enter their conversation. But they all stared at me sympathetically for a moment, then returned to their conversation. I ate in silence.

After dinner I took sanctuary in the lounge, away from the noise and indifference of the transitory dining room. Although the dining room was still filled with happy excited voices and some nondescript background music, in the lounge on the open veranda the murmur was softer. Emanating from the darkness beyond on wisps of cool breezes, I heard the occasional conversations of the wildlife we had all traveled here to observe. I fell in with two proud young men from the East Berlin Safari Club who were not afraid to converse with an American. There were sixteen scattered about the lounge enjoying quantities of Kenya brew and imported German beers. They toasted each other and told of their day's activities, joked, laughed and sang.

"How are you able to travel outside East Germany?" I asked. Their casualness in regard to the supposed confinement behind the Iron Curtain confused me. But these men were born and grew up under the dictatorial and oppressive umbrella of Communism.

"The State approves our club and allows us to travel to Africa and the Orient once a year," they said. "And, Aeroflot transports us at no charge . . . does your country have such opportunities?"

"I'm impressed. From what you're telling me, life behind the Iron Curtain doesn't sound so bad."

"It is for some . . . we have connections."

The Germans' party was becoming more spirited. I had a couple more drinks and excused myself. It was after eleven o'clock and six-thirty in the morning would be here soon, so I headed to my cottage.

On the shelf my toothbrush was sticking out of my toilet-kit. I thought I had zipped the kit closed before I left my room? Curious. I looked inside. Toothpaste, dental floss, aspirins, deodorant, were all there, as was my electric razor. Now if anyone wanted to steal something, the razor was a Braun, a pricey new model. The Black Market would give a good price for an item like a Braun razor.

"Oh my God, I hid my traveler's checks behind the lining." I pulled the lining away from the inside of the kit. There they were. I fingered them. "I guess I didn't zip the bag after all," I mumbled, pushed the lining back into place, removed the toothbrush and paste, and proceeded to brush my teeth. "Too many beers."

The maid did arrange the mosquito netting over the bed. It looked like a voluptuous conical tent, diaphanous, sheer. I crawled into this soft, silken, hedonistic chamber. This sure beats crawling into a sleeping bag, I thought. I rolled around on the sheets. They smelled delicate, felt cottony. My sleep would be luxurious, sensual. The only thing missing was a nubile nymphet. Dream on, I thought, and fell asleep.

An hour before the alarm sounded, I awoke. It was still dark outside. I rolled out of bed slightly hungover. I brushed last night's flavors out of my mouth, shaved, swallowed a couple of aspirins and replaced everything back into my toilet kit, zipped it closed, put it on the shelf and checked it. "Definitely closed," I said. I dressed quickly, because I didn't want to miss the effect of sunrise on Mount Kilimanjaro. I slipped the strap of my Nikon over my shoulder, grabbed my lens case and exited the room.

Since the cooks were already preparing for breakfast, I was able to get a cup of coffee. They gave me a large cup filled almost to overflowing with strong coffee, very black; just what I needed to bring my brain into focus. Outside in the lounge, the chair and table I occupied yesterday afternoon were still there. Amid some distant elephant bellows and the harmony of waking birdcalls, I sat back to await the sunrise.

Traveling toward me about 1,040 miles per hour was the boundary between night and day. Although approaching at a speed greater than the speed of sound, its arrival was imperceptible, diffused. First the light blue dome-like glow appeared on the eastern horizon. Above and around me all was dark, stars shone brightly. The dome enlarged noticeably, and soon the sky above was a white-blue. The stars disappeared, but Kilimanjaro, bluish, misty, stood as if in shadow. There were no clouds anywhere. Well before the sun rose above the horizon, the icecap covering Kilimanjaro's summit reflected a bright ruby gleam. A distinct line separated the mountain's brilliant crown from its darkish, subdued body. I watched this line move down the slopes, awakening the vista. As the day chased the night from the mountain's descent, Kilimanjaro's radiance softened to orange, pink, mauve, and faded purple as the sun cleared the horizon. The day's commencement finished within about fifteen minutes. Once it was consummated the panorama took on its daytime hues of yellow, beige, brown, rust, separated by various shades of green, and the air heated quickly.

I watched the early morning unfold against the Mount Kilimanjaro background and photographed the highlights. The feature was definitely spectacular. Unfortunately, a still camera cannot capture the progression, so my future presentations of this event will appear as a set of staccato clips.

With the sun well above the horizon, Kilimanjaro stood sharp and distinct, a lone protuberance in a desert-like flatland. Its vivid white snowcap contrasted conspicuously against royal blue. While I remained entranced, a few small cloud tufts formed below the apex. They signified locations of avalanching masses of cold air. But my morning was also advancing, so I checked my watch. I had ten minutes to get breakfast. Because of time, a roll and another cup of coffee would suffice. My driver, impatiently waiting behind the steering wheel, was ready to take his two clients on the scheduled game drive.

Amboseli National Park diffused into the desolate Taru Desert located in southeastern Kenya. Its dusty fields of prickly, scrubby brush and shurbs gave it an arid appearance. The vast barren, dry bed of Lake Amboseli enhanced the parks aridity. But contradicting Amboseli's apparent wasteland image were a diversity of open shallow bogs, fens and marshes created by meltwater from Mount Kilimanjaro's icecap. In an attempt to cross one quagmire in four-wheeled drive, the rear tires mired. Sticky, gray clay touched the axle. Although the front tires were on more secure soil, they spun on the greasy mud. The driver tried rocking the van back and forth, but without success. We were stuck. I suggested we get out and push while he attempted to continue rocking. "Oh no. Too dangerous. The elephants . . . " He tried to talk with someone on the radio, but all was static. "If we put the two boards that are lying at my feet under the back tires and push while you attempt to drive forward, we might get free," I said.

"No one is to leave the van. It's the law," he warned.

"Then we will sit here until we're found. That may be days, since we're not on a primary road. And I don't see any elephants anywhere."

He opened the van door. The German fellow and I scrambled out, pulled out the boards from under the seats, wedged them in front of the half buried wheels, and put our shoulders to the van. "Drive," I yelled. The van slid to one side, then the other, but the wheels contacted the boards, the back tires grabbed traction. They rolled forward, pushed the front ones onto dry, solid ground. We were free, but my boots and pant legs were painted in gleaming, wet gray mud. My boots would need to be cleaned before I returned to my hotel room in Nairobi. They were the only shoes I had, but I'd face that problem later. Now it was time to continue the game drive.

We stayed on higher ground, passed hummocks of lush acacia trees, until we bounced back onto the primary road. If it were not for the many downed trees, the wetland might have looked almost oasis-like.

Throughout this marshland, elephants frolicked and wallowed in the bogs and fens, snorted and squirted water from their hose-like trunks. Probably it was the water and abundance of marsh vegetation that attracted the massive herds of elephants to Amboseli. During this morning drive we encountered several herds that contained ten to twenty individuals. Although the elephants were enjoyable and interesting to watch, they took their toll on the landscape. When they migrate about the park and feed, they pull down branches. If the leaves are out of reach, they uproot and push over trees. Also elephants like to roll on the ground and cake themselves with soil after bathing. This behavior created small dust bowls, and in the process, crushed and ground the fragile vegetation where they rolled over and over. Between the drought-like conditions and the elephants, Amboseli National Park resembled the dregs remaining in a south Alabama clear-cut forest.

Winding our way along the maze of roadways back toward the lodge, we passed many elephant herds. One in particular gave us a bit of a scare. We approached a group of eight females and their three offspring feeding next to the road. They were, in fact, scattered on both sides of the road. We moved along slowly trying to get by, but one of the children decided to cross the road, the smallest one, about one meter high, probably within a month of its birth. And, like a child, it was playful. It lollygagged along, cutely coiling and uncoiling its trunk, and puffing dust from the road. Its antics invited picture taking, so we stopped. But immediately, a female moved between the van and the youngster, rolled her trunk, stomped her front feet, and started walking toward the van. The driver shifted into reverse, and, when the female gave a couple of strong, deep trumps, he began to slowly back away. Her bellows alerted the rest of the herd. Ear flapping increased, so did the trumpeting; the adults began to encircle the other two youngsters, but their heads remain toward us.

"Let's get out of here," the driver said. "It would only take one of those beasts to flatten this van. And, a couple appear ready to charge."

The driver doubled the van's speed, in reverse. Clear of the herd, he rapidly turned the wheel to the left and slammed the break pedal down. The van pivoted on its front tires and spun the rear end one hundred and eighty degrees throwing up a cloud of dust. We were flung against the right doors. Our driver must have watched too many car-chase movie scenes. In a moment we were about a hundred meters away from the agitated elephants, and heading in a forward direction.

In about ten minutes we passed through a meadow of waist-high grass that descended downward into a valley. Several hundred meters down the slope to our right, the head of a full-grown, black rhinoceros contrasted against the beige grass. From the distance it looked like a moving silhouette. The horn, distinct, long and tapering, curved backward to a sharp point. Too distant to photograph, I watched this majestic beast through binoculars.

"It's a female," the driver said after he borrowed my binoculars. "And, she's running toward us and does not know we exist. We're too far away and beyond her perception."

A good thing I thought, because we didn't need another hair-rising incident like we had with the elephants. We moved on, since we should be seated in about fifteen minutes for lunch at the lodge.

The mud on my Gore-Tex hiking boots was mostly dry and so hard that I could barely scrap it off with my pocketknife. In this condition Joseph surely wouldn't take them in trade for anything in his Namanga Gasoline Station. I asked the driver if he knew any way they could be cleaned, because I could not enter the lodge with such muddy boots.

When we parked, the driver explained my situation to several maintenance men milling about the parking lot. One walked off. Before I entered the lobby, he returned with a young girl about fifteen years old. She had been drafted, I was informed, to clean my boots. Would I remove them so she could begin to clean them, they asked? Then they informed me that cleaning the boots would take two hours. Not a problem, I said and slipped off my mud caked footwear and gave them to the girl. She accepted them shyly, nodded and disappeared behind the building. I decided to have lunch, but wondered if I'd be allowed to dine in the restaurant without wearing shoes. Well, I was wearing sweat socks.

I finished lunch, strolled into the gift shop, and then, to the lounge. Other tourists gave me a curious look when I walked by. I was sure they were wondering, *Why, is that fellow wandering around the hotel in his stocking feet?* After a couple of beers, I returned to my cabin. Everything seemed in order so I packed my belongings and returned to the lobby and checked out. It was almost time to start back to Nairobi and I had not seen the girl charged to clean my shoes; nor had I seen any of the maintenance men who arranged the cleaning. My driver was getting impatient and he noticed my anxiety. Hiking boots are something of value out here in the bush, I thought. So it would not be unusual if mine were on sale, right now, somewhere in Tanzania.

"Do you think my shoes are clean?" I ask my driver. "I'm a bit concerned."

He asked the bartender if he knew the status of my boots and was told that they were still drying. "Fifteen more minutes," the bartender said.

"What are they doing? Cooking them," I said facetiously. The bartender laughed just as the girl and the maintenance men entered the room. They told her to present the footwear to me. Bashfully, she moved forward and with a timid smile, handed my boots to me.

"I am flabbergasted. There's not a spot of gray mud on these boots . . . none even on the soles. They look like they did the first day I bought them," I said to her though they felt a little damp. My hiking boots had never looked better. "You did a wonderful job," I told her. "Thank you so very much." Her sense of accomplishment and appreciation radiated from her face when I handed her a fifty-shilling note for her effort.

One of the maintenance men gently took hold of her shoulder and said, "Thank the *Bwana* for his generosity." She tried, but her words choked in her throat. She timidly smiled and ran away clutching the money.

My boots were so clean that I hated to put them on and walk across the parking lot. I was afraid that they would collect dust and destroy the cleanliness the young girl worked so hard to attain. But, the driver urged me to hurry along.

* * *

On the way back to Nairobi our driver drove as if he had a hot date that evening. Occasionally, on the forty-kilometer stretch from Amboseli to the paved road at Namanga, we were caught in the contrail of dust from a van or truck ahead, but our van was air-conditioned so very little dust found its way inside. We arrived in Nairobi in record time, but entered the city at the height of the evening rush hour traffic. Our driver took this in stride, but weaving and cutting his way down the almost solidly jammed Kenyetta Avenue. At several intersections he ran the stoplights and traveled along a sidewalk for a short distance. His cutting in front of other vehicles was most frightening. The astonishing thing was that no one became upset. Often vehicles actually gave way by pulling to the side to allow our van to pass through. It was almost as if there were unwritten rules specifying that commercial vans had the right-of-way over personal vehicles.

At last, I disembarked at my hotel, collected my gear and took a final look at the van. Except from being covered with dust, the safari van did not have any noticeable mars, dents or scratches. I tipped the driver one hundred shillings, then asked, "Do you always drive this van?"

He scratched his head. Inspected the note I handed him, and thanked me in his language, *"Asante sana."* Then he answered my question. "Yes."

"You should consider entering the Safari Rally."

He chuckled and displayed a thumbs-up. *"Jambo Man,"* he said and drove off to deliver the German fellow to his hotel.

* * *

I entered my room. Everything was just as I had left it: my day pack in the corner, T shirts still draped on the bed, sandals on the bathroom floor. "It's been a dusty trip, so I need a shower before going to dinner or they might not allow me in the dining room," I muttered at my image in the mirror. I unpacked the kit with my toiletries and found the items I needed. Since I had little cash, I removed the travelers' checks that were hidden in the kit, behind the lining. "I thought I took six? There are only four . . . and I didn't cash any at Amboseli." I pondered a moment longer. "Maybe I did take only four . . . don't know."

Like shuffling a deck of cards, I slid the individual checks from the top to the bottom of the stack and inspected the serial numbers. "They're out of sequence! O-two and O-six are missing," I exclaimed. Someone had rifled through my kit and taken two of my checks. And, they did it in a way that a casual inspection wouldn't immediately reveal the theft. At least the crook wasn't greedy, but to me, two hundred dollars was a significant amount - also to the one who took the checks.

I surmised that the clever thief was probably the maid at the Kilimanjaro Safari Lodge. Aloof, inhospitable, unfriendly, all traits used by purloiners to remain unconnected from a potential victim. Also, her roving eyes inspected all my belongings. She saw a small amount of cash in my wallet when I tipped her, so she probably assumed I had more money stashed somewhere. Being a maid gave her access to my room when I wasn't around and she had plenty of time to snoop. I remembered zipping my travel kit closed before I went to relax in the lounge the day I arrived. The thief opened the kit and left it open after she took what she wanted. I'll have to be more careful.

Although having something stolen is disruptive and makes one feel deceived and betrayed, I knew I could get the checks replaced. They were issued by American Express and my check receipts were up to date. I decided to contact the American Express office Monday morning. Meanwhile, I showered, shaved, had dinner, and slept.

Although this incident made me suspicious of everyone, the staff at the Milimani Hotel had been super. During my almost six-week stay, not one item of my belongings had turned up missing, not even articles I sent to the laundry. I had learned to trust this group of people.

Nairobi's American Express offices were only a short distance from the New Stanley Hotel. I relayed my story to a very personable agent. He then provided me with a standard loss of property form and asked that I fill it out. He left for a moment and returned with two replacement one hundred dollar American Express checks. My curiosity about how a thief could cash stolen checks in a country that strongly monitors its citizens' finances and spending patterns, was whetted. So I asked the agent. While we shook hands, he proceeded to tell me.

"The thief cannot cash the checks in Kenya," he said. "He or she will sell the checks to someone, an intermediary, who will take them to another country, Tanzania perhaps. The checks will then change hands several more times as they pass through the black market. Eventually, they become the property of individuals of supposed unquestionable reputation."

"More like a person with a dubious reputation," I interjected.

"Yes," he agreed and continued the lecture. "These people are respected, honored, but most times feared. They are the henchmen of dictators, rulers, and tyrants. In their country no one will dispute or question their actions, or accuse them of wrongdoing. The checks may travel the black market for months, maybe years, before their value is used. Only the despot can cash them. And he does, when he dines at a restaurant or buys gifts somewhere in the world where his notoriety is known. The restaurateurs and retailers don't question because they fear retribution. Or it could simply be they do not know how to handle travelers' checks, although they have heard of them. Either way they lose, because, if the traveler reports the loss, American Express will have the serial numbers and will not pay."

"For the black market, stolen travelers' checks are valuable articles of trade. The thief and the intermediaries receive about one percent or less of a check's value, while the crooked czars obtain enough to pay for their dalliance and amusement. To the tourists and American Express, the thefts are minor inconvenience, but they hurt those engaged in honest business activities."

"If at the end of its journey, one of the stolen checks could talk, it would probably have a magnificent adventure story," I said.

"How true." We again shook hands. "Enjoy your continued stay in Kenya and don't let this incident discourage you. We are a decent people, but there are many ways to do commerce."

I walked out the door and toward the railroad station to arrange a trip to Mombasa.

TRAIN TO MOMBASA

In the opening scene of the movie *Out of Africa* a locomotive, rhythmically pumping billows of steam, pulls a tail of railroad cars toward Nairobi. Dwarfed by the vast expanse of the savannah, it moves slowly across the motion picture screen. This panorama aptly portrays the lonely open landscape that existed in Kenya's hinterland when Karen Blixen traveled from Mombasa to Nairobi in 1914. This was her first time aboard the Uganda Railway.

The only thing different from the past is that today a diesel-powered locomotive hauls the Uganda Railway train. The rolling stock that follows the locomotive, inwardly and outwardly, appears the same as that which moved materials and passengers on the day that the train made its maiden voyage. Additionally, little change has occurred in the landscape, except near the two major destinations, Nairobi and Mombasa. Both cities have sprawled far beyond their original boundaries.

Ever since seeing *Out of Africa*, I had thought a trip on the Uganda Railway would be exciting and historic. To ride this train is to perceptually go back in time and experience life, as it was when energetic, resolute pioneers were beginning to explore, tame, develop and settle the wilds of East Africa. The British constructed this railway to efficiently accomplish the above activities and provide a conveyance for more rapid transport of materials and people to and from the interior of this territory.

Building the Uganda Railway was no trivial matter. From its inception the project was fraught with controversy. When first proposed by a group of British visionaries, a pragmatic minority found many reasons to reject the notion and vehemently voiced their concerns. The minority believed its construction would cost too much and the British taxpayers would have to underwrite its price. Since the interior of East Africa was an unknown wilderness, the question was who would go there, who would benefit. Basically, it was believed by many that the railway would be a boondoggle to nowhere. During the debates the railway was dubbed the Lunatic

Express. Nevertheless, with the arguments of the majority led by Lord Salisbury, the British parliament funded the project. Their action commenced one of the greatest, and most costly, adventures in British history.

Salisbury asserted that the Uganda Railway would stimulate commerce, open the interior of the East African Protectorate, and end the slave trade. Additionally, the railway would be strategically important in maintaining Britain's control on Egypt and the Suez Canal, and secure for the Kingdom a foothold in the upper Nile Valley.

* * *

When George Whitehouse came ashore in Mombasa in December of 1895 charged by the British government to build the Uganda Railway, he faced a formidable task. Whitehouse, a Brit who had spent his life building railroads and harbors in India, was given complete charge in the construction of the railway. Although he possessed considerable experience, he had never before encountered an assignment like the one that confronted him.

Before any rails could be laid, they, and all the other bedding materials, locomotives, railroad cars, construction equipment, and workers had to be secured. Most had to be shipped from Britain. Because of the considerable weight, especially that of the locomotives, a deep water harbor had to be built. This harbor contained derricks, cranes, and docking facilities that could handle the off-loading from ships of construction materials and rolling stock. Warehouses, roundhouses, and living quarters had to be constructed. Although local men were available, their work ethic did not fit the requirements for this arduous construction project. Consequently, craftsmen and laborers were commissioned in India.

Undaunted by the prospects that confronted him, Whitehouse built a new harbor at Kilindini, on the western side of Mombasa. He obtained the needed materials and crew, and laid a bridge across Macupa Creek. Since the City of Mombasa is situated on an island, the latter provided access to the mainland of East Africa. A little over a year after Whitehouse disembarked in Mombasa, the railway penetrated only twenty-three miles toward the interior. At this point in the railway's construction, Whitehouse engaged Ronald O. Preston, a dedicated, energetic, and responsible railhead engineer who had also gained his work experience in India. Preston took over the day-to-day responsibilities of moving the railhead forward. Even under Preston's supervision it took another year of arduous effort to cover roughly the next one hundred miles to bring the railhead to the Tsavo River.

Preston initially faced difficulties bridging several streams and furrows, but the severities encountered in crossing the Taru desert caused him greater frustrations. At first glance the Taru, a minor desert by most standards, appeared to have few barriers to rail laying. The distance to cross was about sixty miles and the terrain looked flat. But when the ground crews started to prepare the railroad bed, they were faced with a tenacious tangle of head-tall, barbed wire-like ground vegetation. It took days to bushwhack a distance of a few miles. Then there was the lack of sufficient fresh water, a major problem. About ten thousand gallons of water per day had to be brought by rail from Mombasa to supply drinking water for the crews working the railhead. This was more fresh water than Mombasa could supply, so drinking water had to be rationed and the steam locomotives were forced to use brackish water in the boilers. Like the human being, steam engines cannot drink salt water. Locomotive breakdowns caused considerable construction delays.

Then there was the intense heat of the desert. Not only did it increase the demand for drinking water, but the continuous sunlight converted iron rails, fishplates, tie-downs, spikes and other metal objects into branding irons. So the thirsty workers also had to contend with burns and blisters on their hands, legs and bodies caused by handling the materials.

If conspicuous obstacles caused delays in railway construction, imperceptible hurdles brought the operation to a near halt. Drinking untreated water inoculated the workers with a variety of intestinal protozoans, so dysentery continually debilitated the work crews. Because of the septic work environment, any scratches, punctures, and cuts festered into putrid sores. Rains favored rapid development of mosquitoes, so malaria ran rampant through the camps. Another aerial borne pestilence, the tsetse fly, the harbinger of trypanosomiasis or African sleeping sickness, laid waste to all non-native pack animals; the miles between mile forty and two-hundred along the construction route were considered to be the Fly Belt. Also within the Fly Belt were human botflies, not lethal, but definitely demoralizing when the human body became a habitat for developing maggots. Since workers did not wear boots or shoes, burrowing fleas added to the devitalization of the work force. These insects burrow into the skin of the feet and legs, lay eggs and when the larvae hatch, they feed on the cutaneous and integumentary tissues of the host.

Another flea-borne disease, though it did not occur in East Africa, brought construction to a halt. Early in 1897 an epidemic of bubonic plague broke out in Karachi, India, closing the port to the emigration of workers. Since this was the workers' only gateway to East Africa, hiring to replace those lost to the infirmities contracted in Africa came to a stop. With most of the construction crew incapacitated, work on the railway ceased until autumn of 1897, when India ended the quarantine and workers could again be hired.

To the cheers of workers, the railhead finally reached the east bank of the Tsavo River in December of 1897 - a paradise they thought, because of the continuous supply of water. They could bathe, cool off, and have sufficient water to drink. Preston commissioned Lieutenant Colonel J. H. Patterson to oversee the building of the bridge across the river. But, for the next year a pair of lions thwarted Patterson's efforts and dashed the workers' visions of paradise. These man-eaters killed over one hundred workers and natives. Attempts to bag these "devils" proved difficult. The lions' unpredictability caused the frightened, superstitious workers to run away to Mombasa. Also during this time, unskilled workers masquerading as bricklayers, a skill important to bridge building, caused turmoil and insurrections. It took another year and a half for the railway to reach Nairobi, 325 miles from Mombasa.

To reach the planned final destination, Port Florence on Lake Victoria, took another two plus years. It required crossing the great African Rift Valley. The railway would descend the precipitous two-thousand-foot eastern escarpment, cross about eighty miles of a hot, dry valley floor, and ascend approximately three-thousand feet to the summit of the western escarpment. From there the grade descended for the next one-hundred miles to Lake Victoria. By December of 1901, six hundred and fifty-one miles of railroad track lay between Mombasa and Port Florence. Roughly six years after Whitehouse started the venture, the Uganda Railway, as it was named, was completed.

Many accounts have been written and several films produced about the trials and tribulations the British encountered building the Uganda Railway. However, Charles Miller, in his book titled *The Lunatic Express,* discusses the historical and political events that led to the construction of this railway. He presents a detailed account of its construction - almost a day-to-day diary - and the consequences the railway had on the development of East Africa.

* * *

The Nairobi Railroad Station is at the end of Moi Avenue. It still looks much like it did in old-time pictures I saw in Blixen's *Out of Africa* and Elspeth Huxley's *Out in the Midday Sun.* Missing from today's scene are the horse drawn wagons and buggies and the rickshas that once brought passengers and freight to the station. The station seemed more romantic in the films.

I entered the waiting area after running a gauntlet of raggedly dressed porters and beggars. The waiting area was dingy in spite of the intense sunlight outside. Dismal-colored paint, which appeared to not have been refreshed since the station was built, probably absorbed most of the brightness. Except for the abstract images caused by age and deterioration, a board listing the train's arrivals and departures, and the signs above ticket booths and toilets, the walls had no other decorations. I do not think the train's schedule had changed in years. This waiting room was gloomy, but a few people sat, many slept - permanent residents, I assumed - on the few benches and chairs.

I had made reservations and purchased my ticket the day before, but walked to a ticket booth, one of several that lined the sidewalls, to ask how I was to locate my compartment once I boarded the train.

The ticket agent informed me. "Berthing passengers are listed on the side of the Pullman that contains their berth. First Class cars are the three just behind the restaurant car. Since the train has arrived, you may walk to the platform and inspect the cars to find your name, and you may board."

"Thank you." I did as told and found the procedure straightforward and simple, because only the first class passengers had their names listed on a little panel near the door of the Pullmans. The last six or eight cars of the train had no berths and were designated for the second-class passengers. Passengers in these cars had to take potluck seating.

My compartment, Number 1, Berth 2, aboard Pullman Car E was simple but comfortable. It contained an oversized soft, mohair-covered, cushioned bench and a backrest that crossed the entire cubicle. Since the bench was wider than the width of a standard seat, I had to sit forward for my legs to flex at the knee so that the soles of my feet could contact the floor. On each side of the bench was a shallow storage area recessed into the wall, an ashtray, and a fold-down table. The walls were of dark oak paneling. Two small mirrors hung on the wall in front of the bench. The side panel next to the walkway had a sliding entrance door and a small window, the opposite side had a large window. Both windows were framed by curtains. When the backrest was folded upward to a horizontal position and attached to the pair of chains suspended from the ceiling, the bench converted into upper and lower berths. Both berths were curtained to give sleepers privacy. The space under the bench provided storage for carry-on luggage. Lavatories were located at each end of the Pullman car.

When I entered the compartment, I found that it already contained someone's luggage. Confused, I asked the conductor if I had the correct compartment. I followed him off the car to check the passenger list. Yes, I was listed to be in Car E, Compartment 1, Berth 2. The first compartment past the lavatories after you enter the rear door of Car E contains berths one and two, he explained, Berth 1 is the lower and two the upper. If I wanted Berth 1, he said, I could sort that out with the passenger with whom I shared the compartment. He checked the passenger list and mentioned a Dutch sounding surname, which I did not catch, and said this passenger boarded the train in Navaisha. I thanked him and returned to my designated compartment and stowed my bag under the bench.

No sooner had I sat, than the train started its departure. Simultaneously, the conductor came by sounding a triangle. "Last seating for dinner in ten minutes," he said. I looked at my watch. It was seven o'clock in the evening. The train left on schedule.

"*Jambo*." The conductor poked his head into the compartment. He told me that while I dined, he would prepare my berth for the evening. There would be a six-shilling charge for sheets, blanket, and pillow. He would raise the backrest and attach it to the ceiling for no charge. I could splurge and have my bed made for about fifty cents. So I gave him a ten-shilling note. He smiled. I had made a friend. "Please, the dining car is forward, Sir. I will have your compartment prepared when you return. Enjoy your meal."

When I entered the dining car, the first thing I noticed was the overhead fans, six of them. Their paddles rotated rapidly, but each entire fan wobbled prodigiously, out of phase with its neighbors either by design or poor alignment and balance, sending cool blasts of air onto the diners. It was as if at any moment they would break free of their connection to the ceiling and spiral through the car. I felt like ducking my head as I searched for an empty table.

This car, a real antique and definitely part of the railway's original rolling stock from the early nineteen hundreds, had simple tables set along its sides. The aisle, slightly wider than those found on a Boeing 747, progressed forward toward an L-shaped bar and then into the galley. White tablecloths covered the tables. Silver salt and pepper shakers, a sugar bowl, ashtray, and vase containing two or three cut flowers were centrally arranged under the window. Diners sat on straight-back wooden chairs with rattan seats and backs to allow air to freely circulate. The domed, dingy beige ceiling blended with the polished dark wood panels and window frames that made up the sides and ends of the car. Polished brass plates, handrails, and the light fixtures, located in the space between each window, decorated the walls. Dark green-gray linoleum covered the floor.

Apparently most of the passengers awaited the final seating, because there were few empty places available in the dining car. An elderly American couple invited me to join their table.

"Excuse me. I'm Allen Barkley. Al for short. My wife, Cisely, would like you to share our table, because she thinks you have a tight ass."

"Allen, really!" Cisely appeared humiliated and indignant. She looked at me. "I only said that I liked the way you looked."

"Sorry." Allen smiled sheepishly. "I believe it's the scotch talking." He moved his arm across the table toward an empty chair. "Do please join us."

I smiled. "Thank you," I said.

Al, a robust man with profound eyes set in a roundish, weathered face, had long, wavy white hair that trickled almost to his shoulders. It gave him a distinguished, roughish look.

"I'm Cisely." She did not extend her hand in greeting. "Pleased to meet you. My husband is a tease."

Cisely's almond-shaped, playful eyes, small nose, and full lips on a narrow face suggested that she may once have been the teaser also. But now, she too had that "seasoned look," in an unflattering sense. Life appeared not to have complemented this demure, fragile-framed woman. The two of them turned out to be a most interesting and engaging pair.

For the past five years the Barkleys, originally from San Francisco, had lived in Saudi Arabia. Al, a retired freelance foreign correspondent, had covered many major news events in Asia, primarily in Korea and Vietnam. Most of his activity took place during the Vietnam War. Now since his retirement, he said that he had been working on a memoir describing his escapades as a front-line reporter. Cis wrote Gothic romance novels, which contained Chinese, Japanese, Indian, or other Asian heroes and heroines. She explained that Orientals tended to be more sensual than Caucasians and their sexual activities were more novel and unusual. Her readers were mostly Asian; she did not have a large following in the United States, she said.

"I can never return to the U.S.," Al said.

"Why?"

"While we lived in Saudi, I wrote some articles about how the U.S. and the CIA were in cahoots to overthrow the Iranian government. After their publication, a bunch of officious-looking guys from the American embassy stopped by our apartment and confiscated all my notes and my typewriter. Probably they were CIA, but acting like the KGB. They said my articles denigrated the government of the United States and its people, that I vilified my country. And if I ever set foot on American soil, they'd enjoy charging me with treason. 'We could take your passport,' they said, but they didn't." Al paused for a moment and took a sip of his coffee. "Since the Saudis are in cahoots with the U.S., they also asked us to leave their country. Those "ragheads" canceled our visas."

"My God! That's quite a story. So what are you two going to do?"

"No big deal," Al said while tapping the top of his head. "Since I'm alive, I'll have all I need for an exposé on the American-Iranian association locked in my brain. They could chop off my head, I guess. The Saudis do that you know." He chuckled. "Anyway, after Cis and I visit Kenya for a week or two, we'll go on to the villa we bought in Spain. One can live there without any American interference."

Cis nodded. "Spanish men are really sexy, too, so I won't be at a loss for material. We're going to write in Spain." She seemed excited about the prospects of living there. "Do you know that you can get three servants in Spain for the price of one Arab? And they're more reliable. Spaniards are Catholic, as you know. So they live by the Ten Commandments, instead of the teachings of Allah."

"Sounds like you two are in for an adventure."

Walking back to my compartment, I wondered about the validity of Barkley's story. I began to grin because it sounded a bit far-fetched. Many Americans have a complaint with the government. Some keep it to themselves and others make theirs known. Our officials are mostly thick skinned. Although some molt, they rarely seek vengeance. As Americans we have a constitutional right to criticize our government. There are many characters in the world; Al Barkley is probably one of the more contentious.

On the way back to my compartment I passed the conductor. He said that my compartment mate asked him not to prepare the bunks for sleeping because he wanted to sit, read, and drink a beer before turning in. "It will only take five minutes to arrange the compartment," the conductor said. He asked if I would mind.

"No. But a beer sounds like a good idea. Would you bring me one also?" I asked.

Legs bent under him, knees splayed to the side, Derrick sat on the bench with a book in his lap. He looked like an American Indian ready for a powwow.

"Derrick Van Rooijen," he extended his hand. "I guess you are my compartment mate. Sorry for not being about when you boarded. While the train was stopped in Nairobi, I stepped out on the platform to have a fag. I dislike smoking in the compartment."

I shook his hand and introduced myself.

"American? I can tell by the accent. I'm an Afrikaner. Originally from South Africa, but I now live in Navaisha."

"You sound Australian."

"Been living with the English for too long. Van Rooijens have been in Africa for five generations. My family immigrated to British East Africa during the colonial time because the Anglo-Boer War made living in South Africa difficult. So my parents came north and created several farms. That is what I do, farm."

Dressed in a short-sleeved, khaki-colored shirt and shorts with a brown bandana around his thick neck, Derrick typified a rugged outdoorsman. His flowing flaxen hair contrasted with his dark, deep-set eyes and handsome, tanned face. Although small in stature, about five and a half feet tall, his body was muscular.

The conductor brought us the Tusker Beers we ordered. Derrick paid the tab.

"Thank you for the beer. I'll get the next. What do you farm?"

"Crayfish. *Procambarus clarkii.* The same crayfish you Americans farm in Louisiana and eat in New Orleans."

"That's unusual. I didn't think crayfish were found in Africa. Thought they were endemic only to North American."

"You are correct. I brought a bunch of breeders from a group of cooperative aquaculturists in Louisiana some years ago and set them up in Lake Navaisha. They were trying to promote their industry in foreign lands. So that is how I started. Every couple of years the Louisiana Crayfish Aquaculture Cooperative sends me a new shipment to replenish my breeders. The crayfish actually survive in Lake Navaisha so I am able to successfully produce an economically feasible yield."

"Since I'm a crustacean biologist, I'd be interested in visiting your operation, but I'll be returning to the States in two weeks. Let's keep in touch." I drank my beer and ordered two more because the conductor announced the last call for service.

Because I had not seen crayfish on the menu of any of the restaurants in Nairobi, I asked, "Where are there markets for the crayfish you raise?"

"None in Kenya. Except, maybe, the occasional tourist. Crayfishes are not part of the East African culture. Europe is my market. The French, English, and especially the Swedes find them a delicacy. The problem is that I have to truck each harvest to North Africa, Tunis, and make sure it is loaded on a ship to Marseilles."

"Across the Sahara? Alive? In the heat?"

"Yes. My operation has four large lorries equipped with refrigeration units to keep the water about twenty-five degrees centigrade. We have some losses. It is like the cowboys in the American west. They had to herd the steers from Texas to Montana."

"To drive from Kenya to Tunis is quit a trip! How often do you have to drive it?"

"Whenever we harvest, about every three or four months. That is the reason I am traveling to Mombasa today. There I am planning to inspect a freezing facility. If freezing the crayfish is feasible, I can then arrange to ship them via steamers from Mombasa to Europe. It would save time. The drive to Tunis takes about one month, and there is much stress."

"Should work well. Frozen shrimp from the Gulf of Mexico are shipped all over the world. Good luck."

The conductor came back with our beers and converted the bench into berths. Derrick took the upper berth. I did not have to ask him.

"See you for breakfast," he said. "Get up at sunrise because the train will be passing through Tsavo National Park. We will have a great view of the game while having breakfast. Good night."

"Good night."

I did not sleep much during the night. A lurching train, an excited state of mind, neither is conducive to sleeping. Several times during the night the train stopped at a remote village. Afraid that I would miss something, I parted the curtains to see what was going on. Most time I saw the usual, passengers boarding and leaving, mail and freight being loaded or off loaded. I rolled back into the pillow and tried to sleep. It eventually came in laborious catnaps.

When I awoke in the morning and crawled from out of the berth, I noticed that Derrick's upper bunk was empty. After dozing for most of the night, my last hour of sleep must have been deep enough that his departure did not disturb me. I dressed, made my way to the dining car and found him seated at one of the tables. He motioned me to join him.

"Open the window, mate," said Derrick. "The train is going less than forty miles an hour. We are passing through Tsavo National Park, so we can watch for wild game."

I wrestled with the window for a minute, but Derrick, who had often traveled this route, knew where the window latches were. As soon as he flipped them up the window released, moved. The dust accumulated around the frame burst into aerosols. The window slid down into the dining car's bulkhead, creating an open space large enough to jump through. An apparent breeze flavored with the scent of Tsavo's dry, dust laden vegetation gusted in, dispersed the micro-dust-devils and diluted the smell of bacon and eggs. The air outside was soft and cool; the rising sun had not yet filled it with heat.

My eyes momentarily teared when a wind-stream gently blew across my face as I leaned out the open window. I thought about the times when the railroad actually placed a bench at the front of the engine to allow dignitaries to enjoy spectacular views while the train moved along. Winston Churchill and Theodore Roosevelt took advantage of this perk, but they had to put up with a continuous wind in their faces. All I had to do to avoid the stream of wind, while viewing through an open window, was to relax back against my chair. From the comfort of the restaurant car I could sip my tea and enjoy watching the scenery appear, pass and disappear.

With clear and pure resolution, I observed the landscape undulating as the car rocked and rolled over the uneven rails. In front of me the embankments near the railroad bed slid by rapidly in a blur, momentarily obstructing farther views. When the prospect cleared, telegraph poles popped along almost in rhythm with the "clackity-clack" of the wheels as they passed over the expansion spaces that separated the individual rails. The scene sank and rose through depressions, and, in the distance, merged into a great flat expanse of the arid gravel and scrub plain. This range seemed to rotate in front of me, its pivot in the distant mountain range.

In the old days, if one opened a window, smoke and soot from the steam engine's exhaust inundated the interior of the restaurant car. Dignitaries seated on the bench over the cow-catcher did not have a smoke problem because they were forward of the engine's stack. Though the cars on the train tended toward the antique, a diesel locomotive pulled it along. So all that blew in on the wind was a little grit and the biologically scented heat.

Small herds of gazelles, wildebeests, zebras, and occasional giraffes fed near the tracks. When they heard the rattling railroad cars and screeching wheels, they would lift their heads and stare in unison at the approaching train. Almost on cue, the antelopes bounded away. A trail of dust marked their retreat to a more secure distance. The giraffes momentarily looked up and then returned to their meal. Periodically, the locomotive's horn sounded a short blast, which caused me to glance forward. The resounding blare roused cape buffalo away from the tracks, on one occasion, an elephant. For a few minutes, just before the train reached the bridge over the Tsavo River, I watched two female lions crouch and slink along a rise as if they were stalking prey. This dynamic experience, seeing the landscape and nature passing by the open window was like viewing an IMAX film, except that the episodes didn't roll by as if they were in flat space. All perspectives were focused through all dimensions, the entire scene, very real!

The train clattered onto a bridge. Stroboscopic bursts of light canceled my delightful trance as the train passed between the girders of the Tsavo River Bridge.

"This commonplace bridge has much historical significance," Derrick said. "In the spring of 1898 Lieutenant Colonel J. H. Patterson was put in charge of building this bridge. With his considerable experience in building railroad bridges, he should have completed construction in about three to four months. Because of inappropriate equipment to place the girders, a malaria epidemic, a worker strike, and the time Patterson had to spend quelling worker insurrections, it took nearly a year to build it. But those were not his greatest challenges, he gained his fame from the eradication of two man-eating lions that plagued the work camp. These stealthy creatures rebuffed almost all of Patterson's attempts to eliminate them. For most of the year the man-eaters stalked the work camps, which became known as lion *chopshops*, picking off their human prey even under the most heavily guarded situations. This literally threw the workers into a panic."

"It must have been horrible to live under such a threat," I said.

"Yes," continued Derrick. "You would never know who would be the lions' next meal, or where they would strike. Those cunning devils would just boldly invade villages, camps, and heavily fortified enclosures, even take a bullet or two, then return at a later date, and saunter off with a victim. Their ability to avoid capture and death caused the natives and coolies to attribute them with supernatural qualities. They dubbed the lions as *The Darkness* and *The Ghost*."

Derrick sipped his tea, then continued. "A fortuitous encounter early in December of '98 allowed Patterson to bag one of the two lions with what may have been a single lucky shot. Some days later he brought the other one down, but with more difficulty. The lion took three shots and continued to charge. Patterson escaped up a tree and finished him off as the wounded beast tried to climb after him. He accomplished a feat that soldiers and professional hunters were unable to achieve. Patterson became a celebrity with the workers and the railroad committee. The bridge was completed in March of 1899 and railroad construction was again moving ahead. But, during the nine months that those man-eaters terrorized the Tsavo construction camps, they killed over one hundred people. Back then they were as famous as great white sharks are today."

"Only great white sharks have not killed as many . . ." I clarified. "You know, I've seen those lions, or what's left of them. During my college years I visited the Chicago Field Museum and there they were, on display. Back then I didn't realize their significance, because I had never heard of the *Lunatic Express."*

"Yes, the museum purchased them. It is amazing what a good taxidermist can do," Derrick said. "The skins of those lions were torn, poorly preserved, and shot full of holes. The last one shot took seven slugs, several at close range. I heard recently that museum explorers found the lions' lair. In it they found remnants of many human skeletons."

"Amazing! It must have been a gory mess." I continued to stare out the window, fascinated by the landscape. "I wonder if that pair of lions I saw just before the train crossed the Tsavo Bridge were related to the two devils that stopped a railroad?"

"Perhaps." Derrick rose from the table. "I am returning to the compartment to gather my luggage. We will arrive in Mombasa in about an hour."

The train entered the Taru Desert. I remained in the dining car staring out the window, captivated by the landscape. I had read of this small harsh desert. During the construction of the railroad, water trains had to shuttle back and forth between the railhead and Mombasa because the Taru had no water. Besides this, an impenetrable tangle of thorn bushes and spiny vines covered its floor. Adding heat, parasites, dysentery, and a shortage of workers to this intractable, arid desert, it took more than a year to lay the fifty-six miles of track needed to cross this wasteland.

People walking along near the tracks, children nearby waving, greener vegetation, lush foliated trees growing next to shacks made from crates and sheets of corrugated metal, twisted, engineless vehicles rusting away, squalor, and a considerable increase in humidity signaled that the train was approaching its destination. I pulled the window closed and secured the latches as the train began crossing the bridge over the Macupa creek. Since Mombasa is on an island, bridging this creek became the first major obstacle in the construction of the Lunatic Express.

A freshly painted, well-appointed railroad station greeted me when I stepped off the train in Mombasa. Vines of bougainvilleas cascaded from the latticework at each end of the platform. Royal palms graced the lawn near the street. The diesel locomotive's exhaust dissolved into the moisture laden, frangipani-scented air. I crossed the platform and passed through a clean interior waiting room. There were no beggars. Several uniformed railroad workers greeted the passengers and pointed toward available ground transportation. This was nothing like the railroad station in Nairobi. The Mombasa Station gave me an impression of a commuter train stop in a New England village set in a tropical environment. After a handshake with Derrick, I wished him good luck with his crayfish enterprise and waited my turn to secure a taxi to the hotel. Apparently, the Barkleys either left the station earlier or were still gathering their possessions on the train. I didn't see them before I secured a taxi.

THE TOWN THAT NETTLED THE PORTUGUESE

The isle before them stood soon near land,
that narrow was the strait which lay between;
a city situated upon the stand
was on the seaboard frontage to be seen:
with noble edifices fairly planned
as from the offing showed afar the scene;
ruled by a king for years full many famed,
the island and city were Mombasah named.
from *Lusiads* (103) by
Luis Vaz de Camoes.

Mombasa, in its two-thousand-year history, survived periods of adversity, annihilation, rebirth, peace, and prosperity. While many ancient Indian Ocean seaports along the African coast crumbled and rusted into obscurity, Mombasa survived to modern times. Resilient to time and turmoil, this island city along the coast of Kenya evolved into the largest and most modern seaport between the Red Sea and the Cape of Good Hope.

Ships from Phoenicia, Egypt, Arabia, Assyria, Greece, and nations to the east took on, off loaded, and exchanged cargos at Mombasa. This port was listed in a guide to the seaports of the Indian Ocean published by the Greeks in 150 AD and later described in Ptolemy's *Geography*, circa 400 AD. From 900 to 1500 AD, Mombasa became a key Arabian seaport. During this period, immigrants from the Middle East settled the East African Coastal area. These people developed the coast into civilized, prosperous Arab states or sultanates. Collectively, the strip of coast became known as the Zenj Empire or "Zenjibar" (Black Land). Each dominion came under the rule of a sultan. The Sultan of Bombaze - later known as the Sultan of Mombasa - built Mombasa into a flourishing port. Shipments of such commercial items as maize, cassava, cashews, tobacco, ivory, gold, and slaves originated at this port. Over time the affluent diverse population melded into Swahili, translated as the coastal people, the culture that predominates in today's Mombasa.

Vasco da Gama's visit to Mombasa in 1498 brought the first major intrusion of Europeans, the Portuguese, into East Africa. This visit initiated the demise of the Zenj Empire. The Portuguese encroachment into Mombasa brought with it a period of about two-hundred years of turbulence.

Although all other sultanates succumbed to Portuguese occupation, Mombasa resisted. Because word of the atrocities and indignities suffered by villages to the south at the hands of the Portuguese reached the Sultan of Mombasa, Vasco da Gama's ships were met with suspicion when they arrived there. Fearing retaliation, da Gama sailed seventy miles north to Malindi. In this state, ruled by the Sultan of Malindi, Vasco da Gama received a dignitary's welcome. While there, his crew was given time to relax and recoup before they continued their journey to India.

The Sultan of Malindi had ulterior motives for providing this open-arms greeting to Vasco da Gama's ships. Mombasa's strategic location as a port on the lucrative trade route between Africa and Asia, its accessible harbor, and its riches aroused his desires for possession. Though the Sultan had also received word of Portugal's forcible takeovers in the south, he did not have an amiable relationship with the Sultan of Mombasa and he surmised that a collusion between himself and the Portuguese could be turned to his advantage. Fortunately for him, the Portuguese had similar desires. They not only realized Mombasa's potential, but that of all of the East African coast. The Portuguese also knew that they would soon be in competition with the newly formed, privately owned British East India Company, as well as merchants from France and Holland. Therefore, they decided to create their own empire and gain supremacy over Indian Ocean commerce. By capitalizing on the discord that existed between the Sultans of Mombasa and Malindi, the Portuguese, with the latter's help, invaded Mombasa Island in the early fifteen-hundreds. In an effort to bring the city into submission, they repeatedly looted and burned it.

The Portuguese successfully forced other ports along the East African coast to acquiesce. During this time Mombasa did not capitulate and, in fact, thwarted Portugal's strong efforts to gain supremacy over it. So during the fifteen hundreds, Portugal and its Malindian allies invaded Mombasa four times, each time looting, burning, and slaughtering many of its residents. After each foray the town's people rebuilt the city and, even more vehemently, opposed Portuguese interference and intrusion. Additionally, between the Portuguese raids, the Turks also besieged Mombasa, though their attacks met with little success.

At the end of the century Mombasa, frustrated, attempted a counterattack on Malindi, but lost and the Malindian troops massacred the remnants of Mombasa's troops. This made it possible for Portugal to finally take over the city and install the Sultan of Malindi as its ruler.

After Portugal gained dominance over Mombasa, it made the city the capital of its East African empire. To discourage further invasions, Portugal built Fort Jesus on a promontory overlooking the entrance to the harbor. Completed in 1593, the fort's construction was far from a trivial task. Large stones and other construction materials to build this monumental edifice were unavailable in the coastal area surrounding Mombasa and had to be shipped there from quarries in Portugal.

Although Fort Jesus dissuaded intrusion by rival European traders and savage tribes from the hinterland, it did not deter the townspeople who continued to revolt. Portugal maintained control over Mombasa until in 1696, when the Arabs of Oman laid siege to Mombasa and Fort Jesus. This invasion caused the Portuguese to take refuge in the fort. And here they stayed, incarcerated. The Omani captured the city and embargoed the fort for the next three years. Most of those self-exiled in the fort died of starvation and disease. Several minor raids early in the eighteenth century again returned control to the Portuguese, but these periods were very short lived. The Omani finally ousted the Portuguese in 1728 and took control of Mombasa.

For the most part, peace and prosperity returned to Mombasa. During this period the most important items of commerce, derived from inland Africa, to pass through the city were slaves, elephant tusks, rhinoceros horns, and other exotic items. The Omani maintained control under the authority of the Sultan of Zanzibar. Fortifications at Fort Jesus were enhanced and a wall was built to completely enclose the complex.

Once again a European nation took control of the area when in 1875, Mombasa and its surroundings were leased to the British. For eighty-eight years, life remained harmonious. Although Britain, through the Imperial British East African Company (IBEA), administered Mombasa and the surrounding coastal area, the state remained within the Sultanate of Zanzibar. Because of an economic downturn in the IBEA in 1895, the British East African Protectorate was formed and administration of this coastal strip was transferred to the British Colonial Government with Mombasa as its capital. This entity governed Mombasa until 1963 when Kenya gained independence and the coastal state became part of this new African country.

During Britain's occupation, prosperity reigned and Mombasa became a thriving seaport. The slave trade was abolished and, with the construction of the Uganda Railway, the interior of the country was opened and settlement began. Finally, Mombasa was established as the major Port of Entry into East Africa.

HAGGLING AROUND THE CASTLE HOTEL

When Sir Richard F. Burton, the British explorer and author of *Arabian Nights,* arrived in Mombasa's harbor in the 1850s, he described his coming as ". . . derided by black nymphs bathing in the costume of Camoens' Nerieids, and sable imps sunning on the white sands. . . ." My arrival did not generate any banter from the natives, although sable imps abounded and the black nymphs appeared later. My initial greetings to the city came from the taxi drivers outside the railroad station. They were cordial and friendly, but practical.

I arrived in Mombasa without hotel reservations, but with information about the Castle Hotel and Manor House Hotel, two quality inns in the city's center. The taxi driver made my choice. He recommended the Castle Hotel because it is on Mombasa's Moi Avenue, the main street for commerce and excitement. ". . . besides, you can see and feel the pulse of the city from the Castle's Terrace Café," he said. "Being the oldest hotel in the city, it also has much history," he mentioned. I respected his selection and he delivered me to the Castle Hotel.

On the way to the hotel the driver turned onto Moi Avenue, the main east-west thoroughfare through the city where opposing lanes are separated by a grassy, treed median. We passed under a pair of very large elephant tusks that crossed over the lane we traveled. Another set also intersected above the opposite lane of Moi Avenue. These metal sculptures, built in 1956 to honor the visit of Princess Margaret, symbolized the city's heritage as the center of the East African ivory trade. About two blocks ahead stood the Castle Hotel, a brilliant white, four-story structure with arched, balustraded balconies that delineated each story across the front and east sides. Its architecture suggested a nineteenth century Arabian palace. The taxi driver stopped along the side to allow me to enter and determine if a room were available.

A slight twinge of disappointment came over me when I realized the staff was not clothed in caftans, filmy blouses and harem pants; neither did any of them wear slippers.

Where's the Sheikh that's suppose to greet my arrival? I wondered.

The hotel staff was Swahili, not Arabian, and they dressed in typical modern, western clothing like most hotel staffers throughout the world: dark pants or skirts and short-sleeved white shirts or blouses. The desk clerk, a pleasant young man, said that a room was available and asked me to register.

The Castle Hotel's airy, East African colonial-style lobby and main floor were decorated with a wooden ceiling and trim, and furnished in an eclectic mixture of period furniture and accessories. This decor contrasted with the light-colored plaster walls. Built in 1909, the hotel provided elegant lodging for aristocrats and wealthy travelers who came in search of adventure in the newly opened East Africa territory. After spending several weeks at sea, travelers could relax and refresh themselves amid the comforts and amenities the hotel offered before they ventured to Nairobi aboard the Lunatic Express or into the interior to hunt big game. Many of the rich and famous in the early nineteen hundreds lodged at the Castle Hotel. When the excitement of East Africa faded during the two world wars, the hotel fell into decline. Restoration, renovation and modernization made during the 1970s brought the establishment back to its prominence as a first-class hotel in the city's center.

I followed a porter up a stairwell barren of carpeting and decoration to the third floor. The scrape-clap sound, made when our shoes contacted each step, echoed through its recesses. My room was about midway down a dimly lighted, empty hall. When we entered, a cloud of heavy, stale air engulfed us. It was as if the atmosphere in the room contained the heat and smells of many of its past tenants. For thirty-dollars a night and no advanced reservation, it was as if the hotel assigned me a room that hadn't been occupied since the days of the great white hunters.

"It is the air conditioner, Sir." The porter dropped my bags and began fiddling with the device below the window. It awakened with a grinding whir and settled into a loud drone that intensified to a clamorous bumble when the compressor kicked in. Later, I found that the contraption cooled, but removed little moisture. I decided that I could tolerate the clamminess during my short stay in Mombasa. However, when I returned to the lobby and I mentioned the problem to the desk clerk, he contacted a maintenance-crew. They changed the filter and unplugged the drain to release accumulated condensation. The fix left me with a cold and dry room, but with an air-conditioner that whirred, buzzed, slogged and clanked as it went about its business.

Other than the problem with the air conditioner, the room was habitable, but sparsely furnished in austere Danish-modern furniture: a bed, end table, lamp and chair. Unlike my warm, airy room in Nairobi, this one had a functional television set, but my choice of T.V. entertainment was limited. Soccer matches and political discussions dominated the two available channels.

This room came with a private bathroom. The small cubicle contained the usual: a commode, lavatory, and stand-up shower.

The ornate-looking, balustraded balconies that so elegantly decorated the outside of the hotel created a very somber atmosphere within the room. Their scope restricted the amount of outside light that could enter. Before air conditioning, the balconies and the brilliant external whiteness of the building had more than just a decorative role. These features reduced interior heat due to solar radiation during the daylight hours. Additionally, in the old days, guests could open their room's windows. This generated an upward and outward convection that cooled those who sat in the breeze. Early guests could also use their respective verandas where they could enjoy leisurely afternoon tête–à–têtes and sip aperitifs, teas or liquors. But now, refurbished, the windows didn't open and the door to the balcony was sealed. I could only see roosting pigeons when I peered through the window toward the balcony, and a newly formed puddle of air conditioner-drainage water.

Nevertheless the room provided a comfortable place to sleep during my stay in Mombasa. I stowed my belongings, took a shower, changed clothes and went to the Terrace Café, a raised, tiled veranda beneath the balustraded balconies just off the Castle Hotel's lobby. The café faced Moi Avenue. Unlike the vegetated borders around the Thorn Tree Café at the New Stanley Hotel in Nairobi, the Terrace Café opened completely onto the street. Pedestrians who walked past the Terrace Café could, if they wanted, walk through that portion of the café nearest the street, or stop in to take advantage of the shade it offered. To not discourage local foot traffic, tables were arranged behind and between the hotel's massive rectangular support pillars with an aisle that passed straight through the length of the café's interior. This aisle separated the more interior sets of tables from those along the street. Often walkers stopped and rested at tables between and around the pillars.

While I sat for lunch at a table in the inner part of the café, I noticed that most of the noon-hour walk-in crowds gathering around the pillars were businessmen from surrounding office buildings. But two, sometimes three, of the tables along the outer margin of the café were occupied by lone, young to middle-aged women who would order a drink and nurse it for several hours. Waiters did not interfere with these women after they had purchased their drink. My waiter informed me that the women were prostitutes. He could, if I were interested, arrange an afternoon and evening of splendor and excitement. "What an interesting proposition . . . but no thank you," I said.

The diversity of people and the smells and sounds of traffic moving past the hotel while I lunched heightened my urge to explore. From where was all this activity coming? I wanted to find out what lay beyond the Terrace Café and Castle Hotel. So after lunch I asked the concierge for a little guidance.

"Mombasa is dangerous," she said. "Stay on the main street. If you go onto secondary streets do not wear watches, rings, jewelry, or carry a camera. Wear your oldest clothing. . . . Tourists can stroll in safety along Moi Avenue to Arab Town, Fort Jesus, and to the railroad station." Chilling advice. I decided to stay on Moi Avenue.

There were about twenty portable tables arranged haphazardly on the sidewalk along the three blocks between the hotel and the crossed elephant tusk sculptures. Some contained handicrafts of local artisans; others displayed toiletries, books, T-shirt, spices, and other small commodities. Several tables were staffed by solitary proprietors trying to sell their wares. Other tables had two or three eager, sharp, casually dressed young men hanging around. These fellows haggled with potential buyers and tended to follow them along the street for a short distance trying to make a sale.

Haggling, the face-to-face negotiation during the acquisition of something, is an expected way of street and market bargaining in this part of the world. In the United States we either pay the ticket price or take a less contentious method of negotiation toward obtaining a better price. But in East Africa and the Middle Eastern countries, haggling is a way of life.

While in the Masai Mara, I found Masai girls to be sly hagglers. They placed the object of interest in the hand of the buyer then allowed the buyer to first quote a price he or she was willing to pay. Of course the quoted price was always insufficient, so the seller gestured discordantly to show that the quotation must be increased. If the buyer tried to return the object, the seller refused to take it. She continued to sign an upward signal with her hands, arms and body. When the exchange appeared to be failing, the girl would become more familiar, touch and caress the buyer's arms or shoulders. Soon the bout became a sensuous contest between the language of the buyer and the vernacular of the seller. Neither totally understood the words of the other. This contest continued until a compromise occurred or the frustrated girl retrieved the bangle and tried to sell it to a less frugal tourist.

A Pakistani proprietor in a back-street copper shop in Nairobi told me that he felt disappointed if the buyer accepted the price he quoted and didn't haggle. He believed that tourists who don't haggle discounted his culture through their ignorance, because they deprived him of a challenge. But, on the other hand he did recognize the advantage of tourists' ignorance. "If I tell them a price and they pay it," he said, "I make lots of money. Since I expect buyers to bargain, I always begin by asking more for the article than what it is worth. If the price is not questioned, and I am paid, it would not be prudent for me to tell such buyers that they are paying too much. Sometimes I feel guilty, but not so much as to ruin my day. I would rather the buyer disagree with my price and argue. Haggling is a game of verbal conflict. It can become a very heated contest.

In the end we either agree or disagree, but we respect each other's decisions, shake hands, and always part as friends."

This method of bargaining is energizing and exciting. What a great way to buy a few souvenirs, I thought. So I wandered into this milieu of exchange, but not before setting a five-dollar limit (about 80 Ksh) as my maximum amount to spend.

At about the third or fourth table I stopped to admire a display of bracelets. My interest in handcrafted jewelry quickly caught the attention of several roving peddlers. Before my wristwatch flicked to the next second, two were at my side hawking the quality of their products. One fellow had fastened onto the lower length of his arm a variety of wire bracelets. One particular design, created from pieces of thick and thin copper wires braided together and intertwined with similar sized segments of aluminum wires, stimulated my interest. I had seen these worn by some safari guides and other men in Nairobi. They seemed to epitomize East African machismo. I pointed to one. "How much?"

"Two-hundred Kenyan shillings."

"Thank you." I moved on.

The other fellow had a display box of more authentic-looking native-made bracelets created from colorful Arabian glass beads, seeds, wood, shells, or a mixture of these strung on pieces of very thin wire or strands of plastic-like fiber. These bands appeared to be authentic, simple and fragile. Additionally, this seller had some arm bands made of braided elephant hair. Although these are prized for their uniqueness and supposed mystical quality, to me these fall into the same category as bangles made from ivory, sea-turtle shell, or any product that results from the slaughter of wildlife.

Out of curiosity I asked the price of an elephant hair bracelet. One thousand shillings (about $75.00 U.S.) was the quotation. Since I have seen these ornaments on wrists of many young tourists, they were in demand. The sale of one elephant hair bracelet would bring the seller, even if he is haggled to a lower price, an income of more than is normally earned by an average Mombasan in a month. So it's no surprise that these street peddlers are dressed better than most people.

He tried to place one of the elephant hair bracelets on my wrist. "No. I'm not interested. They're illegal where I come from," I said and pulled my arm from his grip. "How much for those?" I pointed to several bands made of seed mixed with Arabian glass beads.

"Since I have not sold anything today, I will give you the choice of three for one hundred and fifty-shillings." He circled his finger over the bracelets in which I showed an interest.

"They're not very well made," I said and pointed to the clasps. "Look, these will easily come apart and I will lose them." I move away, but toward the peddler with the copper wire bracelets. I turned back toward the seed-and-bead guy. "Twenty shillings for the three."

"No," he said. "I cannot buy a Coke-a-cola for that price. Get real . . . as you in America say." He turned and thought for a moment. "Seventy-five shillings for the three that is half of what they are worth . . . and I cannot go lower. I have to feed my family."

"I'll give you twenty-five shillings for the three, and no more," I called back and started walk toward the hotel. As I moved slowly away I fixed my eyes on the fellow with the copper wire bands. The quality of his bracelets seemed better. We made eye contact and he came forward.

"Perhaps this one will interest you?" He removed one of the six-strand copper and aluminum braided bands from his arm and snapped it onto my wrist. "My wife made this, but she will not be happy if I sell it. It is her favorite . . . but for one-hundred and fifty shillings I sell."

"Nice, but too much. Besides I can't take something your wife prizes. When she finds it missing, she'll probably get mad and konk you on the head with her club." He smiled while I took the bracelet off my wrist, examined it, rubbed it against my pant's leg and viewed the metallic contrast between the apparent warmth and coolness of the metals. "I'll give you 150 shillings for two." He clutched a bracelet tightly, looked at me in disgust and retreated behind a nearby table to rethink his strategy.

The seed-and-bead man took my hand. "Fifty shillings. I have children to feed."

Maybe he has children, maybe not, I thought. But he does have to make some money for his efforts. And, I do want those bracelets. The one with what looked like wheat seeds arranged crosswise to strands of green beads is the one I wanted to wear myself. It would finish off the Great White Hunter image I fancied. *What vanity.* I smiled to myself. I opened my wallet, withdrew a fifty-shilling note and gave it to him. His face beamed. He handed me the three bead bracelets and receded down the block.

Before I had time to close my wallet, the peddler with the wire bracelets again appeared at my side. I am sure that he saw the edges of several more shilling notes extending from my wallet and observed the success of the fellow who sold me the bead-bracelets. I sensed a rivalry between these two guys earlier when they vied for my attention. So probably, my money and competitive jealousy stimulated him back into action. He held the two braided wire wristbands in front of my face. "Two hundred shillings . . . and I cannot take less."

Without making eye contact, I started to walk toward the curb to cross the avenue and go beyond his territory. There were other vendors on the other side. He jumped in front of me, out into the traffic. To avoid hitting him, a truck and a taxi came to a screeching halt. Apparently, from comments I heard after, such behavior in this stretch of the avenue is common. Even so, the drivers of the vehicles shouted advice laced with African profanity.

I removed a hundred-shilling note from my wallet and flashed it at him.

"You are a criminal," he shouted. "I am almost killed and you offer only a pittance for my work. I feel you do not like my art and I will starve if I accept your poor offer." He ranted and waved the arm that held the bracelets around in the air defiantly until the truck driver shifted into gear and started forward. The peddler jumped back onto the curb, dejected and disappointed, but continued to stand tall.

I smiled, felt proud of myself for resisting the temptation to give in to his sales pressure. His outbursts and spirited display, a final enthusiastic ploy to capture a sale, didn't work. Looks like I won, I thought, but I don't have the bracelets I wanted. So I felt a little guilty for leading this haggler on. He worked so hard. "Fifty shillings for your effort and a hundred for the bracelets," I shouted after him.

With his back toward me, he yelled at the top of his voice. "You are still a criminal." He turned and faced me. He smiled. I saw that his spirit had lifted. We made the exchange and shook hands. As he left, he said, "You drive a hard bargain. Come by my table tomorrow and I will have more for you to see."

After several more encounters with the street vendors, I spent about a total of fifteen dollars and invested a couple of pints of adrenalin for a trove of trinkets, most of which I had little intention of buying. I also spent a bit more than I had planned, but what I purchased would serve as souvenirs to give friends and relatives when I return to the United States.

I also bought several necklaces crafted by native artisans. Two primitive-looking ones were composed of a single strand of beads from which several pounded-copper leaves hung. Several tiny, blue glass, droplet-like pendants dangled from the tip of each leaf. A couple of necklaces had tightly coiled copper spring-like pieces linked by colored beads. From this primary chain many strands of interlocking copper rings hung vertically below the wearer's neck and draped over the clavicles. I also found two brass choker chains. One design contained hundreds of very thin overlapping leaves that cascaded in a triangle over the suprasternal notch and made a metallic "shushing" sound as the wearer walked. The other had a similar design, but was made of strands of hundreds of thin overlapping dime-sized coins. This one looked, and felt, heavier because the metallic scarf was designed to fall further below the neckline and cover a larger area of the upper chest. This one also shushed when it moved, but at a higher pitch. Either of these could have been worn by Scheherazade, or maybe a harem dancer. I also acquired five camel-tooth necklaces. Each had an authentic camel's tooth pendant clasped in an imitation gold holder that dangled from a black fiber string necklace. Like the shark-tooth necklaces worn by surfers and SCUBA divers, the camel's tooth is another display of masculinity seen in East Africa.

From a vendor across the street from the hotel I bought another unique gift, a snake box. It was made from a pinkish, satiny, marble-like mineral called soapstone, mined near Lake Victoria. Snuffbox-sized, this container had a little rodent-looking handle sculptured on top. If someone pushed against this handle, a pseudo-secret door slid open and out shot the head of a cobra. I thought the snake box would make an ideal paperweight, and a surprise for my curious friends.

Shortly after 4:00 p.m. I returned from my haggling experience and walked through the Terrace Café to get a beer before going to my room. Allen and Cisely Barkley, the elderly couple I met on the train from Nairobi were sitting at a back table. Al waved excitedly. "Richard, join us," he said. "Did you notice anything unusual during your walk?"

"Nothing out of the ordinary," I said. Although, while walking back toward the hotel, I did notice several small groups of clean-cut, white young men walking along the avenue. About a block from the hotel near a little park, four or five of these tanned, muscular males, sporting crew-cuts and dressed in clean polo shirts and Levis, appeared to be engaged in lively exchange with a couple of nicely dressed, eager young native women. Groups of vigorous, but innocent-looking, white men were rare in Mombasa, so seeing them is unusual. They certainly weren't missionaries. Their behavior seemed controlled by an overload of testosterone. This post-pubertal condition manifests itself in young males; they try to connect with anything wearing a skirt. All guys go through this situation, but these boys appeared seriously afflicted.

"Good grief, Al! Those guys are Americans, aren't they?" I said. "What are they doing here?"

"Yes! Yes!" Al bounced in his chair. Held tightly to the edge of the table. He used his left leg to push a chair toward me. "Sit. Let's watch the excitement develop."

"What're they doing here? "Where'd they come from?"

As I started to sit, two taxies pulled up and stopped in front of the Terrace Café. More Levi clad vitality aggressively poured out. For the next ten to fifteen minutes several more taxies unloaded more lusty passengers. Soon the scent of Old Spice permeated the café.

"The American Navy has landed."

"They're not in uniform," I said.

"The uniform is too conspicuous, so the boys do not wear them on liberty outside the U.S."

Al slid his chair back, swung the beer bottle to his lips, drained its contents, slammed the empty onto the table and vigorously motioned the waiter to bring another round of drinks. "Three navy ships tied up in Kilindini Harbor this morning. The waiter told me that Mombasa is expecting about six-hundred sailors, because that's how many received a twelve-hour liberty pass to straighten their sea legs in this city. Richard, take a look around." Al swept his arm around. "Don't you find this excitement invigorating?" Al's fervor livened. "What energy! This place is charged. Don't you smell the lust?"

"Allen, Allen, relax! Take it easy." Cisely tried to calm him. "I know you'd love to be out there sparring with those fellows, telling risque stories, lying about your conquests, propositioning those hot little nymphs, but you're married. . . and you're too old."

Transfixed on the events that were occurring on the avenue, I did not realize that the café had filled. Sailors and young women were everywhere. Groups of guys and groups of women waiting to make connections stood on the sidewalk next to the café. In the aisles between and around the tables mixed groups gathered. Some just hung about and watched their buddies entertain their newly made friends.

I knew where the sailors came from, but *where* did all these *women* come from? When word hit the streets that several American ships were anchored in the harbor women came into the city from everywhere. The majority were in their twenties, but there were many in their teens. All anticipated the free food, drink, and monetary compensation that came from serving foreign sailors on leave. I looked about the café, my view of the avenue, virtually obscured. What a crowd. I overheard three guys at the next table weighing a proposition to buy a round of drinks for five girls that moved to their table.

"Damn they're bold!" Cisely shooed two wantons away from Al's side, when they decided he needed to buy each a beer. "Get lost, he's too old for you," she said. Al and I laughed.

A sudden commotion on the opposite side of the café caught our attention. Two sailors in a fist fight thrashed about the area. Tables and chairs near them overturned as the two scuffled around the floor. One of the combatants crashed a beer bottle against a pillar just as a couple of shore patrolmen, night sticks brandished, broke through the crowd and disarmed him; this ended the fracas. None too soon, because several Mombasan policemen arrived looking stern, angry, and in the mood to haul everybody to the hoosegow. Instead, the drunken fighters were pushed into the back of a jeep by the shore patrol and removed from the scene. They'll complete their liberty in the bowels of some ship, I thought. Quickly the activity in the Terrace Café returned to its original electrified furor once the furniture was righted.

In a burst of uncontrolled energy, Al slapped me on the back, hugged Cisely and shouted, "It's like during the last days of Saigon, when we had only a few hours to evacuate. Everyone, Americans, Vietnamese, and even the stray dogs, were trying to find a way to leave that hellhole. It was the last chance the South Vietnamese women had to rope some poor unsuspecting GI into getting them, their kids, parents, and grandparents out of the city, out of Vietnam, away from the terror that would come when the Vietcong took over the city. Those left behind would face a life of prostitution or soldiering for the Cong, or they'd be imprisoned, tortured, starved and executed for helping Americans . . . a truly miserable way to live. There was a major sense of urgency during the days before Saigon fell. So the women came in from the fields and gutters in droves. Gave up their dignity and made themselves openly available to any western male. Saigon became an orgy of lust driven by fear. Of course, the guys took advantage."

"Did you get involved in all that horror, Barkley?" Cisely looked incensed. "What were you doing *there*?"

"Writing the story. Trying to save my own ass."

"So where's the urgency here?"

"Dammit, Cisely! These sailors have been out to sea, maybe for months, and when they're offshore, all they have to make love to is some centerfold pinned above their bunk or stuck under the lid of their footlocker. Pictures aren't very satisfying. To get laid is their urgency. All they want to do is put in at any port when a storm is evident . . . and there's a definite storm here."

"In the land of AIDS!" Cisely slapped Al on his shoulder. "This is insane, turning all these beautiful young men loose to roll in fields of poison ivy. This is how epidemics are spread. What's wrong with the Navy? Have they no sense?" Cisely's eyes flared.

"They're issued condoms." Al tried to pacify his wife. "Before the sailors are given liberty, the health office instructs them on how to protect themselves."

"Don't give me that bull." Cisely pushed herself away from the table. "Those healthy boys. They look so innocent. I should talk to them. . . ." She stood, but before she moved away, she finished off her brandy and winked at me.

Distracted by the ongoing activity and oblivious to Cisely's actions, Al dallied with a couple of older, curvaceous goddesses that had entered the café. She noticed his indiscretion and bent toward me. She whispered. "He's all man, but an ol' fool. I need to get him out of here before he has a heart attack."

"Good luck. I'm going to get some dinner." I chuckled as I rose and took my purchases from the table. "Maybe I'll see you two tomorrow." I made my way through the crowd to the lobby. The reservation desk was surrounded, several bodies deep by a clamorous mixture of intoxicated sailors and eager looking women trying to support each other and bargain with the desk clerks to secure a few hours of privacy. For them, this was their first exposure to the art of haggling.

I made my way to the hotel restaurant. Several of the twenty or so tables within this more sedate atmosphere were occupied. The maitre'd showed me to a table, but as soon as I sat two young women walked up and seated themselves. They smiled. Announced that they were going to help me enjoy my evening, but first I must buy them a drink.

"I'm flattered, but not tonight," I said. "I'm not a sailor. And I am not interested in sharing my evening. Go to the café. There are many sailors looking for young women." I motioned for the maitre'd.

Disappointed, they left.

A PHOTOGRAPHIC TOUR

The young man said, "You shouldn't go there by yourself," when his course merged with mine.

Shrugging off the advice, I gripped my camera strap tighter and continued to walk toward Arab Town. "I've been around, know what to expect, surely don't need someone, especially a man like this telling me where I can and can't go. I'll take charge of my own affairs," I mumbled to myself. "I've encountered pseudo guides like him before; they're predators on tourists."

Ignoring his presence I crossed the square toward the lane beside Ali's Curio Shoppe and Coffee House, the entrance to the oldest part of Mombasa.

Thoughts of Arab Town have always conjured images of *Arabian Nights' Entertainments*, Aladdin, magic carpets, sheiks, slave girls in harem pants nimbly twirling on cool marble floors amid soft sounds of Arabian woodwinds and tingling tambourines, gossamer curtained chambers emanating exotic perfumes, blue smoke issuing from narrow-necked vases, genies, vivid eyes of black robed women framed between veils and scarfs, scimitar slung eunuchs, exploding dirt and dust behind Bedouin riders, Sindbad, thieves, and concubines. I wanted to smell, feel, and taste this mysterious, mystical, ancient jewel of African civilization, but I didn't want a guide disrupting my fantasies, nor my resulting adventure.

Several cars blocked the narrow street next to Ali's Curio Shoppe. This allowed only pedestrian traffic to enter the street into Arab Town, a place I imagined still existed as it did in times past.

"You know, Arab town is confusing. Tourists get lost. Some never reappear." He approached, extended his hand. "I'm Ahmed," he said.

Ahmed was one of the three young men dressed in Polo shirts and Levis that I had seen relaxing under the acacia trees next to Fort Jesus as I approached the lane entering Arab Town. Otherwise inconspicuous, his clean, strikingly new black and white Reeboks made him stand out. A warning I thought, a sign of affluence probably attained in some unscrupulous way. The shoes lacked the sand-colored smudges that covered the weathered and shabby ones the other young men wore. He had dark skin, a squarish face with prominent cheekbones, thin lips, delicate nose, and a head of short wavy hair. His frame, attired casually in American-influenced garb, cast a handsome image. Had he worn a caftan he could easily be mistaken for an Egyptian or Moroccan. Young men like him, freelance guides, collect around favorite tourist sites in all third world countries. They're clean cut, gracious, charismatic, friendly, intelligent, but artists of manipulation, persuasion, and salesmanship. They possess all the skills needed to empty a tourist's moneybag and commandeer all useful gadgets. And these guys usually work in teams.

"Thank you, Ahmed. You can tell that to the tourists,"

I said. "Arab Town is no different from any other ghetto I've visited."

Ahmed smiled, remained close to my side. We walked through the blockade of vehicles. "A nice outfit. Banana Republic. . . . Yes?"

Subconsciously, I rubbed my hip pocket checking for my wallet. "Are my clothes that obvious?" I asked him.

"I collect catalogs," Ahmed said. "Banana Republic stuff is worth negotiation. . . . You a photographer?"

My photographer's vest with the usual paraphernalia sticking out of the pockets made an unfounded statement. "I like to document what I see."

Our pace took us deeper into the old city. Ahmed picked up my cadence.

"Do photographers usually hire you as a guide?" I asked.

We turned down another narrow street. My sense of direction was becoming fuzzy. Ahmed's presence and constant questions disrupted my concentration. When we passed Ali's Curio Shoppe just after we entered Arab Town, the sky was brightest behind us. Now it appeared as a slit, a skylight, between shadowed buildings. It glowed with equal intensity from all directions masking the position of the sun, diffusing my ability to navigate.

"Sure," he said. "But, they only want to photograph harem girls, topless ones . . . naked ones even better . . . and they pay well. A score like that will keep me off the streets for a couple of days. You see, I'm not greedy."

We continued.

Suddenly, I felt alone. Missed Ahmed. Hadn't heard his voice in the past few minutes? I turned. He had stopped next to a group of boys playing around a puddle. When he glanced my way, random words in Swahili vibrated the air against my eardrums, their meanings garbled by the boys' suppressed laughter and sporadic nods. Ahmed patted one of the boys on the shoulder. That boy then ran through a nearby door. With a wave of Ahmed's arm, the others scattered in different directions.

Catching up with me, Ahmed looked toward where the boys had been and said, "I asked them if they had sisters that wanted to model for an American newspaper photographer. *You are an American* . . . maybe not working for a newspaper, but a photographer, aren't you?"

"No! And, I'm not some sort of pervert either." My adrenalin flared. "I'm not looking for a pound of flesh. If I wanted that, I sure as hell don't want to photograph some twelve-year-old. There are plenty of whores around my hotel, better looking and probably a damn sight cheaper."

I pulled a city map from my vest and flipped it open. "Bug off, before I do something that will get me into real trouble. Find yourself a horny sucker and deal with him. I travel alone."

"Hey, Man. Sorry. I'm a Christian. I don't sell women." He tried to put his hand on my shoulder, but I moved away.

"This place isn't safe." Ahmed sounded concerned. Extended his hand again attempting to make contact. "Really my friend, life is cheap here, but that vest and camera equipment isn't. They'd bring a month's salary to the wretches living here. Sorry I made you angry." Two braying jackasses pulling an open rail cart masked his apology as they passed us.

"What did you say? You'll have to speak up Ahmed, you're competing with a couple of jackasses."

"I'll be your guide. Free!" Ahmed said. "Show you things tourists don't see . . . like the old harbor. No charge! Do you like old boats? Maybe you'd like to buy perfume for a friend in America? I take you to Yusuf the Perfumer. No charge!"

He continued to talk fast, but I considered only his closing remark, "I keep you safe, show you the way out . . . you can trust me."

"*Trust you?* You lost my trust before you were born. Hey, you never had it! And, if you're not going to charge me, how are you going to make a living? By conning me? Pick my pockets? Kidnap me for ransom? . . . that'll be useless. What's the catch?"

"No catch. I'm shamed in your eyes. Not good for business. Must make up, be your friend."

The street we hiked was only as wide as a donkey cart. Pedestrians had to jump into open doorways if a car came along. We came to a small square where alleys, barely the width of my shoulders, entered from odd angles. Interconnected cement buildings formed an escarpment around us. A few were whitewashed. The walls of others were soiled and eroded, colored in psychedelic patterns of cream, beige, and brown. Baroque balconies disrupted several of the façades. Beneath one, on the far side, walked two women completely dressed in black, each holding the hand of the little boy bounding along between them. Two more Muslim women passed in front of us. All had scarfs wrapped over their heads and across their faces. Only their eyes were visible.

"Do you ever see their faces . . . or hair?" I asked.

"They're not to be looked upon. You'd lose your head if you got caught looking at their faces," Ahmed said. "But, they're said to be very beautiful . . . exotic looking, innocent, but dangerous."

"Why dangerous?"

"Because, if they for some reason become involved with you, their men will kill you. And then, kill them."

We walked down one of the alleys. After several angular turns, we came to another square.

"Hey! We've passed that sign before." I said spying the sign advertising Bahari Boutique. "We're walking in circles."

"This is the back entrance to the shop," Ahmed said and continued ahead of me.

"That's how you guys confuse tourists." I stared at the sign, then the building's façade. "Walk a guy around. Talk a lot. Confuse his sense of direction. Then, he has to hire you to get him out."

"Do you know where you are?" Ahmed grinned.

I waved the map. "Won't need your service, but thanks anyway," I said.

"Hey man, suit yourself." Ahmed shrugged and stayed fixed in place while I walked toward a group of Muslim women window-shopping at Bahari Boutique. They quickly dispersed when I approached.

I looked back. "Alone, finally," I sighed.

* * *

The square I entered contained no tourists. As a matter of fact, I hadn't seen any for some time. Clotheslines crisscrossed overhead between balconies and open windows. From them a dynamic colorful, crazy quilt of scarfs, wraps, veils, sheets, and clothing danced in the breeze, obscuring most of the sky. Five pathways radiated from this square, their destinations erased in the shadows of distant bends and twists. I was in the center of a maze.

The air was hot, humid, although I stood in the shade. Water issued from a fountain at the far side. A splash of water in my face would sure feel good, I thought. But, when I looked toward the fountain, there stood Ahmed. I didn't want to get involved with him again, so I passed on the splash. Besides, three men in frazzled shirts decorated with sweat blotches outlined in salt grouped about him. Dust from the street powdered their slacks and sandal-covered feet. They lazed about the fountain, facing him, listening to him. Not a savory bunch to be involved with, I concluded. A subtle movement of Ahmed's head in my direction appeared to support my contention and suggested my likely involvement.

My hands and chest moistened, stomach tightened. I tried to compare the square where I stood with those on the map. There were several. None fit.

A sailor once told me, "When in doubt, follow the wind." Vibrating, pulsating, undulating swatches that formed the crazy quilt overhead beckoned toward a dark lane. I entered. This pathway curved, narrowed. I rounded a bend and emerged on a balcony built atop a precipice that fell off into the bay. Below me floated rafts of dhows, their sails drawn, baking in the sun. Amid a murmur of shouts and commands, ebony men, some raggedly dressed, others scantly clad, scurried and filed, like ants, over decks, into and out of holds and spaces, and across the gangways that connected the dhows, carrying bundles, boxes, bales, and lumber. Along the wharf narrow streams of cargo laden humanity flowed from cavernous warehouses to and from lighters that negotiated the gap between the wharf and rafts and fed the cargo to the swarms aboard the dhows. On an outermost, heavily laden dhow I noticed ten sweaty men straining against an anchor line.

Capstans, engines, and winches, even antiquated types, were not aboard this antediluvian vessel. Its hull appeared strained, consumed, a time capsule from the Ottoman Empire. This Barbarossan sight filled the viewer of my Nikon. Biceps, deltoids, pectorals, trapeziuses bulged when the men pulled against the hawser strapped across their backs. In unison they rhythmically rocked against this cable, straining, relaxing, straining.

Fascinated, I couldn't stop shooting pictures.

The hulk responded. Water slowly parted from the bow. The ancient ship pulsated forward; inching toward the channel, measured by the metered grunting, groaning chants that mingled with soprano cries of gulls and terns.

The dhow's sails began to unfurl. But a green uniform, meticulously groomed, from its beret to a pair of spit-shined boots, appeared in my viewer and quickly obliterated the dhow. The expanded chest decorated with medals and a holstered forty-five millimeter handgun hanging at the waist made me hesitate, but the automatic rifle he pointed at my feet made me take notice.

"That's the old harbor, isn't it?" I said.

"What are you doing here?" His face remained stolid.

"Just stopped to enjoy the view."

"This area's restricted."

"Right. I'll go the other way."

Sheepishly I started to lift my arm in a parting gesture. Momentary concern flared; this motion might convey disrespect. My hand never rose above my belt. Hair on the back of my neck stiffened. My skin tightened. I faded backward toward the cover of the next building. I wished I had the ability to dematerialize. Invisibility would be a godsend at this moment. I rolled around the corner, took a couple of very deep breaths to calm my twitching muscles and queasy stomach.

"Takes his job seriously."

"What the hell!" My back scraped against the building as I rotated on my heel. "Ahmed."

"Have a Coke?" Ahmed laughed, handed me a can. "I'm a good guy now, yes?"

"Your timing is good. Thank you." I took the warm Coke. "What was that all about? Why the security?"

"His guns probably weren't loaded," Ahmed tried to assure me. "But one never knows. Have you ever heard of slavery?"

"Slavery? What about slavery? It doesn't exist."

"Guess you're not married," Ahmed said with a grin, then continued more seriously. "It exists in some form all over the world, but it's kept pretty secret."

Ahmed ushered me down the street and into an open doorway. "Those guys on the dhow you were spying on are from Dar es Salaam . . . some may be from Mogadishu or places in Iraq or India." After a moment of contemplation, he said. "Some might even be English . . . or American. They do not come of their free will. Shanghaied, I think you call it. They're owned by the captain."

"That's a good story. And, I'll bet tourists really believe that."

"Then why do you think patrols are here?" He answered his own question. "To keep tourists from taking pictures."

Ahmed looked at me. "Did you take any photographs?"

"No," I lied. "I'm sure that if that soldier saw me put my camera to my eye, he'd have confiscated it."

Ahmed took me to a window that overlooked the harbor.

"Take some photographs. I'll watch for guards. But hurry."

I took a couple more quick shots, turned and headed for the door with Ahmed on my heels. "Let's get out of here," I said.

After a couple of right and left turns we arrived again within sight of the bay. Salty, oysterish smells laced with odors of rotting sea grasses and algae filled the hot, humid air.

"Have you got a girlfriend?" Ahmed asked.

"Maybe. Why? Do you think I'm thinking of her?"

"Thought you might want to meet my friend Yusuf." He turned into a doorway of a building with a front that appeared to have collected the bullets released during some past *coup d'etat.*

"You might like to buy her. . . ." His voice trailed off as he disappeared into the darkness of the interior. But, I knew how his sentence finished because I saw the sign - YUSUF ABDULLA JAFFER & CO, PERFUMERS - hanging from the second story of the building. I didn't hesitate.

Inside, before my eyes acclimated to the darkness, fragrances of roses, lilacs, jasmine, patchoulis, titillated my nose. One particular scent conjured memories of Nicosia, visions of a lovely Cypriot woman I once met.

"This is a den of love potions, Ahmed," I said trying to look around the room.

"And Yusuf is the enchanter," Ahmed said.

"When do the sirens sing?" I mocked.

"You make joke of my place, Ahmed," a voice issued from a distant corner. "It's OK. You, my friend, bring many customers."

Ahmed introduced me to Yusuf. My eyes had finally accepted the dim light that entered the room though the door from the street and from some back, obscured window. Yusuf sat just outside the glow an overhead bulb cast on a dark wooden table. Drops of sweat beaded on his forehead. Some trickled down his cheeks and caught in his full black beard. All sparkled. A black fez topped his large, basketball-sized head. A striped, black and white, tent-like robe cascading from his shoulders, covered his body. He looked like a massive beanbag phagocytizing the stool he sat upon. A wall of shelves, all within his reach, held thousands of little uniformly shaped, dusty bottles. Each contained a specific fragrance.

"You have friend . . . wife perhaps?" Yusuf said in a low, slow, rolling voice. "What perfume she use? I can make any."

"Opium." I had no idea what fragrance any of my women wore. They all smelled good.

Without looking toward the shelves, or hesitating, he reached for a bottle and placed it on the table, removed the cap and passed it under my nose. "Is this her?"

I inhaled. "Good God, if it isn't, it should be," I said.

Ahmed stood behind me. "He will be our friend Yusuf, and buy some perfume for his lady," Ahmed said to Yusuf.

Yusuf looked up at me. "Seven hundred and fifty shilling for ten drams," he said, anticipating my question.

"That's not even an ounce," I said. "It's a bit expensive."

"I do not sell perfumes like they make in Paris. Mine are of real essence . . . made from old, secret formulation," he said and removed a small bead of cotton from behind his ear. "A small drop will last many weeks."

"If you don't bathe." I said, feeling relaxed, intoxicated. "The aroma is strong, but it will wash off."

"Not if you wear it like we do." Yusuf dipped a cotton tipped swab into the bottle, then removed the cotton and rolled it between his fingertips into a bead. "Put the cotton behind the ear, like this," he said and pushed the bead into the little space behind his ear lobe. "Remove it when you bathe."

"Sounds easy. So why doesn't everyone do it with regular perfumes?"

"It only works if the formulation is like mine." Yusuf smiled. "When behind the ear, the fragrance mixes with body humors . . . becomes aphrodisiac, inflames the mate."

"One scent and I'll want to ravage her, is that what you're saying? Or maybe she'd want to ravage me?" I wanted to laugh, but I knew he was serious.

I turned to Ahmed. "Let's continue my odyssey." Shaking my head, trying to get my bearings, I looked at Yusuf. "I don't have 750 shillings on me, but I will return. Do you have a card?"

He handed me his card. "Thanks for the information," I said. "It was nice meeting you, Yusuf."

"Tourist." I heard Yusuf say disgustedly when I turned for the exit.

We reentered the maze of narrow, twisting streets and alleys. Fresh air cleared my head of exotic scents, but several lingered near the tip of my nose. I'm glad they did, because we began to pass through wafts of putrid, fetid air intermittently scented with curry, cinnamon, or coffee. Ahmed walked ahead of me because I couldn't pass up opportunities to photograph this human incongruity. We rounded a bend and came upon the source of the scented air, a cluttered, bustling marketplace. Vendors on the front-line hawked their wares from canopied stalls, but just beyond, others had toiletries, or boxes overflowing with Michael Jackson T-shirts, or vegetables, aged fish, or loaves of bread spread on rectangular ground cloths. The distribution of peddlers produced a haphazard mosaic pattern of color and texture. Between the rectangles flowed the *mélange of humanity.*

Ahmed and I made our way around, looked at grassy brooms, wooden antelopes, tribal masks, elephant hair bracelets, shell and precious stone amulets, vases, and Avon products. In front of an open-air building, spice vendors shoveled yellow, orange and brown powders individually into small manageable piles. There was no mistaking the brown stuff I approached.

"There's enough cinnamon in that mound to supply all of New York for the next hundred years," I said.

"It's grown in Madagascar," Ahmed said. "You a gourmet of fine foods?"

I nodded. We entered the building, walked past stalls of papaws, mangos, and watermelons, past ceiling-high piles of cashews and coffee beans. I inhaled the pleasant, spicy aromas, but as we ventured deeper into the building the air began to smell like a kitchen after the door to a broken refrigerator full of food had been opened for the first time in a week. On tables, on the other side of a partition that we passed through, lay row upon row of skinned, bloody carcasses of small animals, probably rabbits, and hindquarters, sides, legs, and heads of medium sized animals. All were covered in a layer of flies and their larvae.

My mouth watered, but not from hunger. Lunch pushed at the base of my throat. I swallowed hard to reverse its direction. "Let's get out of here."

Ahmed grinned. "All the hotel chefs shop here."

"Are the flies part of the weight?" I slipped as we made our way out, grabbed the edge of the partition to adjust my balance.

"Those that can't fly," he answered.

I remembered last night's dinner, roast goat. It took several strong, demanding swallows to force my lunch back into my stomach. Muscles along my esophagus continued to rebel. Fresh air, the spasms subsided.

"Thought you were well traveled," Ahmed said in a mocking tone.

"Takes time to acclimate to new cultural habits," I said.

* * *

We emerged from the shadows of another narrow alley after viewing several traditional tourist sites. I squinted against the brightness of a sweeping white marble rostrum. It surrounded the Hindu temple that filled the foreground. Stairs, guarded by a pair of marble lions, rose to the platform upon which, centrally located, was an open-air edifice. A congregation of thirty or forty Indian women dressed in brightly colored saris sat in a single row on cushions along the length of a central chamber isolated from the outside by a row of pillars. A continuous emerald green mat arranged with dishes of rice, vegetables, fruits, and sauces lay in front of them. Several Sudras, dressed in immaculate white Nehru outfits moved about behind the women, attempted to serve them, but mostly poured drinks from silver pitchers. In a far corner obscured in shadow were two minstrels playing violin-like *Kamanjas.*

"Wow, what contrasts. What colors!" I said. "Do you think they'd mind if I took a few photographs?"

"No. I received permission from the Brahman," Ahmed said as he pointed to a tall man in a white robe with a red sash around his waist, standing in a darkened alcove. "He said that it was acceptable to take some pictures, but not to disturb the luncheon."

I attempted to hide myself from those inside the temple as I walked up the stairs and moved along the rostrum outside of the pillars. But since there were no other people near me, it was difficult to be inconspicuous. Trying to be as unobtrusive as possible I almost tiptoed around, stopping occasionally next to a pillar to take a photograph. As I approached and pointed my camera, small groups of women smiled at me, squeezed together, posed, prattled and giggled. After eight or nine pictures I calmly walked from the temple.

Ahmed and I again entered the maze of alleys, rounded a corner and were out of sight of the temple. In front of us stood two of the men I had seen loitering next to the fountain in one of the previous squares that we had passed. I turned, another one walked toward us from behind.

"What's going on Ahmed?"

"How many pictures did you take at the temple?" He asked.

"Why."

"You must pay these gentlemen for the privilege of taking pictures. So, how many did you take?"

"Why the hell didn't you tell me I'd be charged?"

Again adrenalin rushed into my blood. These bastards are trying to hold me up, I thought. Got to have a clear head, keep my control. "How much do they want?"

"One hundred shillings for each photograph."

"Damn it, that's more than it costs to have them processed." I started to move away, but the four closed around me. "Tell them to go to hell. I'm not paying."

My muscles tensed. Sweat beaded on my forehead, lubricated my palms. Trapped, nervous, but I didn't want to show my fear. "You and your buddies can get out of my face or I'm going to call a cop."

"Why do you Americans always try to act so tough, so invincible? You're alone . . . you don't know where you are . . . and there are four of us." Ahmed swung his arm in an encompassing gesture. "And, there are no police. If there were, they wouldn't care." He waited a moment for me to make a move. "We'll get your money, your camera, your clothes, and you'll be another statistic to support your country's paranoia of terrorists. We're not terrorists. It's our business. Tourists expect . . . no, they want to be assaulted. They plan for it so they can go home and tell their friends what a rough time they had. Now relax, pay up, go home, and write this adventure in your memoirs." Ahmed pushed me against the wall of the building.

"But, I'm not a tourist."

"Then what are you? You don't live here."

One of the others, the guy with a scrubby beard and wild hair raised a club and said, "*Bwana nyani. Natnka yeye fedha.*"

Ahmed raised his arm, stopped the swing of the man's arm, and turned to me. "He called you a baboon, wants to beat you on the head. But, he'll settle for your money. I . . . they, know you took some pictures."

"I took three," reached into my pocket for my wallet and pulled out three 100 shilling notes. Ahmed didn't contradict me.

The three guys grabbed the notes and ran.

"One hell of a tour guide you turned out to be. If you have a card, I'll pass your name around. Make sure my friends know who you are." I looked at my watch. "How do I get out of here?"

Ahmed smiled. "We're not done yet. You owe me one-hundred shillings."

"What for? I didn't get any protection. What happened to the no-charge clause?"

"The perfume shop and marketplace are not on my regular tour. I charge 150 shillings extra to show them, but for you, I make you a good deal."

"You're still a crook!" I handed Ahmed a 100-shilling note.

"Great doing business with you." Ahmed bowed, haughtily, grabbed me by my elbow and coerced my walk around the corner of the building. Ali's Curio Shop and Coffee House was just down the street.

"Have nice day." He said, smiled, and released my arm. "Stop by tomorrow and we'll have coffee. Ali serves the best cappuccino in Kenya. I'll buy."

"You owe me. But, you'd probably try to sell me another tour."

"Perhaps."

A THREE-HOUR CRUISE

After breakfast, I examined the Castle Hotel's bulletin board to find what interesting, inexpensive sightseeing activities were available. It publicized everything from church services to massage parlors. I noticed a little strip of paper attached near the bottom of the board. This ad contained a short notice that announced a three-hour cruise around Mombasa Island for an equivalent of about five dollars. This price not only included the ride around the island on a "seaworthy craft," but also the company provided shuttle service from city-center hotels to and from the dock. Since it would cost more to go to a movie, this meager-looking advertisement, written in the broken font of an antiquated upright typewriter, suggested a shoestring operation. Considering this trip made me apprehensive. Yet it was the most interesting activity on the board. I decided to check with the concierge and if he said the jaunt was legit, I'd have him make the necessary arrangements so I could take the afternoon tour.

"Do not be discouraged by the low cost price," the desk clerk said. "It is a reputable tour. Three fishermen started taking their friends around the harbor after they salvaged an old hull. Fishing for them was no longer profitable. So they sold their fishing boat, renovated the hull to carry tourists, and started taking them around Mombasa Island. They are honest, reliable, hard working men. Although they lack formal education, they know the water and the history of the city, and they are very entertaining. You will learn much when you take the tour. Should I telephone them for you?"

His description of this cruise reminded me of some Louisiana Cajun-guided boat trips I once took through the Atchafalaya Swamp. Because of their fishing, hunting and trapping experiences in the swamp, the Cajuns had a fundamental knowledge of the region. When the cruises first started, their tour boat reflected the quaintness of converted workboats. These cruises were not only informative, but also liberally spiced with Cajun wit.

"Yes." I had the concierge make the reservation. When he replaced the telephone receiver, he said, "A driver will be in front of the hotel promptly at 2:15 this afternoon to take you to dockside."

A slight breeze ruffled the leaves of the trees along Moi Avenue. By afternoon, though, this breeze would die and the air would become hot and humid. So the thought of being out on the water excited me. Besides, I'd be able to escape the ongoing vivacity and hustling between passionate sailors and anxious prostitutes. An air of urgency existed among the sailors, because liberty passes were about to expire. While I waited, I had a comfortable lunch in a cool, shaded part of the Terrace Café.

I checked the time. It was a little past 2:00 p.m. I expected that my ride to the dock should arrive at any minute. Just as I finished my coffee, a large, rugged-looking, well-used dump truck parked in front of the hotel and stopped. A big bruiser dressed in muddy jeans and T-shirt jumped from the passenger's side and sauntered into the hotel. I sat back and attempted to figure out some optimal f-stop-shutter-speed combinations to use during the cruise. In so doing, I brought the camera viewer to my eye and focused on the truck.

"Mr. Modlin," a waiter shouted. "Your transportation is ready."

I looked about for a taxi or a limo, but none was in sight. So I placed my camera into my backpack, paid the lunch bill, and walked to the reservation desk. "Where am I to meet my driver?" I asked. The rugged guy from the truck stood near the desk, amid clumps of dried red clay that flaked from his boots as he moved. "If you are Mr. Modlin, I am here to drive you to the boat," he said.

Not a typical taxi driver, I thought. This guy appeared to have taken time from his construction job to pick me up. "I'm Mr. Modlin." He motioned for me to follow and walked ahead to the truck. Apprehensively I followed, climbed into the cab, and sat between the driver and my grungy escort who occupied the seat by the window. This fellow handed me a tour brochure. It contained a brief itinerary and a list of things I should see during the tour. For liability purposes the pamphlet also contained a paragraph from the owner that described the boat's safety features. Although I had some concerns, mainly caused by the unusual mode of conveyance to which I was now subjected, I felt that all would be well once I arrived at the boat; that is, if we did arrive. The driver seemed anxious and concerned because he had to get me to the dock by 2:15. We had only five minutes. In a cloud of black exhaust he barreled toward the corner and whipped around without stopping for traffic. So there was the possibility that we might crash into a utility pole, or another vehicle, or flip over at the next curve. Luckily the traffic in Mombasa was not very heavy, not like Nairobi.

The driver roared east on Moi Avenue leaving a contrail of smoke and dust. He turned and ground down a side street that lead to a ferry dock next to several silos owned by the Portland Cement Company. We arrived at the tour boat dock, just down the road from the ferry, in six minutes. I thanked the two men and tried to give them a tip, but they would not accept it. We shook hands and they drove away. "See you when you return," the driver yelled.

Tied near the end of the dock floated a wooden, flat-bottom, open-hull approximately twenty-five feet in length with about a four-foot beam. Its gunwale stood less than two feet above the water; passengers could wet their fingertips if they so wanted. Had this craft a truncated bow I would have called it an oversized johnboat. Instead it had a proper, albeit broad, bow. Near the front, the sides of the boat angled upward and joined at the prow. Life preservers were stored in a small compartment beneath the deck that covered the boat's forward end. A thirty-five-horsepower Yahama outboard engine powered the vessel. Four wide planks that crossed the interior from side to side provided passenger-seating space. Painted in fire engine red, the interior contrasted sharply with the off-white seat pads and exterior hull. The vessel glistened. It had definitely been recently painted. But on close inspection the impastoed surface showed that the most recent coat of paint covered many layers of old paint that lay beneath. This boat had seen its prime years ago.

The man who sat next to the outboard motor motioned for me to come aboard. He was the captain. I boarded and sat in the empty seat amidships. Great, I thought, because, since I wanted to shoot lots of pictures and the seat remained vacant, I could slide to whatever side of the boat offered the best prospect. Behind me, sat a couple from Germany. A family from Saudi Arabia, the husband, wife, and, I assumed, their three unruly children occupied the forward two seats. I introduced myself, but no one was cordial. Our guide, a deep-voiced, articulate fellow with an accentless command of English, squatted cross-legged American Indian style on the little deck that covered the bow compartment. The crew moved into activity. A quick pull of the cord and the outboard growled to life. Immediately the guide threw the bowline to an assistant on the dock while the captain flung the stern line off. Its bight splashed into the drink and sank next to the dock. Bow waters parted as the boat moved seaward. Our tour had begun. Unconsciously, I started to hum *The Ballad of Gilligan's Island.*

We pulled away from the dock toward open water. Freighters, small cargo vessels, tugs, and other craft with lighters in tow congested the expansive harbor. As our boat neared the main channel, we gave way to the Likoni Ferry. This crowded, rusty sardine-can-like craft, loaded with humanity and vehicles, pushed a foamy crest across its front. Our captain pointed the bow into the turbulence; we sea-sawed through the wake. We then proceeded eastward, and then northward, across the wide channel that connected the waters surrounding Mombasa Island to the Indian Ocean. The little boat yawed and wallowed as we chugged among the swells that rolled in from the ocean. Several splashes of water wetted the bow deck, caused the guide to jump and pad his bottom. Splatter hit faces and an occasional roller exceeded the gunwale. Although these breaches were minor, the Saudi adults appeared concerned, and probably for good reason. With the gunwale so close to the waterline, a good-sized swell could fill and capsize this narrow boat. The Saudi children, on the other hand, invincible as children think they are, cheered, even exaggerated their sway, when a wave tossed the boat. We grownups, who normally sit taller and stiffer, showed the control of a partially filled sausage balloon. We bounced and tossed about haphazardly, out of phase with the wave flow and the boat's deflections. The other adults and I, in our perceived vulnerability, held on to the gunwales with a white-knuckled grip and fought back the throes of momentary nausea. We moved as if in slow motion while the boat veered over and between the three-foot swells.

The captain expertly, and slowly, maneuvered through the momentary tempestuousness along the northern side of Mombasa Island. We passengers, except the children, guide and captain, were more concerned with survival. Little attention was paid to the park-like scenery along the shore, on which the Oceanic Hotel, the New Florida Club, a golf course, and a minor military post named Fort Joseph, were set. As the boat turned and we paralleled the northern shore westward, we were in following seas. The swells quickly dissipated and the ride softened. I readied my camera because during the ten minutes of turmoil, I noticed Mombasa Island Lighthouse, which was still in view. I needed several photos of this monument to enhance my collection of lighthouse pictures. When I started to take aim, first the driver yelled, then the guide; both warned that photography along this stretch was forbidden for security reasons. A photograph of the lighthouse from offshore would also include all, or part, of buildings that housed the Coastal Police, City Police, State House, hospital, and post office. The government considered these buildings sensitive to the country's security.

Ahead, Fort Jesus dominated the rugged rocky, sandy shoreline. From a waterline perspective I could understand the formidability this fort presented to past sea borne invaders. Its white, aged, south-facing wall, with blackish-green vertical streaks falling from the many scallops along its upper edge, rose high above the hill on which it stood. As the boat turned slightly and followed the channel westwardly, a cylindrical turret with a cross on top appeared to rotate into view; beyond stretched the sheer gray-colored easterly wall of the fort. A moldy blackish layer splayed downward from the top of the wall. Great patches of missing white surface plaster along this wall exposed blotches of sand-colored inner mortar and substantiated the antiquity of this structure. This citadel was built in the 1590s by the Portuguese. Although it took only two years to complete, the contractors had to overcome a major obstacle before construction could begin. Proper stone to build this bastion was not available anywhere near Mombasa. So all the great stone blocks that comprised the walls and interior architecture were shipped from Portugal. In the sixteenth century, this had to have been a considerable feat.

Although Portuguese were rogues and tyrants, I felt respect for their tenacity, but not just because they transported their building materials halfway around the world. Yesterday, when I had toured and photographed the fort's interior, walked its walls and grounds, inspected the turrets, and crawled about the rubble of many once enclosed rooms, I learned that when the Omanis invaded Mombasa during the late 1600s, the Portuguese sequestered twenty-five hundred people in Fort Jesus to defend it. This group remained locked in the fort for two years, blockaded by the Omanis. Food became fatally scarce. Water, what little trickled from a small well, was brackish. But starvation and dehydration weren't the culprits that devastated the insulated Portuguese, an outbreak of bubonic plague killed most of the defenders in the first year of isolation. Only about fifty survived and these remained locked in the fort for about another year.

It's amazing that anyone could survive in this fort for a few days, let alone two years. Life must have been absolutely miserable. The fort isn't large enough to hold twenty-five hundred people. It must have been like living in a sardine can that was baking in an oven. When I visited this stronghold, the temperature on the parade ground within the walls of Fort Jesus reached 110° F; because of the high walls, cool ocean breezes were blocked. The dry, dusty inside air smelled hot and stagnant. Sunlight glared off the bright sandy ground and faded mauve-colored walls and dazzled the fort's interior grounds. I would have been blinded without sunglasses. Drinking water, none was available. The ancient well, the only place that once contained freshwater, was dry and partially filled with sand. Before I had entered the fort one of the street guides suggested that I buy a bottle of water at one of the cafes across the street. That was good advice.

As we cruised past Fort Jesus, Mombasa's old harbor and Old Town rolled into view. Again the captain said that photographing the old harbor and its vessels was illegal. Yesterday's trip through Old Town with Ahmed made me quite aware of this. Too bad, because the old harbor with its variety of large, colorfully painted dhows anchored offshore of wharves, several classic old wooden cargo vessels tied to docks, and rickety warehouses, rendered an image from the *Arabian Nights*. From mid-channel the multitudes of almost naked, muscular stevedores, porters, and animated sailors looked like chaotic processions of ants moving on and off the boats, along the docks, and in and out of warehouses. Since the harbor, built about thirty feet below the city, contained no cranes or other mechanical lifting devices, porters carried freight, spices, scented oils and woods, coffee, tea, and produce to and from the truck loading docks above. Everything seemed to function as it must have in the days of Sindbad-the-Sailor. But, perhaps, Sindbad managed his cargo with a wave of his arm and a couple of abracadabras.

Although we cruised about a quarter mile offshore, Old Town provided an opportunity to enjoy several panoramic scenes of the city. A conglomeration of residential dwelling, small commercial buildings, and several slender towers where muezzins cry, overlapped and superimposed upon the landscape toward the center of the city. Some modern skyscrapers in the background marked the center. The whole appeared as an impressionist's attempt to depict an Arabian scene that rises from a turquoise moire, up a hillside, into the royal blue purity of sky. Within the canvas, one can envision whitewashed and pastel rectangles, black portals, stark shadows, ocherous tiled roofs, small verdant patches, and a couple of ornate probes that tower toward the heavens. Though biblical in appearance, most of this place called Old Town was built during the nineteenth century. However, two of the oldest, and still active, mosques are in Old Town: Basheikh Mosque dated from around 1300 and the Mandhry Mosque was completed in 1570.

About a half mile upstream of Old Town near the old Nyali Bridge we arrived offshore of the reputed oldest part of Mombasa, the site of the original settlement, called Mzizima. Evidence unearthed in this region suggested that humans were settled on Mombasa Island in the eleventh century. Although we passed within about one hundred yards of the shore, I didn't see any archeological sites. Probably most of the artifacts were found during the development of this area. Our guide mentioned that this portion of Mombasa contained residential housing and two hospitals.

We passed between the piers that once supported the old Nayali Bridge. Groups of boys were diving from, and swimming near, these pillars. A good day for a swim, since the air temperature hovered around 90° F and the humidity was about 85% with no semblance of a breeze. Several fishermen fished from the pillar closest to shore. Ahead the New Nayali Bridge spanned the waterway. A small boat marina and shipyard stood along the shoreline. Offshore of the dockage two large classic wooden schooners lay at anchor; both were clean and well attended. Most probably they were private yachts. Since we had moved beyond the supposed security, sensitive areas, I could take some photographs. I took several before the tour boat cruised under the bridge. Through a megaphone, the guide mentioned that the highway overhead was the primary coastal highway from Tanzania to Malindi. Driving this highway from the south, however, the traveler would have to take the Likoni Ferry to enter Mombasa because a bridge did not exist on the opposite side of the island.

Once we negotiated the bridge passage the captain cruised around Ras Makamaiwe, a treed peninsula with residential dwellings that housed the city's affluent population. He then returned our boat to a westerly course for a short distance until we rounded the western side of Mombasa Island. Here we entered the Port Tudor portion of the watercourse that encircled the island. Prams, punts, and dugouts were the main form of transport in this body of water. The guide pointed to starboard and said that it extended westward for several kilometers and was used mainly by the locals for commercial fishing.

We passed several fish traps set near the shore. Although primitively fashioned, the design of the traps is very effective. Fish that swim along the shoal inshore waters are forced into the trap when they encounter a barrier to their progress, a fence constructed from the trap enclosure to the shore. This fence was built from reeds long enough to reach from the bottom to above the water's surface so that the fish cannot swim over. Most fish will not attempt to swim through the barrier, so they turn and swim along its length into deeper water and, unexpectedly, into the net trap connected to the end of the fence. Spacing between the reeds is arranged to allow small fish and juveniles the opportunity to swim through the fence to freedom. In the more technological world, fishery biologists and commercial fishermen employ the same capture method when they use Lake Erie Trap Nets, Box Nets, and Fyke Nets to collect fish. The effectiveness of these modern trap nets is improved by the addition of extra leads or wings (fences). These can be set perpendicular, or at angles, to the trap.

I wondered what species of fishes these Mombasan fishermen caught. If I checked out a local restaurant and ordered a fish plate I might learn. Local restaurants normally serve local fish.

The cruise continued along a body of water called Makupa Creek, a two-thousand-foot wide portion of the moat that surrounded Mombasa Island. Ahead was another bridge, the Makupa Causeway bridge. Only this one had a bit of history. Back in 1896 George Whitehouse, the Chief Engineer assigned to oversee the initial field operations required to construct the Uganda Railroad (The Lunatic Express), found it necessary to bridge this creek so the train could travel toward its goal, Lake Victoria, some four-hundred miles inland. The creek was the first major obstacle that the construction gangs encountered. Although facilities were already built and tracks laid, the train could only travel from Kilindini Harbor west to Makupa Creek, a distance of about four miles. Whitehouse made spanning this tributary a priority project, but he ran into some fundamental encumbrances. The structure that crossed the creek must not restrict boat traffic, tidal flow, nor create erosion problems. It took him eight months to build this viaduct and finally the bridge was completed. Whitehouse considered this a major delay in construction. If he had been aware of what lay ahead, he would have thought this snag insignificant.

As the boat approached Makupa Causeway, I watched several cars and trucks on the main thoroughfare to Nairobi, which crossed over our way, when streaks of colorful radiance caught the corner of my eye. I looked toward the center of the island. Across the horizon rose several low hills that appeared as gigantic, brightly colored quilts with their individual pieces fluttering and waving in sporadic confusion with gusts from gentle breezes. As a whole, they looked like as an artistic wrap created by Christo and Jeanne-Claude. Instead, as the guide and driver explained, what I observed was nothing more than laundered bed sheets, blankets, towels, washcloths and other fabrics from the local hotels. These articles, drying upon the hillsides, were laid out by laundries contracted to wash the city hotels' linens and things. In Mombasa commercial laundries took advantage of solar radiation for drying the wash. The sun's rays were free and abundant. Besides, the sun dried and sanitized all in one process. After being washed the items were individually draped over the low, straggly vegetation that grew on the hills. Although this operation was inexpensive, it required considerable space. But this was not a problem, because the knolls near the center of the island provided the needed open space to handle large commercial loads. Even in this humid environment clothes dried rapidly. Again an ancient method bypassed modern technology.

I continued to gaze at this commercial expression of art as we moved toward the Makupa Causeway. Because of my continual perspective, this colorful scene seemed to rotate across the horizon. Hues and tones constantly changed. Its dimensions squeezed, released, twisted and straightened. This dynamic exhibition ended abruptly when the boat passed beneath the bridge.

The captain increased speed as we emerged. We had been touring for over two and a-half-hours and, if the map I brought along was correct, we still had some distance to cover before returning to the dock.

On the starboard we were abreast of Kwamwanaweupe Island. The guide didn't have much to say, except that we should be on the lookout for goliath herons, black-headed herons, white pelicans, and pink-backed pelicans. The vegetation appeared rough and the island deserted of bird life. Too bad, because an island with such a melodic name should have more significance.

Makupa Creek flowed through a narrows, a space about two-hundred feet wide, before its mouth opened into Port Reitz. Kipevu Causeway breached the space between Mombasa Island and the mainland at this point. We passed under the causeway and the waterway expanded into a large basin. To starboard lay Ras Mchangamwe and about fifteen minutes away, on the horizon, was Ras Kikaangoni. (Ras in Swahili means Point and Kikaagoni translates to Flora, so the latter landfall to the west is Flora Point). The captain steered the boat southeastward toward Kilindini Harbor.

In a few minutes we came between Flora Point on the right and the northern most expanses of Kilindini Harbor.

Kilindini Harbor is the most modern, deep water harbor along Africa's Indian Ocean coast north of South Africa. Along Mombasa's western shore are the extensive industries that associate with this harbor: dockage areas, shipyards, warehouses, cement silos, fuel depots, petroleum refineries, and I was told, sugar refineries. Most of Kenya's international commerce, about two billion dollars annually in exports and three billion in imports, funnels through this harbor.

The view from the water definitely showed an active harbor. A small oil tanker, two general cargo freighters, and two large container vessels were in the midst of transferring their cargo. Anchored offshore, several ships awaited berths. But, most impressive, were the three United States naval vessels that unloaded the horde of sailors yesterday. A sense of warmth and comfort came over me when I saw the destroyer and the two support vessels, symbols of a powerful nation dedicated to democracy and to freedom. What these ships represented evoked in me a sense of patriotism and homesickness. Although thousands of miles from home and on the other side of the earth, I felt proud to be part of this impressive presence. I wanted to stand, salute, and sing *The Star Spangled Banner* as we passed.

The huge gray hulls rose high above the water as our captain tried to pass as close as he could to these warships without alerting the vigilant patrol boats. Although I saw a few sailors milling about, activity aboard seemed subdued. Probably the majority was sleeping off the past day's hangover.

We rounded Ras Kilindini and headed shoreward. The tour dock was about a quarter of a mile away. After waiting for the Mtongwe Ferry to cross our path, the captain brought the little tour boat about and pulled abreast of the dock. Our guide, who remained glued to the bow deck for almost the entire trip, energetically jumped ashore with the bowline in hand and bound us to the pier. The captain secured the stern and stepped off to assist the passengers trying to step onto the dock. Our cruise ended.

Although the tour was more than worth the money I paid, I felt disappointed. Normally, passengers talked among themselves. When I travel, I enjoy interacting with individuals from other countries, and learning about them and their culture, but on this trip, everyone seemed uptight, stoic, and into themselves. The cruise felt comfortable, but the boat did roll a little. Maybe the others felt uneasy being in such a small boat, so close to the water, and on such a large expanse frequented by very large ships. Although we were never more than a few hundred feet from shore, from the seat of the boat the vista seemed immense. To the unaccustomed, such a perception may be frightening.

After chatting with the guide and captain for a few minutes, I climbed into the cab of the dump truck for my ride back to the hotel. Only on this trip, I sat next to the open window, rested my elbow on the sill, and waved to those walking along.

ESCAPE TO A COASTAL RESORT

Only three short weeks ago, I had first set foot in Kenya. Never having been totally alone so far from home, in so strange a country, I had walked off the airplane gripped with apprehension and anxiety. Would I have enough self-confidence and fortitude to persevere for six weeks on my own know-how? This question had gnawed at my brain. With no real plans, goals, knowledge of the cultures, or friendly contacts, during those first few days after my arrival, I had had some doubts about my stay in this country. But after being confronted by interesting and unusual challenges, meeting many unique characters, and experiencing exotic scenes and events, I had changed, gained confidence, become self-assured, a significant benefit of this trip; my character had undergone metamorphosis. Once I realized this, East Africa became a comfortable, cordial, enjoyable, exciting place. My anxieties turned to awe and I wanted to see more, especially the Indian Ocean. I arranged two side trips that would allow me to satisfy this desire. Extremely cooperative travel agents at Air Kenya and the representatives at the Seychelles Tourist Bureau kindly helped me plan visits to the coast of Kenya near Malindi and the islands in the Seychelles.

The beaches of Malindi Marine National Park, a small near shore component of Kenya's Marine National Reserve located just south of Malindi, would allow me shoreline snorkeling access to several reef complexes. The Seychelles, a remnant group of islands, resulting from the separation of the Indian subcontinent from Africa and located approximately one thousand miles east of Nairobi, provided an opportunity to visit the middle of the Indian Ocean. Here I envisioned seeing, in the wild, many strange and exotic creatures while snorkeling, maybe SCUBA diving, around the coastal waters of several of the islands in this group.

* * *

Shortly after lunch, on the Monday after I returned to Nairobi from Mombasa, the Air Kenya airplane, a commuter twin-turboprop Fokker F27 with an overhead wing, left Nairobi International Airport for Malindi. This daytime flight excited me because I was curious about the terrain that lay between Nairobi and the coast of Kenya. Although I had traveled over this landscape on The Lunatic Express, most of this trip had taken place during darkness, so I saw very little. Flying during the day allowed me to see what Denys Finch Hatton saw when he flew over this area in the early nineteen hundreds. What impressions I had of this area came from the movie *Out of Africa.* This flight gave me a chance to experience the vistas first hand.

Finch Hatton flew at an altitude of one thousand feet or less, and in a biwinged aircraft with an open cockpit. This allowed him an almost unlimited view. My perspective, from the interior of the passengers' compartment of a commercial airliner, was more restricted. Although limited, the vista I saw was greater, because my flight cruised at 12,000 feet.

As the plane climbed toward its cruising altitude, the land below rolled through agricultural patches and lush swatches of open range. The continuous cloudbank we approached muted the colors so that the irregular geometry of the landscape coalesced into a darkened, drab forest green carpet. This scene faded when the plane penetrated the thick cumulus. Within a matter of five minutes we popped through the outer wall of this gray-white, vaporous mass. For a moment, I felt as if the airplane were suspended in the division between the deep, royal blue heaven and a bright, rugged, burnt-colored earth. I quickly regained the sense of motion when I looked back toward the cloud bank and saw it shrinking into the background. Below, on the ground, the cloud's shadow inscribed a distinct edge that separated the cool, moist, verdant highlands around Nairobi from the drier, stark, reddish lower tablelands. Not much further east, the ground's color distinctly changed to brownish-beige hues. Then as our airplane crossed from the Yatta Plateau into the Tsavo district, the colors of the ancient sediment became sand-hued. Within forty minutes and just before we flew into a small rainstorm, the milieu below turned green. We were over the coastal plain and about to make the approach into Malindi's airport.

Flying from Nairobi eastward to the Kenyan coast is like navigating over a topographic map on which significant variations in land elevation are indicated by different colors. The bands of color, created by variations in soil and vegetation that I observed from the airplane were due to sharp demarcations in climatic conditions caused by changes in land elevation. Flying east from Nairobi, elevation decreased in subtle terraces from about six thousand feet to sea-level.

The airliner flew too high to define any wildlife, although occasionally I think I distinguished dust trailing from some gray-colored spots. These may have been herds of some sort of beasts. If they were, the color suggested wildebeests or elephants. Below the flat plains, fractured by gnarled crevasses, bleak canyons, sinuous traces of dry riverbeds, usually terminated in sharp, weathered precipices or small ranges of jagged mountains. Greenish blurs showed locations in dry river channels that contained some water. We flew over several volcanic vents, from which once flowed the now solidified, charcoal-colored lava. Occasionally, when I looked through the window across the aisle, I caught glimpses of Africa's best known volcano, Mount Kilimanjaro, projecting its peaks above the usual shroud of cloud cover. The airplane decreased its altitude as the pilot prepared for landing. Spread below I saw scrub jungle with occasional clumps of coconut and other palms, Australian whispering pines, large rubber tree-like plants breaking through a low tangled canopy of brush, halyconia-like leaves, probable banana trees, and tall grasses as we shot in and out of turbulent tropical rain events. To the east stretched a diffused bluish haze, the Indian Ocean.

The Fokker landed smoothly and taxied to the small, modern terminal. Heavy, humid air quickly quenched the air-conditioned comfort inside the airplane when the passengers' door opened. The tropical coastal air, unlike the stagnant stuff found in Mombasa, felt comfortable, relaxing. A moist, soft, naturally spiced breeze cooled me as I stepped away from the airplane. Invigorated, I collected my luggage and, along with other passengers, caught the

Air Kenya hotel shuttle. It took us south along the coast for about fifteen minutes, to the Driftwood Club where the Tourist Bureau in Nairobi had arranged my stay. This resort, located a short distance south of Malindi's center and on the border of the Malindi Marine National Park, allowed easy access to the beach and shoreline coral reef features.

The van to the Driftwood Club traveled on flat, well-maintained dirt roads. It avoided the city center. Along the route we passed quaint airy residential cottages, a couple of substantial homes, and lanes lined with red and purple bougainvillea and bright yellow jasmine vines. Fragrant pastel flowers covered the frangipani trees. Coconut palms and other assorted trees and shrubs filled undeveloped lots. Happy children played. Occasionally, delicate-looking adults dressed in colorful wraps waved when the van passed. A delicious ambience, scented with the lusty, peppery smell of decaying tropical vegetation, came with every breath. I had found my place in Africa. I could be happy here.

The van entered onto the grounds of the Driftwood Club and traveled along a cement lane to the clubhouse located near the center of the complex. Clean, airy, and pleasingly landscaped to provide ample shade, the resort's garden-like grounds were surrounded by a low barrier composed of lush shrubbery, which isolated the complex from the beach and surrounding areas. Strategically placed groves of mimosa-like flame trees sported bright red flowers. Their placement identified walkways through the resort's perimeter where guests could enter the beach and town roads. Many trees were in bloom, so the grounds were a floral splendor. Wooden beach chairs, chaise lounges, and tables were arranged in conversational groupings under the trees and thatched roof cabanas, while many portable aluminum chaises and folding chairs surrounded a large kidney-shaped swimming pool. Sunbathers could enjoy their passion in and around the pool, and cool themselves under several conveniently located multi-head outdoor showers nearby. A thatched roof pavilion attached to the clubhouse and constructed from bamboo and cane served as the hotel's dining room and bar. Although it was set on the side away from the beach, diners could easily see the ocean and sunset through the walkways. The main portion of the clubhouse functioned as the guests' reception area. A bathhouse and laundry were attached to the pavilion on the side contrary to the clubhouse. Guests lodged in bandas, small thatched-roof, white adobe-like cottages with dark wood trim. Each banda had a roofed veranda at the entrance. The bandas were arranged in small groups of four or five. Tall coconut palms shaded these cottages. I counted about fifteen guest cottages around the immediate interior of the resort. Rental rates for the ones nearest the beach were higher than those farther away.

I rented one of the least expensive cottages, but had only a short distance to walk to the beach, pool and pavilion. The cottage contained a comfortable bed under a mosquito net tent, a dresser, a couple of chairs, a bedside table and lamp, ceiling fan, and lavatory with the usual equipment and a stand-up shower all within a well appointed carpeted interior. And best of all, it was air-conditioned, a wonderful contrivance, since the heat and humidity were greater here than I had previously experienced.

The afternoon still young, I dumped my luggage on the bed and changed into a pair of walking shorts, a beach shirt, and sandals. I quickly grabbed a bite to eat and hiked up the beach toward Malindi's town center, about three miles away.

With my sandals stuffed in my hip pockets, I walked and splashed through the three- to four-inch wavelets that rolled in from the ocean. I could see far across this turquoise sheet. Circular, spiral, and fleur de lis-like disturbances that appeared on the surface pinpointed locations of coral reef crests and other shoal features where sea life congregates. These were the best places to snorkel. Most were merely about one to two hundred yards offshore. Although a light breeze blew southward, sailors would rate the ocean's sea state just as "Force 0" on the Beaufort Wind Scale. The horizon appeared as a solid, straight line, broken only by three mauve-colored, skewed triangular sails of dhows gliding several miles offshore.

At a far distance, in the direction I walked, I saw some bright colored low buildings, a minaret, and a few thatched roofs. All appeared to be clustered tightly between sand dunes and squat, scrubby vegetation. This view of Malindi remained remote, though I continued my approach.

After about thirty minutes of walking over soft sand and exposed coral pavement, I neared a knoll, higher than, seaward of, and detached from, the range of sand dunes that backed the beach. During most of the walk to this point, the hill blended into the background, but as I approached, it commanded my view, obscured the sight of Malindi. This hill was the highest feature along the entire stretch of beach I walked. Its summit stood about fifty feet above the beach. Waist-high, stiff, intertwined woody brush appeared to completely cover it. Although seemingly impenetrable, I wanted to climb to the top just to glimpse the spectacular views I assumed I could see from its summit. I circled its base to decide if another side might be less perilous to ascend. On the northeast side, just above the vegetation, a substantial wooden brown signboard with beige letters engraved on it spelled out "Pillar to Vasco da Gama." The beige arrow, engraved below the phrase, pointed to a tortuous trail that led up the knoll. Until that moment I did not know such a monument existed. I climbed up the hill avoiding the thorny branches that, in places, grew onto the path.

What a special opportunity, I thought, to be able to visit, maybe walk over the same ground, where over five hundred years ago, one of the world's notable explorers set foot. In elementary school I learned that Vasco da Gama, in 1497, sailed from his homeland, Portugal, to India. Unlike Christopher Columbus who had also sailed from Lisbon five years earlier on the same quest, Vasto da Gama successfully found the lucrative, sought after, sea route to the land of silk and spice in the east. Only a few years after his return, the world's oceanic trade routes to the Orient were established.

World explorers have always fascinated me. I had to see Vasco da Gama's Monument, although I knew that his visit completely changed the East African coast, culturally and politically, and threw the area into turmoil for the next three- to four-hundred years. The consequence of his exploits changed the balance of power forever and turned the course of history. Recently, historians have painted Vasco da Gama and his crew as miscreant adventurers who plundered most of the ports they visited along the East African coast. So why would anyone, in this part of the world, want to commemorate such a disrupter of tranquility? A brief account of this area's history answered my question.

Before Vasco da Gama arrived in Mombasa, word of Portuguese transgressions in coastal cities and villages to the south reached the Sultan of Mombasa. This news generated suspicion. So, when da Gama's ships arrived, the Sultan limited their anchorage to the outside harbor and covertly planned to rid the world of this menace. Vasco da Gama realized his peril, quickly hauled anchor and sailed north to Malindi. Here, the Sultan of Malindi, an enemy of Sultan of Mombasa, warmly welcomed the explorer and his crew with ceremony and hospitality. He offered them refuge and rest, but secretly his disposition contained an ulterior motive; he wanted to use these foreign vagrants to invade Mombasa.

Malindi provided the Portuguese a future, secure, way station to support their shipping attempts to India and beyond. So the Portuguese accepted the hospitality of the Sultan of Malindi. Malindi's proximity to Mombasa also furnished the Portuguese with an opportunity to satisfy a more immediate desire. They wanted to secure Mombasa's protected deepwater harbor and bring it under Portugal's rule. Malindi offered the Portuguese a strategic location from which they could, if they wished, invade Mombasa. So for the next seventy years, the Portuguese, with the aid of Malindi, made many forays to Mombasa. They continually ravaged the city. Finally, around 1582, the Portuguese took authority over Mombasa and made the ruler of Malindi governor of the conquered city. So it should be no surprise that a monument to Vasco da Gama is found near Malindi.

I reached the top of the knoll, entered a grassy clearing divided by the shadow of a twenty-foot, tapering column. The monument's surface was roughened with peels and patches of chipped, molded whitewash. Weathering showed that this memorial was sculpted from stone similar to that used to build Fort Jesus in Mombasa. A Christian symbol of a cross, superimposed on a circle crowned the pillar. The whole structure stood on a large, cuboidal base whose edges and angles had smoothed with time. I walked around the structure to see if there were any inscriptions to suggest its age. I also wanted to select the best location to photograph this tribute to

Vasco da Gama. Neither the pillar, nor its base, contained inscribed information. To my surprise, what I found were four shirtless guys sprawled about the foundation stone, relaxing in the shade of the pillar. Clearly, they had established rulership of the monument's base. Photographing the memorial from its shadowed side would provide the longest perspective and would allow me to capture, in a single frame, the complete monument from top to bottom with the ocean in the background. So I asked the men if they would mind moving for a moment. I wished to take a pure, uncluttered picture. "No," they said. They wanted to be in the photo, but they said, if I paid them, they would move. I quickly realized that their presence added a living component to this otherwise obscure, neglected memorial. So my picture of the Vasco da Gama's Pillar included the living examples of Malindians.

From the summit of this knoll, the highest point in this immediate geographic area, the landscape easily integrated into a spectacular, holistic scene. To the east I could see across the turquoise fringe behind the reefs to the royal blue open ocean. About three miles to the south, roofs of the Driftwood Club's cottages, parts of the clubhouse, and the patterned arrangement of the coconut palms, were clearly visible. Behind me, to the west, lay the chaotic tangle of coastal jungle. And, northward, a carpet of green and flowered patches mixed with the whites and pastels of anthropogenic geometry that defined the town of Malindi. From the city's center the coastline extended north to the horizon as a low sandy cliff and narrow beach. I assumed, except for the popular resort island of Lamu, the beach remained desolate and undisturbed all the way to Somalia and beyond.

Satisfied, I came down the hill and continued my trek toward Malindi, now less than a quarter of a mile away. I walked off the beach path onto the paved street that continued along the town's beachfront. Ahead a small, white, three-story hotel stood alone on the block. This building perplexed me. Its facade seemed normal. Yet, no matter from which angle or at what distance I viewed this building, it appeared to be a facade and nothing more. As I approached from the left, although nothing obstructed my view, I could not discern the building's sidewall. I passed across the front and looked back, and its opposite sidewall also eluded me, yet I could clearly see the facade in all its detail. Baffled, I walked a short distance down the next cross lane to view the building from behind. Illusive mystery solved. If I were able to see the structure from above, its roof would be in the form of a severe acute triangle. Its sides angled back so sharply that they were nearly imperceptible from almost anywhere across the hotel's front. I wondered whether the architect had planned the optical illusion, or just designed the structure to fit on an unusually shaped piece of property. I wondered what its interior looked like, but I never entered the building to find out.

A beautiful, stark-white mosque occupied the property in the next block. It had a moderately sized minaret with a turquoise teardrop-shaped bulb on its top. The colorful pinnacle was in sharp contrast to the white tower. This was one of the buildings that I had observed from Vasco da Gama's memorial hill. The minaret's crown was the only color on this place of worship. The grounds, within the low wall that surrounded the complex, were beautifully appointed with tropical flowers and bushes. Farther along the street stood a strip of small shops. Next stood a café with a gravel parking space in front where two well-used mini-pickup trucks were haphazardly parked. A black wrought iron fence reaching to the top of the café's first story, overgrown with bougainvillea and wisteria-like vines, enclosed the dining area.

Perfect! Just what I needed, I thought, a cool drink.

Inside I could see that the vines grew over the iron fence and attached themselves to the ceiling. Their ends hung down into the restaurant. An interesting effect, and it hid all the blemished, aged, probably rotting, overhead woodwork. A quaint place where several local men sat drinking and eating. I found a table near the center of the space and ordered a Tusker Export and a bottle of water.

The gate to the outside opened and in walked a tall, sturdy, mahogany-colored man with a gnarled face. He had to be over seven feet tall, because he had to bend forward as he passed through the standard-sized door opening. Tussled gray hair and graying stubble projecting from his face put his age at greater than fifty. Powerful, muscular arms emerged from a tattered, sleeveless denim shirt that looked like it was about to rip open across his enormous chest. He wore a pair of heavy, elephant-colored, soiled work pants secured around his hips with a thick, eroded leather belt, and a pair of worn sandals over his dusty feet. When I saw this giant of a man, I could understand where ancient travelers and writers received inspiration to create the legends of Herculean and Cyclopean characters.

He stopped at one of the tables near a door, one occupied by a couple of casually dressed business-types. The men were dwarfed by this colossus, whose head almost scraped the rafters. With his arms hung at his sides, I could see that the third and fourth fingers on each hand were missing. This made his bulky hands and remaining stubby fingers look like a pair of stone crab pincers. He just stood next to the table, did not make contact with those who were seated, but arrogantly stared straight ahead. Apparently, these men had had previous encounters with this giant. One of them held up a five-Kenyan-shilling note and the giant pinched it between a thumb and finger and stuffed it into his pocket. He never spoke a word nor made acknowledging gestures, but moved on to the next table where the same scenario played out. Finally I was next in line. He lumbered toward my table. Since the others were locals and I was a tenderfoot and the only white man in the place, his approaching presence made me anxious, nervous; he intimidated me. So I decided to ignore him. Maybe he would move on, or say something. What did Odysseus do when he encountered his giant, Polyphemus? He overpowered him, bound him, and escaped. Looking at the face of the gargantuan that stood next to my table, aimlessly glaring through the vegetation that hung in front of him. Could I do that? No way! I almost blurted out. My body felt hotter than the surrounding air. I fidgeted. Although my disregard for him continued for about five minutes, it seemed to last for hours and his composure did not change. He calmly remained steadfast to his mission. Finally, we made eye contact. I handed him a bill of an undetermined amount that I pulled from my pocket. His eyes softened and the corner of his mouth moved slightly upward. He took the bill and moved on.

After he moved to the next occupied table, I felt a strong urge to relieve myself. But first, I diluted my adrenaline-high with the beer that remained in the bottle. When I returned from the men's room, the giant had departed the café and, on my table, I found a fresh bottle of beer.

"Thought you might need another cool one after the situation you just got yourself into," said a young man as he approached me from the direction of the bar. "He's harmless, the big guy." He flicked his head toward the door and smiled. "He's the town beggar, but is also hired to do odd jobs. So most of us know him and give him our small change. But, because of his enormous size, he intimidates the tourists. I think he enjoys doing that."

"Well that's comforting to know," I said. "This beer is refreshing, will settle my nerves. Thank you. I seem to know you from somewhere. Do I?"

"I work at the Driftwood. Carried your bags to your cottage. When I finish for the day, I come here to relax with some friends, but they did not come this evening."

"Oh yes. What time is it? The sun seems to be setting."

"About a half-passed five. There is about another hour before sunset and darkness."

"I didn't know it was this late . . . need to start back. It will be dark by the time I return to the hotel. A three-mile walk through the sand will take about an hour. Then I must shower before dinner, so I might be late."

"Finish your beer . . . I'll drive you back. You should not walk after dark. Other giants might get you, and they might not be as friendly as the one you just met." He laughed and sat with me until I drank the beer. We drove back to the hotel in the twilight.

ELECTROCUTION

The friendly, off duty bellhop dropped me off at the Driftwood Club's lobby entrance. I thanked him for the ten minute ride. "Order the lobster tonight for dinner. They are fresh," he said, waved, righted himself in the truck's cab and drove off. "Have a good evening," he yelled back.

On the way to my cottage I passed a waiter and asked that he bring me a beer. I wanted to relax on the veranda and catch the last rays of sunset before I showered and dressed for dinner.

There seemed to be a period of quiet as the earth turned toward twilight. I watched beams of light pulse through the branches and foliage of the trees that lined the beach. Over a period of ten minutes, the sky's color diminished from an intense bluish-orange, through mauve, to wine with streaks of red. The whole deepened to a dirty blood-color after the sun passed below the horizon. During the sun's finale, sounds became mute. I could feel the vacuousness. It was as if all creatures took a silent reverential moment. But after the sun vanished below the horizon, life's noise returned. Electric and staccato buzzes, some powerful, others faint, the orchestrations of crickets and other insects stimulated various lizard species to stalk the musicians. Small, dully colored reptiles seemed to appear next to rocks and on walkways. Whistles, chirps, and occasional hoots of feathered predators augmented an exquisite but tedious insect symphony. Infrequent bass notes were added when some fruit bats dropped from their perches and throbbed skyward. Though harmless, silhouetted against the darkening sky they looked like vampires winging toward some haunted castle.

I finished my beer while a foot-long lizard on the nearby wall swallowed his meal. "My turn for dinner," I mumbled to myself as I returned to my room to shower and dress for the evening.

The luggage lay in disarray where I had dumped it earlier. No gremlins or elves or maids had hung anything while I was out. Seeing the clutter, I felt guilty. I could hear my mother's commanding words, "Hang up your clothes before you go out to play." Most times I didn't listen, instead blasted out the door to capture the all important after school playtime. Oh well, she's not here now, but, like a good boy, I stowed my jacket and pants. Otherwise they would look like I had slept in them.

After I took care of these domestic duties, I stripped to my shorts and entered the bathroom. It looked bright and new. The usual stains one finds were absent and the tiles shone as if freshly waxed; their soft pastel shades enhanced. Even the grouting was spotlessly white. Bright chrome fixtures projected from a polished lavatory and the immaculate wall behind the shower stall. Even the grate over the shower drain gleamed. Nowhere did I see encrusted soap scum, mold in corners or paint peeling. Bathroom cleanliness, I believed, is a hotel's finest attribute. The housekeeping staff must be dedicated and hard working, I thought as I looked around.

My face reflected from the mirror over the lavatory. The sun had lightened my hair and my skin had tanned. I looked healthy, rugged, and felt lighthearted, the rejuvenating powers of the African climate. "Too bad, this trip will soon end and I'll be back to reality and, compared to my adventures in Africa, the pedestrian life in Huntsville, Alabama," I said to my reflection. This adventure will be history; something to tell my kids about, if I ever have any.

I lightly slapped my cheeks and ran my hands through my hair. "No time to become sad," I said to the dude in the mirror, while I unconsciously turned on the faucet to wet my hands so I could slick back my hair, a habit of mine while I contemplate matters before a mirror. "This adventure still has three weeks left."

"Wow!" I snapped my hands out of the flowing water so hard that my shoulder muscles stung in pain. "That was one helluva jolt," I cursed. "I must have built up quite a static charge walking on the beach or watching the sunset." The muscles in my arms felt tender and shaky. Why didn't I get zapped when I turned on the faucet? It's metal. Any static electricity I had stored should have discharged at that moment. Instead, it happened when I put my hands into the water issuing from the spout.

Carefully I inched a couple of fingers of my right hand toward the emerging spate, trying to avoid touching any of the metal on the fixtures. As soon as they came into contact with the water, I could feel my muscle fibers become electrified. Although the feeling was subdued, strings of burning sensations streaked through my skeletal muscles. These traveled from my fingers, up my arm, around the right shoulder, down the right side of my chest, at the groin the tingling split and continued down both legs to the soles of my feet. These were not shocks due to static electricity, because the muscular paroxysm was continuous rather than a pinpoint sting like I received when I touched my cat's fur on a dry day.

With my hands in the water flowing from the faucet, my body seemed to become an electrical conduit. I was grounding an electric current. Since my hands were now wet, I generated the same sensation when I touched the metal spout, but not when I contacted the handles, although they, too, were mostly metal. So I could turn off the water without getting electrocuted. This I did, and stepped back from the lavatory.

What an interesting way to do in an unwanted guest. I wondered if Agatha Christie ever visited the Driftwood Club.

I stood perplexed there in the bathroom, still in need of a shower. An electrician at this time would have been very helpful, but I didn't want to call for one because I was naked, in a strange place, hungry, and a bit unnerved. With the water flow turned off, curiosity prompted me to again touch the spout. Nothing. No shocks, although my hands were still wet.

Maybe a fugitive charge had jolted me, I thought, but my brain remained shackled to this phenomenon. It tried to dissuade me from attempting any more encounters with flowing water in this bathroom. It disturbed me to think that with my hands totally immersed in the water flow, the beat of my heart could have been arrested.

I wondered if this enigmatic shock occurred in other cottages? Did not seem so, because everyone I'd seen at this resort appeared carefree and in control. No one showed signs of sustaining an electrical shock, although I'm not sure how such an episode would manifest. Barring death, I supposed they'd appear shaky, have frizzled hair, and eyes about to pop from their sockets. Yeah, they'd probably look like the cartoon character who stuck his finger in an electrical socket. How am I so fortunate as to have this mystery occur in my cottage? I mused.

Now how could an electrical event like this be created? I checked around the sink for possible electric wires that might be lying against the pipes. None. Although I'm not an electrician, I had taken several courses in basic physics. So my jumbled brain tried to sort out some reasons that might explain this mystery of electrical conductance.

Could some bare electric wires be touching the water pipes that ran within the walls of the cottage? I pondered this possibility. Testing this hypothesis would require tearing down the walls. Seemed like a drastic way to find out, and I'm sure the management would not be too happy. Besides, if electric wires were in contact with the pipes and I touched any of the metal fixtures on the sink or shower, I'd be shocked. Since this didn't happen, the bare-wire assumption was false.

When I tasted the water that remained on my hands and learned that it was salty I realized that the stuff that poured out of the faucet was brackish water. The bottled water the hotel provided for drinking supported my find.

Brackish water is nothing more than diluted seawater, so it's loaded with charged particles, or ions, such as sodium, chloride, calcium, magnesium, carbonates, and many others. This stuff can conduct electricity and, potentially, it could generate electricity.

Because brackish water flowed through the cottage's water system, I concluded that it could be the culprit causing the shocking experiences. I based this speculation on the notion that electricity is the movement of charged particles. So, when all these ions were being propelled along with the flow of water coming out of the tap, under the proper environmental conditions an electric current might be generated. Although I've experienced brackish water issuing from faucets many times before, I have never been shocked. Perhaps in past situations, the critical elements did not come together as they did this time. Therefore, if my hypothesis were correct, the water coming out of the tap would function like an energized electric cable. So, when I put my hand into the flow, some of the electric current would be grounded though my body into the tile flooring.

This hypothesis I could test. I should be able to wash my hands without being electrocuted if I wore my hiking boots. The rubber soles would act as insulators. So I tried this.

Except for the my shorts and boots on my feet, I stood naked next to the lavatory. I turned on the faucet and stuck my hand into the flow. No zaps, shocks, nor flashes. Everything functioned normally. The problem solved, I removed my boots and planned to take a shower.

"Whoa!" I jumped out of the bathroom. Suppose the shower water is also electrified, I thought. I'd get one hell-of-a jolt, totally blasted. My body would convulse and I couldn't free myself from the shower.

I stepped next to the shower, touched the on-off handle. No shock. Next I touched my finger to the shower's spout. Nothing. I licked the tip of my finger and did the same. Again, I had no sensation of an electric current. All seemed well, so I rotated the handle and very carefully advanced toward the spray. But before I could put my hand forward to test the shower water, the spatter hit my thighs. At first it felt normal. Then as my legs wetted, the drops impacted like glowing match tips. My legs pulsed to my feet as each stream hit. I grabbed the handle and quickly rotated it to the off position, but not without feeling as if my arm had been slugged. "Damn!" I yelled at the wall. "If I have to wear my boots to take a shower, they're going to get soaked." I moved away from the aquatic dynamo. Now what, I thought. I could wear sandals. That might work.

So I put on sandals and again entered the shower stall. Slowly I turned on the water and let it dribble across my arm. "Wow! This might work," I said. "Feels like only water."

I fully rotated the handle and stepped into the spray. There was just enough time to grab the washcloth and soap before the impinging spatter began to feel like a bombardment of glass shards. Stinging vibrations zipped to my feet. I stiffened. Momentarily frozen, I felt myself bounce against the wall as if I had been thrown there by an invisible giant. Gasping for breath, I slid down the tiles of the wall opposite the shower stall. My body burned, quivered, my muscles seemed to liquefy. For a moment I sat on the floor and tried to pull myself together. The sandals worked until they became soaked and an efficient electrical connection was made.

When we were very young, my mother used to give my brother and me sponge baths. This would work, I fancied, if I wore my boots. So I put them on, collected my courage, stood naked next to the washbowl, and scrubbed and rinsed myself with the washcloth. Even so, I couldn't avoid getting water on and into my boots, inducing an occasional momentary tingle from the electric phantom.

When I arrived, somewhat clean and refreshed, at the pavilion before dinner I informed the manager of the electrical problem at my cottage. He contacted the duty electrician. When he arrived, the three of us immediately marched back to my abode and into the bathroom for an inspection.

"Turn on the water," the electrician said. When the water started flowing, he stuck his hand into the stream. "I don't feel anything." Impatiently, he went around the room, shining his flashlight into every nook and cranny, touching all metal objects with his hands, and sticking the probes of a multipurpose voltmeter into the several electrical outlets and sockets. "There is nothing wrong here. *Now,* can I return to my coffee?"

"You've got to take off your boots," I said. "Stand barefoot. Then stick your hand in the water."

"Take my bloody boots off?"

I'm sure he judged me to be presumptuous for telling him to remove his boots, because the big guy looked at me doubtfully as if to say, "I am the hired electrician and I know what's to be done." Besides, he probably thought I was suffering from fits of delusion because his inspection showed my complaint to be unwarranted. Nevertheless, he took off his big, heavy boots and walked to the shower. The water was still pouring out of the spout. Barefooted, he shoved both hands into to flow. "Oooooh."

The manager and I helped him to his feet. Slugged soundly by the invisible electric monster, it took him several minutes to realize that he still had all parts of his body connected. After he composed himself, he said, "We seem to definitely have an electrical problem here. It is like the other times, but this is the strongest shock I have ever felt."

"So other guests that have been electrocuted here before?"

He rubbed his hands together as if they burned. "It is going to be hard to pinpoint, because it occurs in different locations around the resort. About a week ago it haunted cottage number eighteen. Maybe tomorrow the mystery in your cottage will disappear. But, I can't say. Or, someone else, in another cottage, or in the laundry room, will feel the sting. I do not know. It's a real phenomenon. A frustrating one."

"I'd like to move you to another cottage, but we're completely booked," the manager said. "You can use the showers by the pool in the morning. But, you will have to wear a bathing suit."

"Not very private," I commented. "I really prefer privacy with showers."

"Sorry, Sir, but that's the best we can do. I do not think you will mind. You will find that several young women enjoy taking their morning showers by the pool. I am sure you will fancy their company."

"Do they wear bathing suit?"

"Yes, bikinis . . . but only the bottoms. Maybe you will make some friends."

"A bit rousing for the early morning, don't you think? Sure beats coffee." I chuckled. "I'll survive, although it's an imposition. And, I don't have privacy. At least, my room charge should be discounted."

"Sir, I'll arrange for the resort to provide dinner while you stay. You may order anything from the evening selection. We will also include a cocktail. Will this suffice?"

"Yes. That will be acceptable."

We all shook hands and they walked away toward the clubhouse. I closed the cottage door and headed toward the pavilion and dinner behind them. The electrician scratched his head while he walked, as if in contemplation, then he turned toward the manager. "George," I overheard him say, "We have got to find out what is causing those electrical shocks. This phenomenon could be bad for business."

George replied that the problem had plagued the Driftwood since he was hired three years ago. But, it hadn't ever debilitated anyone. "Damned aggravating . . . and it just could kill someone," he said. "Suppose one of those ancient dowagers that visit here received the shock you did tonight? That was one hell-of-a jolt you took. The old gal probably would not survive. She would be fried." George put his arm over the electrician's shoulder. "How did it feel?"

"Like getting kicked in the back by a mule. My fingers are still tingling."

"When the others complained, the electrical charge had not been so strong. You need to check this one out. Put that cottage on the list and see what can be done. We have to correct this problem." They entered what I assumed was the business office and closed the door.

There weren't many diners in the restaurant. I seated myself. It took about ten minutes for the waiter to arrive. He handed me a menu. All dinners included soup or salad, an entree, dessert, and tea or coffee. The waiter told me that he was instructed to take my order and, after dinner, take the charges to the office. He repeated what the manager had told me earlier, that I could order a cocktail and any dinner on the menu. Any additional drinks or dessert liquors would be charged to my room. However I could pay for them at the bar, if I wanted to.

"Can I bring you a cocktail?" He asked

"Scotch on the rocks." I felt the need for something to neutralize my frazzled nerves.

"Is the lobster fresh today?" I asked the waiter when he returned and served my cocktail.

"Absolutely, Sir, the boys brought them in this afternoon. They are best prepared split and broiled. Shall I bring you one? "

"Yes. What's included with the dinner?"

"Soup or salad. This evening's soup is cucumber. The entree comes with rice, potatoes, or boiled cassava, complimented with a medley of vegetables freshly flown today from England. Dessert is flan."

"Flan, you say? Must be Kenya's favorite sweet? It comes with almost every dinner." I didn't wait for an answer, but instead sipped my scotch and contemplated the selections. "I'll have the soup and boiled cassava. Haven't had cassava since I visited Jamaica."

"Sir will not be disappointed. Thank you." He marched off toward the kitchen.

Although I'm not an aficionado of spiny lobster (the Maine lobster *Homarus Americanus* is sweeter and more flavorful) I enjoyed the meal. The waiter brought the check. There were no charges listed. "Are you the guest who was electrocuted?" The waiter asked.

I nodded. "What do you know about the phenomenon?"

"No one knows the origin of the electricity . . . or where it might occur. It seems to favor the cottages next to the Malindi road." He removed some of the dishes. "The house electrician once thought a buried cable had broken along the road and electrified the ground water. Then, when the water flowed under a cottage, it imparted its electricity to the metal objects, like water pipes, that passed under the cottages. Work crews excavated the area and found nothing, no wires, no ground water."

"I have worked here for the last ten years," the waiter said. "And only once did a guest become injured and have to be flown to a hospital in Mombasa. Some of the old folks think the Royal Army did something to the area when they were based here during the Second World War. But, historians say the Royal Army camped closer to Mombasa."

The waiter stood back, started to voice another speculation, but stopped. He looked at me with dubious, suspecting eyes, as if anticipating my disbelief of what he was about to say. He said it anyway. "Some of us think it maybe aliens." He stood proudly, as if aliens were the true culprits of the resort's mystery.

"A strong possibility." I humored him. "Martians no doubt?"

"That's right Sir. Can you think of a better solution?"

"I'm going to step out onto the beach tonight and I'll let you know if I see anything unusual. It's a clear night and the stars are bright, so maybe I'll spot some alien creatures lurking about or a UFO of some sort."

"Thank you, Sir. You are making a joke, but you are being kind. Many of us believe in such things." He picked up the last of the dishes and retreated to the kitchen. I signed the check.

I strolled beyond the yard in front of the pavilion, around the swimming pool, and through the trees that lined the beach. When I reached open sand, I walked diagonally away from the resort toward the water's edge. Almost invisible ghost crabs sidled away from my path. Although moonlight provided very little light, bright sparkles reflected from the crystalline wavelets that metronomically rolled onto the beach. Electricity contributed little to this neon fantasy of light that flashed and glowed from the calm, black surface of the water. Aliens to the aerial world of humans, planktonic bacteria, dinoflagellates, ctenophores, polychaete worms, micro-crustaceans, and some fish able to emit light energy by chemically splitting molecules of luciferin, delivered mesmerizing, momentary displays of bioluminescence from beneath the ripples and from the waves that curled ashore. Myriad pinpoints of starlight danced in place on the black carpet that separated two biologically incompatible worlds. Off to the east electricity showed its face. Miles in that direction flashes of lightning illuminated the heavens, but except for an occasional shooting star there were no phantom lights streaking across the darkness.

I'm south of the equator so, I surmised, I should be able to see the stars of the Southern Cross. I wanted to see this set of stars, because navigators in the southern latitudes use them to navigate, like seamen in north use the North Star. They should be in the sky if I looked southward down the beach. There they were, the entire set just above the horizon, the four stars that seemed to illuminate the points of an invisible cross. The grouping actually contained six stars, but those at the points were the most obvious.

On the way back to my cottage, I wondered when navigators first realized they could use the North Star and the Southern Cross as references to determine their relative location north and south of the poles. Did Vasco da Gama use this aid? What about Christopher Columbus? They probably did, but their east-west locations frustrated them. With modern technology and electricity these heavenly landmarks have, except in emergencies, been for most practical purposes, relegated to the status of historical artifacts. Should some catastrophe zap civilization back to a time before computers, electricity, satellites, GPS systems, and telephone wires, could modern mariners find their way? I pondered this question as I walked toward my cottage. I have met some sailors who probably could.

Two male domestics were leaving my cottage as I arrived. They wished me a good evening. When I entered, I found that they had turned down my bed. They had also sprayed the entire interior, under the bed, and every crevice with the most powerful insecticide I had ever inhaled. It immediately gave me a spiking headache. "They're out to get me. First electrocution, now I'm being gassed." To clear my sinuses, I retreated to the veranda and reclined on one of the chaise lounges. Would I ever see the sunrise, I wondered? About two o'clock in the morning I awoke, with surprisingly few mosquito bites, and reentered my cottage. The inside air had cleared, so I crawled into bed and found refuge under the mosquito-net tent.

COLONIAL ARROGANCE WITH SENSUOUS PACIFICATION

My wrist watch alarm startled me. After an almost sleepless night of tossing and turning, I had finally fallen asleep about five in the morning. The rhythmic high-pitched bleep shocked me from an unrestful coma. It took minutes for my eyes to clear, but, when they did, my awareness of the surroundings was still hazy. “I'm shrouded in fog,” I said. Then I remembered the mosquito netting that veiled the bed. Flailing and pitching during the night, I had become tangled in this gauze. I rolled my feet slowly toward the floor as I separated them from the netting. Because of my jumbled mind, dark specters and coils that appeared on the floor registered as spiders, scorpions, snakes, or other ferocious critters that might consider me a fair target. Restless sleep and thoughts that lingered from the shocks of the previous evening made me edgy. With caution, I continued to clear myself of this misty tent and escaped the bed.

Although the air conditioner cooled the cottage, I felt sweaty, flustered, and as disheveled as the mass of bedclothes next to which I stood. My body needed blasting with a barrage of fresh, frosty water to reconnect its senses. So I rummaged through my luggage, found the nylon Speedo bathing shorts I had brought, and donned them. Not much covering my secrets, I thought. *Whatever.* I took a bar of soap, grabbed a towel, threw it over my shoulder, and strolled toward publicity.

Besides the raucous harmony of bird sounds, the only other indication of animal life around the resort at six-thirty in the morning was the night watchman asleep and snoring on the bench outside the pavilion. Though just below the equator, the morning air was cool as was the spray from the showerhead, which tingled refreshingly without any of last night's electric demons. I turned the handle to full on, stuck my head under the flow, and moved under the spray. The discharge splashed through my hair, sloshed over my face, and hundreds of streams and riffles caressed and enveloped my body to my feet. Revived, enlivened, I felt newly created. I soaped myself all over, and began to rinse, until I remembered that this shower was very near the swimming pool. When thoughts of soap suds trailing off me, flowing across the shower's base, and spilling onto the surface water of the swimming pool, my stomach contracted. I looked down and sighed a breath of relief. The foamy rivulets streamed in the direction opposite the pool, into a small furrow, and into sandy oblivion.

Clean and invigorated, I walked back to the cottage. Where were those topless maidens, I wondered? Oh well, there's always tomorrow.

I dressed in traditional walking shorts, bush shirt, and sandals, organized my clothing, but left the bed in disarray. The maids knew how to reassemble the sheets, blankets, pillows, and mosquito netting much better than I. They would also clean the bathroom and shower. I wondered if they knew about the electrical problems. Maybe I should leave a note to forewarn the housekeeping staff, I thought. Their supervisors, however, may have advised them of the problem, so the staff probably was already aware. But, if they weren't and received a couple of jolts, my complaint would be supported and the resort might even write off my room charges in addition to the dinners. But, that would be beneath me, so I left the note. I picked up my journal and walked to the pavilion where breakfast was being served.

During the most active part of the day, the Driftwood's clientele appeared to be typical beach loving, sun worshiping vacationers. They could be seen enjoying the resort's grounds and adjacent beach. Tanned, fair-skinned, bikini-clad, muscular men and endowed women, in pairs or solitarily, flaunted their physiques about the grounds, idolized the sun, and cavorted in the swimming pool. Parents, pallid traditional European types, attempted to contain their raucous, prepubescent, scantily dressed progeny. Apparently attracted to those seeking solitude, the latter screamed and roughhoused within the range of disturbance. Waiters, servants, grounds keepers, and several vagabond beach bums knitted this vacation population together. But when I entered the restaurant

I found, instead, a stiff, stoic, atmosphere with an ambience one would expect to find in a stodgy resort in the British Isles.

Some women dressed in modest, pastel colored or flowered cotton dresses occupied several tables. Their fingers and wrists were decorated unobtrusively with rings and bracelets, and in their ears they all wore plain-styled earrings. Several had their hair tied in a bun. The hair of the others was artlessly straight. When they raised their cups to sip a beverage, I saw them elevate, slightly, their little finger. Three of the women sat alone. At one table, to the right of one of these solitary diners, lay a journal or novel. I fancied these women to be grand dames, dethroned queens, or maybe just spinsters. The others sat in pairs, probably mothers and daughters traveling together. Most were slender, austere-looking women. All appeared to have passed their fortieth birthday, but several were much older.

Built some years ago as a private club, the Driftwood seemed to maintain, at least in the early morning hours, its old colonial British *mise–en–scène.* An aura of pseudo aristocracy seemed to surround this group of breakfasters. I nodded toward several of them occupying tables along the far wall as I seated myself in the middle of the room. Each responded with a tempered nod of greeting.

The waiter arrived and I ordered a basic breakfast: eggs, bacon, toast, sliced pawpaw, orange juice and tea. I fiddled with the silverware while I waited for my food and found that I was missing a butter knife. Since no one occupied any of the tables around me, I reached over and took the butter knife from the setting at the next table.

Shortly after the waiter served my breakfast, an elderly couple seated themselves at that table. They were well dressed in casual tropical attire. The man wore pressed gray trousers, a white shirt accented with a paisley ascot, and a blue blazer. Dressed in a khaki skirt, a short-sleeved silk blouse, and a scarf tied about her neck, the woman appeared soft, fragile, attractive, but plain. Her pale face had angular features and sad eyes. Her abundant gray hair, tossed stylishly in soft waves, hung below her ears. Probably in her late sixties, she was younger than her partner. I estimated his age to be about eighty. A full scalp of gray hair lay in waves and curls atop a large, chubby head that sat on a short thick neck and broad shoulders. Drooping cheeks, full chin, a pug nose, and intense dark eyes highlighted by gray, bushy eyebrows lent a martial character to his ruddy, seasoned face, a true remnant from Kipling's India. I noticed when they approached their table that both were short, but she was slightly taller than he. From a distance he resembled Winston Churchill. Both appeared alert, in control, and surrounded themselves with an air of confidence.

Before the waiter arrived, the lady daintily unfolded her napkin and laid it on her lap. He, however, removed his napkin from the table and snapped it open in front of himself. As the cloth flung forward, it grazed the water glass just enough to turn it over. His companion gasped. It was empty. So he momentarily disregarded it and stuffed an end of the napkin between the placket midway down his shirt and smoothed the rest across his lap.

"Darling, you must be more careful," she said as she attempted to reach across the table and catch the glass before it rolled off.

He grunted, reacted more quickly than she. Grabbed the glass, righted it, and said, "They have many. They can afford to lose one." Then he started to meticulously arrange the silverware in front of himself. "What is *wrong* with this hotel?" He grumbled. "My setting is incomplete! I do not have a butter knife." He scrutinized the table top, scanned the room, looked at me, turned, and directed his eyes toward his companion. "The last time I was in London, I asked the travel agent to find us first class accommodations. She assured me that the Driftwood was just such a place, the best in the area . . . 'reminiscent of the colonial days,' she said. *Bloody hell!* It is obvious that that travel agent has never seen this place. Do not these people realize that our ancestors civilized this country, taught the natives to eat with forks and knives instead of their hands. Our ancestors were aristocrats. They would not tolerate being treated with the commonness this Spartan restaurant is providing. This place is nothing more than a beach shack, a hangout for beach bums and hostlers." He lifted the overhanging edge of the tablecloth. "Look at this! Cotton. Should be linen." He lifted his dinner plate. Examined it. "The least they could do is serve a visiting countryman on Spode or Doulton, instead of this trash produced in the Orient."

He shuffled the forks and spoons from side to side. "Plated metal! Not even silver-plated. Paltry utensils, they are. And, damn it! I do not have a *bloody* knife . . . Sarah, call the servant!" His voice drummed across the room.

I sat, spellbound, during my neighbor's conflict, contemplating the tea leaves in my cup. I didn't look up. I'm sure that if I were a psychic, the leaves would tell me that I'd soon be involved with this old English crank. Since no man would direct to a lady friend, mother, sister, or lover, such a tirade of arrogance I assumed that Sarah must be his wife. Composed, she raised her arm and motioned to one of the young African waiters who stood near the kitchen door. She turned toward her husband and drawled, "Darling, calm yourself. You are not at the Ritz. This *is* a beach resort. And, I find it quaint and refreshing. I will tell the young man to bring you a knife."

Ayoungmansubservientlyapproachedandwalkedunsuspectingly into a harangue about the role, manners, and behavior of servants when they're in the presence of members of the gentry. The poor waiter stood as if at attention, his mouth open, fingers stiff against his thighs, listening while this old coot ranted about the proper way a table should be set. He heard such comments as, ". . . did not we teach you proper treatment of your superiors?" And, ". . . I say, it is no wonder that the structure of this country has fallen apart since we gave you your freedom." From the young man's apprehensive expression, I'm sure he felt like crawling into a hole or running away to the kitchen, rather than listening to the old guy's declamation. The old man's face reddened, beads of sweat appeared, his haughty discourse intensified, became cruel, bigoted.

Enough, I thought. Who the hell does this jerk think, he is? No one has to listen to his kind of bullshit. It's time to quell this pompous ass, I thought. I seized the knife I had been using and thrust it toward his face. "Excuse me *Governor*, but is this what your *Grace* is looking for?" With my napkin, I wiped the butter off the blade, while I leveled the tool in front of his nose. "The waiters had nothing to do with the missing knife. They set your table properly, but my knife was missing. So, before you two entered the room, I took the knife because I needed it and didn't see the need to harass the staff. Had I known you'd become so choleric, I would have taken your entire service. Then, you might have gratified us with a heart attack. Now, apologize to this waiter, and your wife. You're an embarrassment."

Some gurgles and grumbles issued forth from deep within his well-insulated larynx. He sat straight back in his chair, almost flipping himself over, and slammed both fists on the table. "Barbarian from the colonies!" He said to me in several frustrated puffs, and then, said nothing more.

I turned to his wife. "Beg your pardon, Madame. I didn't want to upset your morning. You're quite gentile and should not have to put up with such nonsense." I stood, placed fifty shillings on the table to cover my breakfast and picked up my journal. "Have a pleasant day."

She smiled as I left. By the time I reached the exit I could hear her berating the old man for his behavior. As I pushed open the door, I overheard her say, ". . . your world no longer exists, my dear. Your troops have long since died so you have no one to command, my love . . . only me."

Unfortunately, bigotry exists no matter where one travels. It's too bad that some perceive themselves as superior to others.

I never saw that couple again. Although the old man revealed his prejudice openly, others I met at the resort were subtler. Such confrontational incidents, I learned later, were rare but apparently a few aged guests who visit Kenya from Britain or Europe expect to be treated as if they were to the manor born. They still perceived Kenya as a protectorate of Great Britain and wanted to be attended to as if it were forever so. While I was there, the hotel's staff of African descent indulged the guests. Waiters, bellhops, busboys, and maids did whatever they could to cater to the pomposities and whims of persnickety older travelers.

Outside, the sea breeze continued to blow. It cooled the air, and several groups of chaise lounges remained in the shade. Since my journal needed updating, I decided to recline, relax, and record my earlier observations and feelings. But the distractions were too great. Topless water nymphs cavorted in the pool. Several slowly rotated and sensually caressed their bodies as water from the shower - under which I had stood earlier - enveloped them. A couple of semi-naked beauties reclined on the chaises at the edge of the pool. Their bodies, lubricated with suntan lotion, reflected an erotic sheen. The play of stark shadow and sunlight over these voluptuous, frolicking enchantresses emphasized their not-so-secret virtues. Shakespeare, had he seen this *au naturel* scene, would have written *A Midsummer Morning's Dream* instead of his amorous comedy where all the action takes place after dark.

What started as a morning in conflict, turned into a forenoon of prurience. My mind became cluttered with lustful thoughts. I felt like a satyr. I didn't want to write in my journal, I wanted chase nymphets. After several deep breaths, I stood and walked toward my cottage happily knowing that I wore walking shorts rather than my tight-fitting Speedo bathing suit.

BEACH ANTICS

When I first walked onto the beach, the sand felt soft as warm, coarse powder. As children sometimes do while they wade through a shallow pool I sloshed each foot forward as I moved toward the water's edge, allowing sand to flush between my toes and sift over my feet and shins. Each step would momentarily bury my foot in this warm, dry medium. But toward the middle of the beach, where the sand became mixed with black granules, this play became painful. The gray, gritty mixture baked rather than fondled. The heat grew intense, my soles felt as if they were blistering. My steps turned into a series of rapid leaps toward the wave-doused shoreline.

The beach off the Driftwood Club and to the south is considered a fine-particle beach. It is characterized by a very gradual slope toward the water and beyond, low wave activity, a wide expanse of wet sand mixed with organic detritus that decreases and dries inland toward the berm (a low ridge created by sand deposited by wave action occurring during the height of the high tide). Behind the berm, the beach progresses into a scorching dark layer, which is where I had burned my feet. The black sand in this region becomes diluted and eventually disappears into the very fine, clean sandy powder deposited on the upper beach by the wind. This exposed portion of the beach extends into the sparse vegetation growing on and between the primary dunes.

The intertidal zone lay between the water's edge and the berm. About two-thirds of it off the Driftwood Club contained wet sand. The extent of this wetted area depended on the degree of slope, tidal stage, and wave action. As I walked south, the slope gradient flattened, so by the time I reached a small bay the area of wet-beach extended inland about one-fourth of a mile from the water's edge. Here the beach was composed more of soft silt than sand. At this point a wader could walk out into the water for a considerable distance without soaking his or her belly button.

Fortunately, the tide was low during my stroll so I was able to explore the intertidal zone and examine pieces of driftwood, shells, coral fragments, seeds and seed pods, crab exoskeletons and fish bones, and an occasional coconut left behind when the tide ebbed. Few items of human origin occurred in this beached flotsam. Though not abundant, the many clamshells scattered about suggested a diverse bivalve population. Alive, they provided fodder for several snail predators. I found a couple of empty shells of murex snails, oyster drills, olive snails, and moon snails. In a pool of standing water, next to a chunk of coral, were two colorful cone snails. Since these could inflict a fatal sting, I looked carefully to determine if they were alive. These snails possess a protrusible proboscis armed with a tooth modified into a barbed, venomous stinger. The snail uses the weapon to immobilize its prey. But if the cone snail happened to be picked up by a hapless bather or beachcomber, the individual could be injected with neurotoxic venom. The potency varies with the species but all are debilitating and some can be deadly. The cones were alive; I examined them very carefully, from a distance. Beneath another coral rock and under some of the driftwood that I overturned were aggregates of smooth, shining cowries, a snail for which humans have found many purposes. Before the invention of money, early peoples of African and Oceania used the cowry shells as a medium of exchange. To the early traders, they became known as money snails. Cowry shells have also been employed in the creation of jewelry and ornamentation for apparel worn by African royalty.

The lower intertidal zone is maintained wet by an abundance of interstitial water (water that flows, because of capillarity, within the interstices between grains of sand). This zone creates a habitat for many small and unusual infaunal organisms. Curious about the kinds of critters that live buried in the wet sand bordering the Indian Ocean, I scooped several handfuls of the material. From these digs scurried whitish mole crabs, greenish-red polychaete worms, brightly colored cocina clams (shiny, little surf clams), translucent beige amphipods, and dark, dull-colored dove snails. In one handful, a six-inch, blue and white ribbon-shaped nemertine worm slid free. The disturbance I created caused several mud crabs and swimming crabs (relatives of the famous blue crab found along the Atlantic coast) to unearth themselves and sidle in directions away from where I dug. This zone held quite a zoo. It provided a great feeding ground for the many plovers, stilts, and other shoreline birds that ran along in front of me, probing the sand.

In deeper water near the mouth of the bay a number of fishing dhows lay at anchor. Abandoned and mired in the mud closer to the beach were two wooden hulks. On some of the planking, but darkened by age and rot, the original paint remained visible as red, blue, yellow, and wine colored smears and streaks. Although weathered badly, on the once colorful hull nearest me I could still see carved just below the gunwale and on the rails and bowsprit the intricate filigree and scallop patterns that had decorated this dhow. Since I have a passion for almost anything that floats, sails or swims, it saddened me when I saw these once proud, aesthetically appealing vessels moldering on this mudflat. Though they were beyond repair, I would have loved to salvage either of them, take it home and restore it. But being practical, I photographed it into immortality.

The rotting dhows added to the already spectacular ocean view enjoyed by the affluent owners of some houses built on an inland rise just beyond hammocks of tangled coastal bushes, low deciduous-looking trees and palms. When I strolled around the bay toward Malindi Point, I could see various aspects of these attractive houses; the most unusual was a second gabled roof. These roofs, which completely covered the primary roofs of the houses, were constructed of thatch and supported on large poles. It was as if each of these rustic houses were built in the middle of a gazebo.

The thatch canopy, I was later told, kept a house cool by shading it. The canopy also allowed air to flow through the space between it and the house's primary thatched roof.

This method of cooling is based on the simple fact that hot air rises. As the canopy was heated during the day, the air above also became hot and was convected upward. This action caused the cooler air in the space below to diffuse through the thatch to replace that which dissipated. Similarly, since the primary summit of the house was also thatched, air on the interior of the house replaced that lost from the space under the canopy. Much like a passive attic fan functions to vent hot air from an attic, the updraft created continuous, cool air circulation in the interior of the house. A salutary way to use Mother Nature.

The fellows who worked the desk at the Driftwood Club had told me that the coral reef formations off the club's beach were mostly buried or scoured, therefore not too interesting. Although there were about seven ridges seaward of the beach, most were too deep for snorkeling. The best area to observe underwater life, I was told, was off Malindi Point. That area seemed to attract more marine life because the water was clearer and the coral ridges were less disturbed and rose higher above the bottom. Also the area was only five to six feet deep, a better area to snorkel.

Malindi Point, roughly two miles from the Driftwood Club, was a rounded sandy bulge that jutted a half mile into the Indian Ocean. To the north it formed a shallow bay. I hiked around this indentation to get to the point. Except for several native spear fishermen tethered to dugouts some way from shore, there were no other swimmers. About a mile south I saw a pair of men walking northward. Nearer, several groups of people sunbathed at the base of the dunes.

I donned my swim booties, hung my Nikonos underwater camera around my neck, and waded into the water toward the first coral ridge. When the depth reached about three feet, I antifogged my dive mask, slipped it over my face, stuck the snorkel's mouthpiece into my mouth and bit down on the tabs. Holding the camera next to my chest so it wouldn't bounce off the bottom when I submerged, I fell forward. With a splash, I sank into the warm water, and immediately popped back to the surface and started to swim toward the coral ridge. Normally I would have propelled myself along by moving my swim fins, but I did not bring them to Kenya. They were too bulky. So I swam slowly holding the camera against my chest. Kicking with my booty-covered feet provided little force. Although awkward, I used my free arm to help in my progress. When the water's depth exceeded the length of the strap, I let loose of the camera. This allowed more balanced and less exhaustive swimming behavior. I could now use both arms to move me along.

Ahead I saw the whitish-gray, porous, pockmarked, gnarled coral ridge. It appeared as a low wall extending upward about three to four feet from the bottom. Water depth seaward of the reef was about five feet. A turtle grass meadow, interspersed with clumps of live hard coral, broken strands of soft whip coral, giant sea anemones, and clumps of brown, green, and red algae covered the bottom behind the reef. As I floated above this greenish-blue, three-dimensional, fantastic, alien world, a great diversity of fishes swam with, below, and in front of me. Although I am not familiar with Indian Ocean fish species, I recognized some common types by their shape. There were parrot fish, more brightly colored that those found in the Caribbean Sea. At a distance a pair of triggerfish worked the coral ridge wall, while yellow and black butterfly fish nosed in and out of the turtle grass. A pair of magnificently colored angelfishes rolled on their side to monitor my intrusion into their world. Schools of silvery herring-like fish, probably sardines, swam just below the surface apparently trying to avoid some jacks that zipped around beneath the schools. The only unusual species that I observed were a couple of large gobies. These bottom dwelling fishes were robust and about six inches long. The gobies that I am familiar with from the Western Atlantic do not grow bigger than two inches.

When I neared the coral reef, I found that most of the corals were dead. I saw only the rocky, coral skeletons encrusted with clumps of algae and patches of sponge. However, a few small protected sections and crevices had some small live colonies, but the more exposed areas were barren. This is a common feature of coral reefs that become established off beaches open to the full fury of the ocean. Here, the existence of hard corals is tenuous. During storm events, formations in the shallows nearest the shore are scoured by sand and eventually buried. Those in deeper water are able to survive longer.

Pinkish tentacles of several large, robust anemones danced in the gentle ebb and flow currents near the bottom.

Swimming in and out of one anemone's tentacles were three little pink and cream clown fishes. The only time I had ever seen these fishes alive was in an aquarium. Wow! Here they were in person, not four feet below me. Though underwater light was diminished and turbidity somewhat elevated, I wanted to photograph these anemone symbionts. But to obtain a photograph where the subjects could be recognized, I had to dive down and get closer to the actors. With insufficient weight to counter positive buoyancy, I struggled to remain submerged long enough to compose the shot. This took a lot of lunging, plunging, rolling, and splashing. To observers on shore, I must have appeared like a spastic dolphin. Nevertheless, success comes to the persistent. I did get some photographs. When these films were finally developed and the photographs printed, the pictures portrayed pinkish blurs in the company of fuzzy-looking fingers; abstract expressions that would condemn an artist to further starvation.

After that episode I slowly floated toward the shore. Exhausted, I emerged, slid back my face mask and saw the two men that I had observed earlier on the beach far to the south of Malindi Point, standing near the water's edge. Dressed in well-pressed khaki uniforms with dark identification patches sewn on their shirt sleeves at shoulder level, I recognized them as park rangers. They were waiting for me. Neither seemed confrontational. Their presence was friendly, but official.

"What were you doing out there?" The robust fellow asked.

"Snorkeling. Taking some underwater pictures."

"Can we see your permit?" The other asked.

"What permit?"

"To snorkel, SCUBA dive, do anything in the water, you need a permit. You know this is a National Park?"

"Yes. I know, but I wasn't aware I needed a permit to be here, or to go into the water." At first I felt concerned, then annoyed. Alone, and definitely not a native of the area, I suspected that I was being singled out, because as I waded ashore I noticed that these rangers didn't ask the sunbathers lying on the beach if they had permits. These officials didn't even pay these sun worshipers any notice. Maybe they were residents and I, a dripping wet, spent tourist carrying snorkeling gear, appeared vulnerable. Nevertheless, I thought, if a permit is required, everyone should be asked for one.

"No one at the hotel mentioned the need of a permit when I told them of my plan to snorkel," I said.

"Maybe they are not aware themselves."

Perturbed, I rotated and pointed toward the black free-diving figures spear fishing along the second coral ridge. "What about those guys out there? They're spear fishing! Aren't they? Killing fish in a national park. Do they have permits? Isn't it illegal to kill animals in a national park? I wasn't *killing fish*, only photographing them."

Calmly, the robust ranger said, "They are native fishermen, so they are allowed to spearfish in the park. It is how they feed their families."

These park rangers tried to be congenial, rather than magisterial. They were probably taught to be cordial, but also determined when confronting tourists. I assumed that I was being fleeced, *legally*, out of a few bucks so these rangers could buy themselves some beers. However, it's highly possible, I thought, that they might really be doing their job. At all the other national parks I visited in Kenya, I bought a permit, so why not here. Embarrassed, I asked where I could buy a permit.

The slim ranger smiled and produced a small pad from his vest pocket. "I will issue a permit for today and you can return to the activity you were enjoying."

"How much is a permit?"

"Twenty shillings."

"Well as you can see, I'm only wearing these little bathing trunks." I snapped the elastic band that held up my Speedos, ". . . and a T-shirt. I didn't bring any money with me, since I have nowhere to carry it. And, the hotel is about two miles up the beach."

"Without a permit, you will not be able to go back into the water."

"It's late and I will have to return to the hotel. But, tomorrow if I wanted to snorkel again, where can I purchase a permit?"

The slim ranger turned and pointed down the beach toward a low beige colored building about two miles south of where we stood. "At our offices in the building with the blue roof."

"You know that is a four-mile walk from my hotel. But, I will come by tomorrow morning and buy a permit for the day and pay you for the one I needed today."

"Very well." They both smiled, nodded their heads and looked as if they had successfully accomplished their job.

I took my mask off my head, secured my camera so it wouldn't flop against my chest, waved, and started back toward the Driftwood. "See you all in the morning."

After about five minutes, I turned and saw the two rangers sauntering southward toward their office building.

My flight to Nairobi was scheduled to leave in the morning at seven o'clock, so I would never see these rangers again. I felt a little guilt, but no one had informed me about the need of a permit to snorkel in the waters off the beaches around Malindi. The price of national park permits in Kenya is a pittance and is, no doubt, used for ranger salaries and park maintenance. Had I known, I would have purchased one.

By mid-afternoon I returned to the resort, rinsed the saltwater off myself and the snorkeling gear, unloaded everything in the cottage, collected my journal and a pen, and found an empty chaise lounge near the pool. I ordered a Coke and, although distracted by a couple of topless young women, started to record the events of the past several days. But directly across the pool from me, sat an even more interesting distraction. Poised cross-legged, in the middle of a bright colored oriental rug, was a roundish, heavy-looking, chocolate-colored, Buddha-like man. From his polished, mostly baldhead hung a black, tightly braided ponytail. Because of his slanted, almond-shaped eyes and rotund body, he could have passed for a medium-weight Sumo wrestler. A glint from some metallic pendants that dangled from his ear lobes caught my eye. He was shirtless, but wore what appeared to be red, yellow and white striped harem pants and a pair of black slippers. He sat with his hands resting on his thighs and arms relaxed in a yoga-like position. His portly body glistened. The King of Siam, I thought, but definitely not the taut and muscular figure Yul Brynner made famous.

Around him romped a number of pre-school-aged roundish, oriental-looking children dressed only in colorful diaper-like shorts. Some splashed about in the pool near him. When they did something unusual or accidentally invaded his space, his stern face softened into a stoic smile. He especially became animated when the splash from a child's dive, a "belly-womper," drenched his body and rug. With apparent concern for the child's safety, one of the women who seemed to be attending to the monarch's needs rushed to the edge of the pool. But before she could do anything, the man started from his statue-like posture, jumped into the water, lifted the giggling, sputtering child into his arms, and placed her on the side of the pool. He then returned to his rug. The anxious attendant knelt next to the rescued diver and appeared to whisper a reprimand, because the child's laughter turned to a series of stifled blubbers. While this scene played out, two other women doted on the man, toweled him and anointed his body with, I guessed, suntan lotion.

I assumed these vigilant women were either his wives or some sort of servants. Dressed in vibrant, airy, sarong-like gowns, snugged tight around their chest by the knot tied between their breasts, they resembled Polynesian hula girls. What an unusual group of people, I thought, and wondered where they came from. Where does one find such unusual, kaleidoscopic characters? I fantasized. They probably arrived on the scene aboard a magic carpet, or perhaps a royal dhow skippered by Sinbad himself, from some mysterious eastern province fabled in the stories of Richard F. Burton. I noted this daydream in my journal and continued to study the activity around the pool.

Three women dressed completely in black, in traditional abaya-styled garments, scarf and veil, diverted my fantasy, when they sneaked from the beach onto the resort grounds. I watched them scuttle toward the palm tree boundary along the far side of the resort. I pondered their intentions. I also questioned how they tolerated walking the beach under the intense equatorial radiation on this humid, one-hundred degree day. These must be fervent women dedicated to their Islamic faith, I thought.

I watched the three lightless illusions float stealthily through the shadows of the palm grove toward the rear of the pavilion near the laundry where they disappeared. Within moments, three nymphets in their mid teens, one wearing a bright red bikini, another a blue, and the third a yellow top and black bottom, came scampering from the direction of the pavilion toward the pool. They jumped in, frolicked about splashing each other, screaming and giggling for about ten minutes. Then they emerged and seated themselves on the side of the pool and dangled their feet in the water. I wish I could have understood their impish pattering because it seemed so lively. The more endowed girl in the blue bikini mooched a cigarette from a couple of men that were sunbathing near them. Suddenly she froze, began flailing an arm toward the beach. Outwardly concerned, she whispered something to the others. The three immediately became distressed. I looked in the direction of her gestures and saw a group of Arabic-looking men approaching the resort. I looked back toward the young girls. They had cleared the scene. Some red, blue and yellow blurs caught my attention. The three colors dashed behind the pavilion. The men, who looked to be in their late teens or early twenties, neared the resort's beach access and stopped in an area outside the club's property. They seemed to show interest in the swimming pool and its surroundings. They chatted among themselves, two shook their heads, another laughed. After a moment they turned and continued their stroll in the direction they were initially headed, away from Malindi.

So where were the wayward sirens? I looked around and saw them, again garbed according to the dictate of Allah, moving cautiously among the palm shadows toward the beach. When they emerged onto the beach, they ambled toward Malindi, away from the young men.

The contrary comportment of these Muslim girls made me smile. They really didn't do anything wrong except bypass, for a moment, some of their religion's repressive mores. I guess no matter what the situation young girls throughout the world appear to follow the philosophy that Cindi Lauper proposed in her 1983 hit, *Girls Just Want to Have Fun*. I too, had had a fun day.

EMERALD PARADISE: THE SEYCHELLES

Voices around me drowned in the monotonous drone of jet engines. Although I had a window seat on Kenya Airline's Boeing 707 between Nairobi and the Seychelles, extensive cloud cover obscured everything below. Being sealed in this crowded, stuffy airliner for the past two hours had tucked a hypnotic blanket over my mind. My consciousness drifted. My eyes kept closing. To stay alert, I tried talking to my seatmates, Doris and Sam, a middle-aged couple from Los Angeles.

Doris and Sam's trip to the Seychelles had an unusual twist. Although they planned to honeymoon in the islands, they were not, as yet, married. Since this marriage would be the second for both of them, they wanted to make it unusual, something to be remembered. So they planned their wedding ceremony to occur in some place other than Los Angeles. "Anywhere but there," they said. When I asked how they decided on the Seychelles, I learned that it had nothing to do with the Islands' beauty or their sensuous reputation.

When Doris and Sam became engaged, they vowed not to go through the exhausting ceremony and reception of a typical wedding. They didn't want the hassle. Besides, Sam said such events were for the enjoyment of parents, relatives and friends. He said that when he and his first wife married, the shindig burned them out. They were so tired that when finally alone, they couldn't enjoy their wedding-night. Doris gave Sam a sorrowful look, punched his shoulder and said, "That's not going to happen to us."

Doris said that when her friends learned that she and Sam were to marry, they wanted a full-blown party. So to placate them and avoid any disappointments Sam and Doris threw a "prewedding" reception. It was during this gathering that a pin-the-tail-on-the-donkey-like game determined that the wedding would take place in the Seychelles.

Witnessed by all their friends, Sam blindfolded Doris, rotated her several times, handed her a streamer with a pin and sent her walking toward a large map of the world that hung on the wall. When she bumped into the wall map, Doris stuck the streamer's pin into the middle of the Indian Ocean. Sam said that everyone yelled because he and Doris were destined to go on a cruise and be wed by a ship's captain. But Sam's inclination toward seasickness dissuaded the two from the cruise. They then decided to marry on the nearest piece of land. The Seychelle Islands won the toss.

"What a romantic adventure. Only you Californians would think of doing something like that," I said. We all laughed.

I felt the airplane bank slightly. As I looked out the window, I saw billowy layers of cumulus clouds disintegrate into cottony shreds and puffs. Below, a large emerald mass surrounded by several smaller gems floated on an aquamarine background. These jewels rotated, appeared and disappeared as the airplane maneuvered between clouds in preparation for landing.

"We're about there," I exclaimed.

My two seatmates flattened me against the back of my seat as they leaned across to get a glimpse of the Seychelle Islands. "What a beautiful place," Doris said. "Where will we land?"

"On Mahe, that's the big island below us," I replied.

"Do you think we'll find a priest or minister to marry us?" Doris asked.

"Doris, move your head so I can see those islands." Sam literally pushed Doris into her seat. "All we have to do is find a church . . . shouldn't be much of a problem, they're all Catholics down there."

"Sam, you get so excited," Doris said. "You're just like a little boy. . . . That's why I love you, but don't be so pushy. You can't see anything anyway. Besides, you'll crush Richard."

"Sorry, Rich. Just so there's no hard feeling, I'd like you to come to our wedding," Sam said. "You let us know where you're staying and we'll contact you with the location of the church . . . when we find one."

We all relaxed and sat tight against the seats as the plane zipped a few feet above the water toward the end of the runway. After the airplane landed, we were instructed to remain in our seats and not move into the aisle until told to deplane. The cabin door swung open and in marched a quartet of officials with cans of insecticide. They proceeded to spray the interior of the plane, passengers and crew.

The woman in the mosquito patrol told me that, although mosquitoes were common in the Seychelles, they weren't infected with malaria. So the job of the Seychellois decontamination team was to keep the islands free of this disease. They did this by fumigating everything in sight on all flights from the African mainland.

Once we exited, all passengers filed under a canopy to await clearance through immigration. The procedure was similar to what I expected. It didn't differ from the arrival procedures I had experienced in other tropical island countries around the world. Since I had all the proper documentation and was familiar with the process, my entry went smoothly and without anxiety. Besides, in the waiting line, Doris and Sam entertained me. They were a fun loving couple that seemed to enjoy being the brunt of each other's jokes. But Doris continued to be concerned with finding a church and someone to officiate at the wedding. Sam assured her that they had the required marriage license, but would have to wait out the three-day residency period. So Sunday he'd start looking for a local shaman to conduct the wedding. In the meantime, they could look for a location for the ceremony. But I noticed that Sam was distracted. He was more interested in renting a vehicle to take them to a hotel and for transportation on the island. While they haggled about the car, I pondered the quality of the room I had rented, sight unseen, in the least expensive guesthouse on Mahe listed by the tour agency in Nairobi. After I heard several passengers comment about the availability of choice lodging at moderate prices, I became more dubious about the choice I had made. Since I did not place a deposit, I could change after I saw the place. Sam and Doris said they'd drop me near my lodging. The map showed it just off the road to Victoria, the capital of the Seychelles, where the two of them were headed.

Sam rented a Mini-Moke, a four-seat golf cart-like vehicle covered by a pastel colored canopy and powered by a small gasoline engine. The little motorized phaeton had no space for luggage except the back seat. Since the prospective bride and groom had brought everything but the kitchen sink, the back seat quickly became fully loaded. I wondered whether they were just getting married or planning to homestead on the island. Luckily, a Mini-Moke has flat Jeep-like fenders, so I was relegated to the right rear fender. Since no space remained to stow my duffle bag, I had to hold it on my lap with one hand and with the other keep myself from sliding off the fender. Sam assured me he would corner the vehicle with great care so I would not fly off.

Mini-Mokes are not highly powered. They slow considerably on an uphill grade but descend with a whiz. It took us about twenty minutes to travel the four or five winding miles from the airport to where the road to my lodging crossed. Since the trail to my bed and breakfast ascended steeply, Sam worried that the Mini-Moke would have trouble going up the hill. And if it made it he feared that he might not be able to break the contraption's downhill free fall toward the main road sufficiently before Doris, he, the Mini-Moke and luggage would fly off into the ocean. The main road into Victoria paralleled the seawall and there weren't any barriers. I agreed to walk the remainder of the way to my lodging and thanked Sam and Doris for the ride.

"We'll be in touch," Doris shouted as they puttered off.

I only encountered Doris and Sam one more time, at a crosswalk in the tourist district of Victoria. They had found a church, they said, and planned to marry on Monday. Since I'd be on one of the other islands Monday, I congratulated them and voiced my regrets for not being able to attend. I never saw the two of them again.

After they left me at the crossroads, I trudged a quarter mile up an exhaustive forty-five degree incline and found the guesthouse where I had reserved a room. Soaked in perspiration, I rang the doorbell several times over a period of about ten minutes. No one answered. Frustrated, I mumbled, "Where's the proprietor? I had a reservation so someone knows I'm supposed to arrive." I walked around the house and decided I'd wait. I seated myself in a deck chair on the patio. The ocean vista was beautiful. There didn't appear to be any other guests. The place was empty, yet the doors were wide open. While I relaxed and cooled, I noticed that the house needed repair. The patio was in disarray. Things like shovels, boards, broken chairs and old barrels were scattered about. I looked into the kitchen. It had the ambience of a flophouse. After two hours, I hiked back down the hill to check out the guesthouses along the main road next to the seafront. A good decision, because

I later found out that the guesthouse on the hillside had a reputation for not living up to its responsibilities. I learned that the proprietor overcharged, double rented rooms, rarely changed the bedclothes, and on several occasions didn't provide breakfast.

Catty-cornered from the cross-section of the main road and the trail I had just descended, I espied the Harbor View Guest House and stopped to check room availability. Mrs. Collie, the proprietress, said that one of her eight rooms was available and suggested that I inspect it before registering. The room had a bed, table, lamp, chair, large fan, and was across the hall from a shared bathroom. And the price was right. I booked the room.

Although small, the Harbor View had an attractive, open-air dining room with a view of the harbor, a small but complete bar, and it was only about a mile from the center of Victoria. The route into town turned out to be a pleasant stroll. But if I didn't want to walk, the local bus stopped in front.

Although the normal hour had passed, and I had not had lunch, Mrs. Collie said she'd whip something together. After I off loaded my backpack and belongings, she directed me to a table in the dining room.

While sitting and waiting for the food, I became aware of a soft, musical, metronomic, swooshing sound emanating from the deck-bar area, a single tone, no variation, no intonation, but rhythmic. It sounded as if someone were laying a beat for a jazz composition. Fascinated and curious about this beat, I looked around the wall to learn what was generating this "catchy" rhythm. To my surprise I saw a maid polishing the wooden floor. She had the front of her skirt rolled up and pinned to fold at her thighs freeing her legs. Hoofing back and forth in a short scooting dance, her steps scraped across the floor in a definite pattern. Fashioned to her sandals were coconut halves, the instruments she used to polish the floor. The coconut's rough, fibrous outer husk provided abrasive for cleaning, while the inner nut supplied polishing oil. If a talented musician had heard this rhythm, he might have improvised a lively melody from the "scrapy-polishy, scrapy-polishy" sound.

When I returned to the table, rice, bread, fresh greens, and a strange casserole awaited me. The casserole smelled and tasted heavily of curry. It contained green, red, white, black and orange bits of vegetables suspended in a gravy-like sauce. Bite sized chunks of a sweet, chewy, slightly fishy, gray-colored product constituted a meaty component. The concoction filled a porcelain bowl. Not until I recognized some suckers attached to one of the meaty pieces did I realize I was enjoying a bowl of curried octopus. It surely beat a grilled cheese sandwich. My lunch became an epicurean delight. I ordered a glass of white wine.

Although the Seychelles, like most exotic, tropical escapes, are fancied as pleasure domes for sensual and hedonistic enjoyment, the cultural mixture of French, English, East African, Indian, and Oriental makes them a gastronome's playground. I'm far from being a gourmand of exotic foods, but I do enjoy native dishes. This trip provided one of the most unusual meals I have ever encountered in my travels. Long before I visited these islands, I read that the Seychellois ate fruit bats or flying foxes. After lunch I asked Mrs. Collie if any of the restaurants on Mahe served fruit bats. "You mean *chauve-souris*," she said. "No, not many people eat, as you say, fruit bats anymore. But some Seychellois, especially the old Natives, still prepare it for traditional meals."

She looked at me and noticed my curiosity and disappointment. She then said that if I were interested she could prepare a fruit bat dinner. In the morning, she would ask the old man, a Seychellois who did odd jobs for her, to catch some bats. This would take a couple of days, since catching these animals involved stringing several curtains of nets in a field near some mango or banana trees frequented by fruit bats. These nets, I learned, looked much like the mist nets used to capture song birds for ornithological research, but their construction and mesh were more substantial. Mrs. Collie told me that her younger son would help the old man arrange and pitch some nets in the proper field. If they were successful, I'd have a *chauve-souris* dinner Saturday evening. That would satisfy my curiosity, I told her.

Since it was late in the afternoon, I decided to skip dinner and explore the area near the Harbor View Guest House before dark. I could grab a snack when I returned.

Lush vegetation, palms and varieties of exotic trees, bushes, and flowers grew wild along the road that ran toward the center of Victoria. I followed the road for about a quarter of a mile until it turned inland and passed through a park-like landscape. On the left the prospect ascended steeply up the mountain, similar to the one I had trekked up earlier when Doris and Sam dropped me off. But instead of supporting cottages and a dilapidated guesthouse, the two-thousand-foot mountain that was the center of Mahe was richly blanketed with rainforest vegetation. At a sharp curve in the road the mountain walled against the road's left edge. A stream washed from a crevice, flowed under the road and meandered through the ground cover of grass and pink-white flowers that carpeted the open forest. I could see that it spilled across a small beach and emptied into the ocean several hundred feet away. A sweet, pleasant perfume issued from these woods. I stopped to watch, and listened to, the many colorful, as well as some drab, exotic birds that flitted about the branches. Although I considered myself an advanced birdwatcher, I could not identify these species.

As I stood watching the birds rustle about the trees and smelling pleasant fragrances, I realized how Indian Ocean traders of the past knew, before sighting land, that they were nearing these islands. They could smell them. Not only are ambrosial aromas produced by such exotic plants as frangapani, ornamental peppers, citrus, and orchids, but aromatic spices such as cinnamon, vanilla, tea, and coconut are commercially grown and processed here. It's no wonder that the balmy evenings of these islands have generated such a sensuous reputation. The air is flavored with aphrodisiac scents.

When I returned to the guesthouse dining room, a waitress took my order for fried fish fingers, coconut-flavored rice, a salad, and a beer. An enticing bouquet of frying foods and coconut, slightly flavored with cigarette smoke, filled the café. The side of the room that faced out toward the harbor opened onto a deck. Subdued indirect lighting came from eight ceiling-mounted lamps. The two lamps over the exit to the deck cast light downward. All the others projected light away from the corners onto the adjacent walls. This arrangement created two discrete ovals of illumination on the upper part of each of the three walls. The ovals did not overlap. Although not an extremely unusual method of lighting a restaurant interior, the consequences of this arrangement had an interesting influence on the local reptilian population.

As I relaxed at my table, while awaiting the meal, my eyes became transfixed on the bright ovals on the wall in front of me. When I stared into the brightest area, everything outside the oval appeared black, invisible. But, when I turned my head slightly and my eyes became accustomed to the surrounding shadows, I noticed that the penumbra was filled with many green geckos. These little lizards were polarized, fixed against the wall nose to tail, into two or three incomplete rings that encircled the spots of light. Where the light beams stretched toward their source, the geckos filled the penumbral triangles from their base to the apex in rows of decreasing numbers; the row along the base of the triangle contained four to five individuals. The corner two lizards splayed away from the row and blended with the circles. A single, steadfast individual guarded the spot nearest the lamp at the triangle's apex. Their heads all pointed toward the light spot on the wall. During the night, as long as the walls remained lighted, they were transformed into an M. C. Escher-like mural.

Periodically, several of the lizards would break ranks, vigorously run into the light, and perform a staccato-like dance, then return to the original position. When I saw this behavior, I realized that the geckos, which are nocturnal insectivores, were taking advantage of the room's lighting pattern to catch insects. These glow-spots simplified lizards' lives by attracting prey for easy capture. What a headline for *Technology Today,* "Seychellois Green Geckos Use Human Technology to Secure Food."

The next two days I spent my time sightseeing. I walked to Victoria, a small colorful, well-appointed city, the commercial center and capital of the Seychelles. I found it to be a friendly place inhabited by very handsome people who spoke English with a French accent to tourists and French among themselves. Throughout history, governance of the islands has flip-flopped between the United Kingdom and France. The Seychelles gained their independence from Britain in 1976 and became the sovereign nation known as The Republic of the Seychelles. Ties to Britain can be seen in Victoria where an approximately twenty-foot tall replica of Big Ben dominates the city's main square. Victoria is connected to France through its food and language.

There are no full-blooded Seychellois. The people are considered Creole, an admixture of African, French, English, Indian, and small compliment of other Asian genes. They closely resemble the people I have met in Belize, the only English speaking country in Central America. Although many of the culinary gratifications of both countries reflect Creole flavors, those in Belize are more closely aligned with tastes from Africa. One would think this should also be so in the Seychelles because they are so much closer to the dark continent. Instead, Seychellois cuisine is more like the *nouvelle cuisine de Français.*

My lunch at the Marie Antoinette Restaurant, an upscale restaurant on the road up the mountain from Victoria, reflected this French influence. I ordered the fish of the day, baked. When the fish arrived, I was a bit surprised because it was a colorful Christmas wrasse. The only other wrasse I had eaten previously was a cunner, a dark-colored fish commonly found in New England Harbors. In the tropics, fishes of this taxon become highly colored, which is often nature's way of advertising a harbinger of some type of toxin. Wrasses feed directly on hydroids, algae, coral polyps, and other types of organisms encrusting rocks and pilings. The tissue of any of the foods a wrasse may eat has the potential to house symbiotic algae. Many of these produce a variety of toxins. So when a fish eats a jellyfish, it can assimilate a toxin. Although most toxins do not causes ill effects to the fish, in humans they attack the nervous system and greatly debilitate an individual's senses. In large concentrations they can be lethal.

Nevertheless, my plate contained a Christmas wrasse attractively and appetizingly displayed. Though baked to perfection, the turquoise and red strips that colored the fish maintained their brilliance. Its head was arranged on the dish in its proper location but partially separated from the body. The tail was still attached. The fish lay upon a bed of rice and was encircled by a medley of fresh vegetables and scalloped potatoes. Indeed a culinary delight, but I told the waiter of my hesitation to eat this fish. He knew the fish's potential to carry some sort of toxin, but assured me that everyone eats Christmas wrasses, as well as other species of wrasses, so long as they are less than eight inches in length. Juveniles, he said, did not concentrate sufficient quantities of the toxin to cause problems and wished me *bon appétit.* I consoled myself with the thought that some alcohol would, no doubt, denature any existing toxins, so I ordered a glass of white Bordeaux. The meal was exquisite and I suffered no ill effects. In fact, I felt more invigorated as I returned to the city's center, probably energized by the wine or the down hill trek from Marie Antoinette's.

While on the island of Mahe, I spent most of my time doing what tourists normally do. Victoria contains many fine restaurants in all price ranges, but more interesting are the little craft shops and galleries. I took a bus that groaned its way up and over the steep mountain and coasted down the other side into the Beau Vallon beach area on the northwest side of the island. Here a large, white, sandy beach stretched along a roadway shaded by very tall Australian pine (*Casuarina*) trees. I saw many sunbathers and swimmers, although the beach did not appear crowded. A few of the women on the beach wore swimsuits, but most preferred to sun *au naturel.* When I stopped for tea at the Beau Vallon Resort Hotel, I met an American couple who worked for the American Embassy. The young woman wore a standard two-piece swimsuit and her male friend, a pair of Speedo swimming trunks. They explained that one could identify American females because they either were not topless, or they were well tanned except for conspicuous white breasts and strap marks.

With this in mind, I saw few Americans in and around the hotel's swimming pool or on the beach. Most everyone else showed little guilt at flaunting about in the nude. P. T. Barnum was correct, however, when he said that a partially clothed body is more sensuous than a naked one. After viewing the parade of completely or partially naked sun worshipers for about ten minutes, I realized the appropriateness of his philosophy. It seems when bare truth is displayed, once hidden imperfections assume dominance. Although the female body has great appeal, seen thus en masse my desires were not heightened.

I returned to the Harbor View Guest House in time for dinner. On tonight's menu, *chauve-souris*. The trappers caught a half dozen flying foxes, so I, and the other guests as well, were going to have the special meal I had requested. I felt a bit squeamish and sad because, on the hike into town, I had seen several of these animals. Although they appeared like little Draculas hanging from the electric wires strung above the road, they really were innocent, harmless creatures about the size of a toy terrier. They hung upside down, asleep, their wings wrapped about their body like a cloak, with only their fox-like head protruding below. On the hoof, they were more adorable than appetizing.

As with the octopus, the animal in the casserole was not identifiable, but the meat was dark and sweet. It might have been any species of rodent. The taste resurrected a long lost memory of a flavor I savored in my childhood. The dish tasted a lot like muskrat stew my mother once cooked. Except the *chauve-souris* was more highly spiced than my mother's stew. She used the same recipe in preparing rabbit or squirrel, so all these animal dishes shared a similar taste.

Mrs. Collie complimented her dish with vegetables and rice. I chased each oily mouthful with a swallow of beer. Though initially palatable, the taste of beer, spices, and sweet, musty bat persisted throughout the evening and into the next morning.

* * *

While in the Seychelles I wanted to visit Praslin and La Digue, the other nearby commercially important islands in the archipelago. So while I was walking about Victoria Center, I had stopped at one of the city's main tourist agencies, Mason's Travel. The agency arranged a flight to Praslin, and reserved a place for me to stay. If I wanted to travel to La Digue Island, I could book passage directly aboard a schooner sailing from Praslin. The travel agent at Mason's suggested that I spend only a day on La Digue, because she said that the only excitement on this island, except for the exquisite beaches, was the copra plantation. Nevertheless, the whole quest sounded like one of the romantic trips portrayed in the defunct TV series

Adventures in Paradise. I decided to put this trip on my agenda for the next day.

So after my epicurean adventure with a fruit bat and a sufficient time at the bar to allow the meal to meld itself within my digestive tract, I returned to my room to pack my belongings. Since Air Seychelles allowed only two kilograms of luggage. I packed lightly and efficiently. The airplanes that serviced the island were small, with little luggage space, and passengers were charged if they exceeded the weight limit. My backpack weighed in at about seven pounds. I paid extra. Hey, I needed to take my toothbrush and extra film.

The plane flew out at ten in the morning. The flight lasted fifteen minutes. I barely had enough time to blink.

My hotel on Praslin, The Britannia Hotel, located a short distance from the airport in the town of Grand Anse, was actually known as the island's five star restaurant rather than a place of lodging. About a week before my arrival, six guest cottages were completed behind the restaurant. Since the cottages were brand-new, I was offered a reduced rate to be a "guinea pig" guest. The smell of drying mortar and paint lingered during my entire stay. But I couldn't complain, because breakfast and lunch were also included in this special "introductory" rate.

The interior of my cottage, a single large room, was airy, beautiful and comfortable. A commode and lavatory were separated from the room by a tiled wall, but a slightly depressed tiled area extended into the main room. This depression served as the floor of a "curtainless" shower. Although I had encountered showers such as these, which soaked the entire room and most of its contents, in Italian hotels, the one at the Britannia worked. But still skeptical from my experience in Malindi, I gingerly tested the pipes and out-flowing water before I decided to rinse off. Here I did not encounter an electrifying experience.

Except for a couple of taxis and tour vans, no other forms of public transportation were evident on Praslin. Bicycles were out of the question for trips beyond the town. A rugged mountain formed the interior of the island, over which crossed a paved road. But a network of rugged dirt trails crisscrossed the mountainous areas.

I came here to explore and I needed a vehicle. The hotel arranged a rental car from a private individual who had two Isuzu jeeps. He graciously and excitedly delivered one of his four-wheel drive vehicles almost to my doorstep.

The jeep gave me the freedom to negotiate the rugged, mountainous inland and coastal roads of Praslin; well, most of the roads. I found that even a four-wheel drive vehicle does have its limits. Early in my excursion, I tried to force the jeep, while locked in four-wheel drive, to climb a furrowed, rock strewn road up a tortuous razorback buttress that had an incline of almost fifty degrees. The road was slightly wider than the width of the jeep with no extra space on either side if I needed to turn around. It resembled a donkey path rather than a road. As I drove upward, the front end kept rising, angling higher than the rear. I felt as if at any moment, the vehicle would flip, pitchpole, backward end over end. Gravity strongly pressed me into the back of the seat. Through the windshield, I saw blue sky and only a sliver of the mountain's summit. Only a couple of hundred feet more, and I'll be over the top, I thought as I floored the accelerator, but the engine groaned, coughed, and choked toward a stall. And the trail angled more steeply. It became acutely obvious that I had no choice but to back down. When I looked out both side windows, I couldn't see the bluffs beneath me. Frozen in my seat, I saw only the open space across the canyons to my left and right. Behind me, a narrow sandy colored ribbon, slightly obscured by a dust cloud thrown up by the tires, snaked down the knife-edged protuberance. Dread! Panic struck me hard. I shifted into reverse and eased the jeep backward. If one of the tires drops off the edge, I'm history, I thought. Acrophobia kicked in. I began to remember many obscure details from my past. Ridiculous questions popped to mind. Would the brakes hold while I backed this buggy down? If not, who'd get charged for this jeep? When I finally reached the bottom, which seemed to take a lifetime, I tried to bury my face in my hands, but couldn't. My fingers were locked onto the steering wheel. Every stitch of clothing I wore was soaked. Sweat seemed to flow freely from my every pore. I turned the jeep around and slowly drove back to the hotel.

What I had attempted to follow was a route that, on the map, appeared to be a shortcut to a very secluded beach named Anse Lazio. What the map failed to show were the changes in elevation. Also it did not show that the road was only passable on foot or horseback. So much for trying to take a shortcut.

During the rest of my visit on Praslin, I drove on paved roads or flat dirt trails along the shore. I found a safer picturesque route to Anse Lazio that took me over the mountains southward to Baie Ste. Anne, around the bay, then along the east shore to Anse Boudin. The paved road ended at Anse Boudin, but a dirt road continued over flat ground through the coastal forest to the secluded beach on the northeast side of Praslin. When I arrived, not only did the scenic beauty of the area impress me, but also the sensuous activity that was occurring there.

Four extremely attractive models cavorted and posed amid the sand and waves at the far end of the beach before a company of photographers. The photographers advanced and retreated, stooped and reclined, twisted and curled in accord with the models' movements. With each flash and snap of action, bundles and ribbons of blond hair flung and flailed above male and female heads as if the genders danced in ardent competition. From the distance of my perception only the clothing distinguished the obviousness of the sexes, since both had long blond hair. Khaki colored cargo shorts and unbuttoned flaring field shirts separated the exquisitely tanned photographers from the lithe enviously sun kissed, leggy models. The models wore only minuscule bikini bottoms. Two of them periodically added demure bits of apparel, such as pastel-colored wide brim hats and scarfs, during their dynamic dalliance before the cameras and video recorders.

The girls quickly covered their breasts and turned their backs toward me when the jeep rolled into the scene. Their modesty lasted only a few minutes, because a shirtless guy in baggy white pants, scarf and a panama hat yelled something. He, no doubt, was the director, because the models quickly returned to frolicking before the cameras. Momentarily surprised and embarrassed that I had invaded this sensuous scene, I backed the jeep into the forest behind the beach.

Beautiful, healthy, well tanned topless women were commonplace in swimming pools and on verandas and beaches of all resorts in the Seychelles and along the coast of Kenya. Consequently, a hedonistic ambience seemed to envelop these places. In such an atmosphere most visitors, except puritanical Americans, lose their inhibitions and bare all. Additionally the Seychelles and other remote idyllic islands have been used as backdrops for many visually diverting projects for magazines, advertising, and films. After a few days in the Seychelles being stimulated by the many exposed feminine bodies, I became somewhat desensitized to their allure. Nevertheless, the appealing models at Anse Lazio began to aggravate my libido. I wanted to stay and watch the shoot, but prudence suggested that I leave. I drove to Anse Boudin, the beach near where the paved road began, to do some snorkeling.

When I returned to the hotel and dinner that evening, the film company from the beach, all prim and properly dressed, was dining at the Britannia Restaurant. I learned that the group was from Germany here to produce advertising videos and photos. They didn't speak much English and seemed to socialize only within their own group.

At Anse Boudin I snorkeled in the channel between the island of Curieuse and Praslin. Underwater in the channel, beautiful well-developed coral colonies covered the bottom. A neat aspect of this area was that the colorful underwater wonderland was approachable from shore and the reefs were at a depth accessible to free diving. Later I rested on the white sandy beach and looked around. Curieuse, a private island about a kilometer from Praslin, must have had a small settlement because a short distance from where I lay on the beach a school bus stopped to discharge a group of children. The children boarded a small open boat and were transported to Curieuse.

I spent several hours snorkeling and photographing some colorful anemone fish, unicorn fish, a diversity of butterfly fishes, and two striking black, white and yellow banded Moorish idols. As the Moorish idols glided gracefully over beds of finger corals, the tips of their dorsal fins trailed away like long white streamer. But the most unusual fish that I saw, I observed as I rested on the beach mesmerized by the wavelets that curled onto the sand. To my surprise, I saw a sight that didn't initially register as real, several small beige-brown, mottled fishes emerged from the wavelets and slithered toward a boulder about two meters away. I watched them make their way across the hot, dry, open sand to an algal mat that grew at the base of the rock. When I realized that I wasn't being overcome by sunstroke or thoughts of seminude women, and knowing that I was not underwater, the images finally registered as real fish. These were mudskippers.

Mudskippers are fishes about four inches in length, with a blunted forward projecting face, protruding alert eyes, and a dorsal fin firmly raised to attention. Using their pectoral fins as legs, they can come out of the water, walk short distances across land areas, and climb roots of mangrove trees and other moist solid objects on shore. As long as these fishes remain moist, their gills can extract oxygen from air as well as they do from water. They resemble gobies and are usually classified in the family Gobidae. Since they feed on gnats and other small flying insects, the collection of detritus and algae at the base of the rock made a perfect "landfood" restaurant for these amphibious fishes.

On the way back to the hotel I stopped at Vallée de Mai, a National Park, home to several plants and animals that exist nowhere else on earth. One of these plants is the legendary coco-de-mar. This palm has an interesting folk history.

During a time back in the past when places beyond the shores of the "civilized" world were poorly known, any mysterious object of unknown origin that washed onto a beach was considered by uneducated humans to be a thing sent by the gods. So a coconut anatomically resembling the size and shape of the lower third of a female torso in such detail as to include a properly located clump of pubic hair easily became a precious treasure. To the ancients it symbolized female fertility and sexuality. Since the coco-de-mar was a token sent by the gods, only sheikhs, maharajas, and pharaohs were allowed to possess them. These idols were thought to carry a prophecy from the supreme beings, and only demigods could decipher their messages. So when found, the coco-de-mar was immediately taken to the ruler.

I am glad that our perception of supreme beings and religion has changed, because I wanted a coco-de-mar as a souvenir, a felicitous symbol of the Seychelles. But since this fruit was produced by an endangered species, weighed forty plus pounds, and was too big to fit into my suitcase, I settled for an eight-inch wooden replica, which I purchased in Victoria.

The coco-de-mar palms grow on a slope not far from the entrance to the Vallée de Mai. A forest of mature and juvenile trees can be found just off a trail reported to be over one thousand years old. When I walked beneath these trees and looked upward, I felt as if I were playing some strange form of Russian roulette. The gigantic double coconuts dangled above my head. One could do some major damage if it fell on me.

This National Park has a system of excellent, well-marked, interpretive nature trails. Growing inside are not only examples of the flora found in the Seychelles, but also plants found on many neighboring Indian Ocean islands as well as on Madagascar and continental Africa. Blossoming bromeliads and orchids abound, as do other rare and beautiful tropical flowers. Since the park is situated on a slope, visitors do a lot of uphill walking. In the heat and humidity this can be a bit stressful, but well worth the time and effort. This is the only place on earth that one can see and hear the black parrot. These birds are not exceptionally reclusive. I saw one within the first fifteen minutes that I was there. The Vallée de Mai is a bird lover's paradise. A large diversity of bird species resides or passes through this park. In addition to the many varied and brilliantly colored birds, most of which I could not identify, I saw the rare blue fruit pigeon. And this was the only place during my entire visit to Kenya and the Seychelles that I encountered a sunbird. I couldn't identify it specifically, but its brilliant metallic feathers and curved bill were quite distinctive. Although larger, these birds resembled hummingbirds.

* * *

I took a day trip to La Digue Island aboard an old, restored, interisland schooner. To my disappointment the ship lumbered along under power, although the winds were sufficient to sail. Because of scheduling constraints, the use of the engine was considered to be more efficient than the aesthetic alternative of billowing sails. It didn't take an economist to understand the financial foolishness of having a ship's crew spend two hours hoisting and setting sails for a thirty-minute voyage. So the ambience of sailing a tropical sea voyage had to succumb to transporting passengers quickly and on schedule between points A and B. Nevertheless, the trip was fun.

Except for a couple of trucks, there were no motorized vehicles on La Digue. Transportation around the island was via bicycle or ox cart. I rented a bike and cycled around the island and on several roads that cut through the island's interior. There weren't many real highlands, so pedaling a bicycle was easy.

After touring most of the island, visiting a copra plantation (the island's major industry where coconuts are commercially grown), and stopping for lunch at the only restaurant, I bicycled to Grand Anse. (Most of the islands in the Seychelle Archipelago have a Grand Anse or Big Beach.) Grand Anse on La Digue is one of the most picturesque beaches in the Seychelles, literally a living postcard of a tropical paradise. Gigantic walls of granite boulders, naturally stacked and fitted together so precisely that they looked as if they had been assembled by experienced masons, defined the lateral boundaries of Grand Anse. These walls stood ten to thirty feet in height and extended seaward for several hundred feet. Aeons of wind and water have smoothed the surfaces and edges of these giant pink-gray boulders. In between the walls an expansive sandy beach sloped moderately from a green coconut palm forest to the brilliant turquoise ocean. Large curling rollers, created when ocean swells funnel and compress between the walls crashed onto the beach with exploding force and dissipated into white, iridescent foam that rapidly coursed up the grade toward waiting bathers and, just as quickly, retreated.

Since the ferry wasn't to leave for about two hours, I decided to lie on the beach and catch a few rays of sun. Though I didn't bring my bathing suit, I wore a pair of dark blue bikini-like briefs. So why not do as the Romans do, and strip to my underwear, I thought. On this beach, with half the women naked or topless, no one will know the difference. So I found myself enjoying the sun and sea at a site slightly away from the masses, stripped to my pseudo Speedos.

I had lain there for less than an hour when an ox cart loaded with about a dozen elderly women and two nuns stopped fifty feet away from me. The guide spoke German, but I understood, from what he said, that the women would have about thirty minutes to enjoy this beach. Most of them stood at the brim and looked at the waves. Others explored the flora behind the beach, and three walked to within ten feet of where I lay. I estimated their ages to be about fifty or sixty. Since I had staked my claim earlier, I felt somewhat intruded upon. Nevertheless, the beach *was* a public beach and a tourist attraction, so if they wanted to spend a few minutes sightseeing next to my underwear-clad body, they had every right. I assumed they'd look around, take some pictures and move on.

Not so! In fact, I wasn't prepared for what happened next. The three talked amongst themselves, became somewhat giddy and animated, and striped off all their clothes. Every stitch! Then they ran down the beach, jumped into the surf and romped about for a few minutes. One by one they scampered back up the beach to their pile of clothing, shook out their hair and proceeded to dress. When again fully clothed, they returned to the ox cart. Not once, during their quest for refreshment from the heat, did my presence inhibit nor distract them. To them, it was as if I were invisible. These were definitely emancipated, free spirited women. I wondered how the folks back home would view this incident. No doubt, we Americans would be shocked. We're a bit too conservative to break free of modesty like these elderly German women. I definitely was taken aback.

After a while I dressed and returned to the ferry dock. The trip back to Praslin was more boisterous than the voyage out. A group of middle-aged French tourists, who appeared to have visited La Digue primarily to party, continued their party onboard the schooner. Well oiled from an abundance of wine, they sang loudly and danced on the foredeck. Two of the men played recorders while a rugged, tough-looking woman attempted to sing songs made famous by Edith Piaf. As she sang and evocatively gestured, the crowd, especially the men, egged her on. She got so wired from the attention and horseplay that about half way across the waterway she threw off her blouse and jumped up onto the bowsprit and intoned even louder. Interestingly, she actually could sing. Her voice sounded somewhat like Piaf's, but more gravelly when she tried to warble. But most impressive at this moment was the sight of her facing into the wind topless on the bowsprit, breasts jutting forward, legs frozen in mid-stride as if she just broke free of starting blocks, arms extended high above grasping tightly to the forestay, and her blond hair blowing aft tumultuously. Her guttural trills mixed with the moan and clatter of vibrating shrouds as she belted strains of Piaf's famous *Hymne A L'amour.* She looked like the ship's figurehead, a siren protruding from the bow. When she finished, her performance raised a cheer of rousing whistles, shouts, and toasts, and a fusillade of empty wine bottles tossed into the harbor as the schooner approached the dock.

Once on shore, the inebriated party quickly dispersed and disappeared. I jumped into the Isuzu and drove to a west facing beach to catch a last glimpse of an African sunset, a fitting end to an exciting day and nearing conclusion of my African adventure. In a week I would be on my way back to the United States of America.

* * *

After breakfast I sat in the Britannia Hotel's courtyard waiting for the owner of the rented Isuzu. I checked my watch. Surely, he'll be here shortly to pick up the vehicle and drive me to the airport I thought. I was booked to fly back to Mahe and then on to Nairobi.

The Africans say that, ". . . if you leave a footprint in the sand, you will return to Africa." I put my foot down firmly beneath a frangapani tree, just off the Britannia Hotel's parking lot, and left a solid imprint. Then I collected some flowers from the tree, arranged them around the footprint, and photographed the impression. I wanted to remember the moment and preserve evidence of my visit to the Seychelles and Kenya. Someday, I will return.

HOME ON THE WINGS OF TERMITES

Checking out of a hotel after a long-term stay in a country that has a strong bureaucratic culture usually takes considerable time. Clerks can spend inordinate amounts of time meticulously completing audits, checking and rechecking their arithmetic and filling out piles of officious-looking forms. Then all this paperwork has to be approved and signed by the managerial staff, and eventually the guest. I started this process early, immediately after breakfast. Sometime during the day I'd have to reserve a taxi to take me to the international airport. But as it happened my final day in Kenya turned out to be pleasant and relaxing in spite of the glut of mid-level bureaucrats.

My flight back to the United States was not scheduled to leave until one-twenty in the morning. I'd actually be leaving Nairobi early Monday morning, more than a whole day away. So I essentially had the entire day before I needed to arrive at the airport. I had arranged with the Milimani Hotel to retain my room through Monday, even though I would actually leave the hotel Sunday evening around 11:00 P.M. The clerks would complete the checkout process during the day and I could sign all the paperwork when I returned later for dinner. My day was now free.

I had arranged to spend this day with Anne and Michael, the sister and brother I had met on the camping trip in the Masai Mara about three weeks earlier. They wanted to take me to lunch at the Carnivore Restaurant. Without being summoned, I knew they had arrived because their coming disrupted the peace and quiet that normally existed around the hotel on Sundays. The old wreck of a Fiat, which Michael purchased to provide transportation during his extended visit in Nairobi, backfired as it came up the hotel's driveway. The explosion and the jet of heavy black smoke the vehicle released before its engine died caused a flurry of activity among the hotel personnel. Actually, I think they were trying to run for cover. Michael emerged from the cloud with a wrench in hand, flipped open the hood, seemed to tighten something on the motor's block, wacked the carburetor, and slammed the hood closed.

"How are you this morning Richard," he said? "I hope you are hungry." I nodded as I said hello and got into the vehicle. Anne sat confidently in the backseat. Michael seated himself behind the wheel of the Fiat, turned the key and the engine quickly started.

"This vehicle has a few idiosyncrasies," he laughed and waved to the fellows gathered in front of the hotel as he drove toward the avenue.

Lunch at the Carnivore Restaurant was a fitting conclusion to my East African adventure; I was delighted that Anne and Michael chose to take me to this unique Nairobi landmark. The Carnivore is one of the very few restaurants in the world that is allowed to serve wild game from the herds that roam the plains of East Africa. Can you imagine a restaurant in the United States listing hartebeest or zebra on the menu? If there are any, they're known only to a select few.

Anne and Michael agreed that a meal at the Carnivore would be a proper and unusual sendoff. But none of us realized just how unusual this lunch would be. When we arrived I expected to find a bevy of tourists. Instead, we walked into the restaurant amid the revelry ending one of the world's most grueling automobile races, the annual East African Safari Rally, and there were very few tourists.

* * *

I had seen some of the colorful race cars that completed in the East African Safari Rally, decorated with advertisements of their various sponsors, limp across the finish line in Jumo Kenyatta Square a few days earlier when I returned from the Seychelles. The evening of the day that I returned to Nairobi I had wandered toward the square and was caught up in the end-of-the rally festivities. A large crowd had gathered for this event. Race cars were still crossing the line and whenever one did, excitement rippled through the throng. While I watched, the boisterous crowd parted, allowing a muddied Mitsubishi and a Subaru to enter the square. As they entered the cars moved between a gauntlet of cheering and whistling fans.

When the vehicles came to a halt, they were encircled by the hordes. Once the driver and navigator exited, the crowd treated them as if they were winners. Teammates shook and sprayed Champagne into the air. Much of it spattered the drivers' jumpsuits. Fans sprayed themselves with beer. Apparently, everyone considered any driver and race team member a winner if they drove their car across the finish line and into the square.

The Safari Rally is one of the most punishing cross-country competitions in automobile racing. For three days and four nights racers are confronted with rugged mountain roads, flooded riverbeds, treacherous terrain, wayward wildlife, bandits and rebels. The challenge becomes one of completing the course, not necessarily for winning, but crossing the finish line in one piece. This 3000-kilometer course winds them through Kenya, Uganda and Tanzania. Barring accidents, the vehicles take the greatest beating; human discomforts are considered minor. Although they're built to sustain the rigors of the East African terrain, the bush, heat, dust, rocks and ruts brutalize the vehicles. Since auto repair shops are few and far between, any mechanical failure must be fixed by the cars' driver and navigator. I read later that several cars were actually destroyed by rebels.

In between the arrival of racecars, the crowd milled around the square eating, drinking, and lounging about. Throughout the square, gaily-decorated flags signified the various countries from which contestants came. The waving banners of automobile manufacturers, tool companies, STP, Coca-Cola, Tusker Beer, Sportsman cigarettes, leather jackets and pants, advertised the Safari Rally sponsors. One advertisement displayed a bevy of contorted models wearing skimpy bathing suits. I wasn't sure what statement that ad wanted to make. Flimsy kiosks, constructed around the periphery of the square, sold most of the items advertised, except for the cars and models.

The entire texture of this event was engulfed in a mist of acrid auto exhaust, cigarette smoke, vapors from meats and corn being grilled, human sweat, onions, stale beer and urine. Mixed within this atmosphere, the merriment of the crowd and the energy and dynamism that characterized the finale of the Safari Rally was contagious. Although many of the revelers were somewhat sedated from imbibing too much spirits, by two o'clock in the morning the party seemed to be at its crest. I decided to return to the hotel because several unsavory characters in tight miniskirts began to cast their eyes in my direction. I hailed a taxi for the three-block trip.

* * *

Even though the Safari Rally had ended, the merriment of private parties greeted Anne, Michael and me as we entered the Carnivore Restaurant. In their brightly colored nylon warmup jackets, neck scarfs, and amid flying banners hung over the tables, several racing crews, along with all their support personnel, wives, girlfriends, and children, were celebrating their wins, race completions or losses. The racing team from Sweden, at the table near us, flaunted a large silver bowl filled with blue and yellow flowers that depicted their country's national colors. Interlaced through the arrangement were silver ribbons. Miniature Swedish flags decorated the table. It looked as if the Swedes won some prize, because they boisterously toasted each other, sang national songs, and hugged and kissed their partners. When I looked around the restaurant, other racing groups were behaving in similar fashion, so I could not discern who were the losers and who were the winners.

As we departed the Carnivore, I stopped to congratulate the Swedes on their supposed win. They told me that they took third place. However, their happiness didn't stem from the win, they said, but from the fact that they were able to complete the rally with no injuries and with a vehicle that remained relatively intact.

Before we departed the restaurant the Swedes invited us to join them in a toast to the drivers. With a shooter of flavored vodka, I raised my shot glass and voiced a hardy *Skål*!

Michael suggested that we spend the remainder of the afternoon watching horse races. Anne and I agreed and he drove the short distance from the Carnivore to the Ngong Racecourse, home of the Jockey Club of Kenya.

The British brought their favorite pastime with them when they appropriated British East Africa. During the development of the city of Nairobi in 1904, the elite were competitively testing their horses under the auspices of the East African Turf club. In 1921, Lord and Lady Delamere and other prominent individuals established the Jockey Club of Kenya. Besides the Delameres, the new horse racing club's membership listed such historical celebrities as the Honorables Berkeley and Galbraith Cole, Sir Northrup McMillan, an American millionaire who was knighted by the British Crown for valorous service in World War I, Captain C. B. Clutterbuck the foremost East African horse-trainer, and his famous aviatrix daughter Beryl Markham. Markham actually became the first woman licensed as a trainer of thoroughbreds in Africa under English Jockey Club rules. The club members initially raced their horses on a motley course constructed north of Nairobi. Eventually, four hundred acres of prime real estate off Ngong Road was granted to allow the club to build a racetrack according to the racing specification of the United Kingdom. Since its opening in 1954, Ngong Racetrack has hosted such famous jockeys as Lester Piggott, Willie Carson, and Dick Saunders, the latter a Grand National winning amateur rider. Because of the potential for contracting African horse sickness, only horses bred from African stock race at Ngong Racetrack.

We arrived just after the horses for the day's first race were paraded around in the paddock in front of the club house. We made our way into the bleachers to watch the first race. Not being familiar with horse racing nor its vocabulary I shied away from placing bets on this race. Michael seemed to understand the betting process and explained some fundamental details. We tried our luck on the second race.

Michael suggested that I scrutinize the entry list and examine each horse's weight, past winning record, and status of the jockey before picking my favorites. Most importantly, he told me that if I bet on a horse to win, it has to win the race for me to obtain prize money. But if I bet on the horse to show, I will collect winnings if the horse crosses the finish line in either of the top three positions. Now you can place a bet, Michael said, but don't forget to memorize the stable's colors so you can follow your horse's progress during the race. When I decided on which horse would win me the pot of gold or at least some beer money, the next step was to find a bookie. The track didn't have any betting booths. Bookmakers roamed about the grounds and were easy to spot, because they walked around waving fist-fulls of tickets in one hand and bills of currency in the other. I found the bookmakers to be eager, no nonsense, business types who took your money and didn't chitchat about the race. Wagering started a half hour before the race and continued until the horses entered the starting gates.

Michael provided more information about the strategies of playing the ponies than I cared to absorb. So when I selected three possible horses running in the second race, I picked them only because their names fascinated me and not because of any of their statistical or quantitative attributes.

A fat bookmaker stood by the bleachers near Michael, Anne and me. I said to him, "I want ten shillings each on Zizania, Gondola Girl, and C'est ci bon to place." He took my fifty-shilling note and kept the change, his tip he said.

"Guaranteed to win, yes?" I asked when he handed me the chits that contained information on my bet.

"Never can tell," the bookie answered and turned to another customer.

The starting gates flashed open and the horses ran. "Who did I bet on?" I yelled to no one in particular. I looked at my stubs to determine on which of the horse I had placed a bet. Suddenly, the race was over. It didn't matter who won, because my horses placed fifth, sixth, and seventh.

Michael selected an almost-winner. His horse came in fourth. It didn't pay anything. Oh well, on to the next race.

"Only four horses will run in the next race," Michael said. "It's the run for The Delamere Gold Vase. We should be able to win something on this one."

Landmark, Taberin, Y Not, and Mariner were the names of the horses scheduled to run this race. I wagered ten shillings on each to win. Unfortunately, all were rated as excellent thoroughbreds that had won many races, so the betting odds were low. So what, I wasn't here for the money but the excitement and thrill of the race and an opportunity to be with friends. I was also learning a bit more about Kenya's culture. Besides, in this race I could cheer for all of the horses. My winnings would definitely cover the cost of several rounds of beer no matter which horse won.

During the third race the sky began to turn ugly and rain threatened. After six weeks of dry, clear weather, the rainy season now moved into Nairobi. Since the windshield wipers on Michael's car didn't work, he wanted to beat the storm back to the city. But it was faster and we had to drive through the middle of a torrential downpour. Michael kept his window open to allow him to reach out and move the wipers. He steered with his right hand and moved the windshield wipers with his left. His efforts were of little avail, because we still couldn't see a car-length ahead. The rain hit the windshield with the vehemence of a stream blasting out of the end of a fire hose nozzle. Although there were few cars on the roads, Michael's actions were a danger to all of us. So I opened the window on my side and worked the wipers while he drove. By the time we arrived at the Milimani Hotel, the storm had abated to a continuous drizzle which stopped just before we walked through the main entrance. Soaked, we left a trail of water through the lobby on the way to the bar. We needed to warm up and dry out. My winnings bought us several rounds of brandies.

After about an hour, Anne and Michael wished me a bon voyage. I went to my room and changed for dinner. My flight wasn't scheduled to leave for another five hours, so I had plenty of time before leaving for the airport. Nevertheless, I packed my belongings before I went to dinner.

When I returned to my room after dinner, I found that I had left the lights on. Normally this would not have made a difference, but tonight my room became the focal point of a termite jubilee. Thousands of inch-long, black, ant-like insects were flying through the sliding door access to the balcony that I had left open. Stimulated by the day's deluge, the reproductively mature, subterranean, African mound building termites had sprouted wings, exited their caverns *en masse* and swarmed above ground in reproductive orgies. Attracted by the room's lights, multitudes of them flew in. When I entered, thousands of airy–fairy, isinglass-textured wings wafted into the air. Appearing weightless, they were blasted upward from the floor, bed, dresser, tables and chairs by the sudden puff of wind created when I pushed the door open. From the doorway I watched winged individuals flit about, land, and begin running. Some pursued, while others tried to escape. But as soon as a male captured a female, the two connected, head to tail, and jettisoned their wings. They then scurried, in tandem, locked in coital bliss, searching for a proper habitat where the female could propagate her offspring and become the queen of a colony.

Though totally harmless to humans, a room full of confused flying, crawling termites bothered me. Yet many East Africans consider termites to be a delicacy and look forward to these massive swarms. They collect and dry them and resupply their coffers with these nourishing, candy-like tidbits. I had an opportunity to taste dried termites. Their flavor was sweet.

The primary sustenance of termites is anything vegetable or made from vegetable matter, like wood, grass, paper, and cotton or linen cloth. What these vigorous tandems were searching for was a proper nest site loaded with food. So I became concerned, not so much for the room nor its concrete walls, but for the furniture, bed, rugs, and, most importantly, my belongings. I gingerly entered the room. Even so, every step I made crunched many enraptured couples. They were everywhere. I quickly closed the sliding the door and drew the drapes. The maneuver only slowed their access. I looked above the drapery rod. Six weeks in this room and I had not noticed the unscreened, baffled vents placed above the sliding doors. Can't close those, I thought. The termites were flying in through the vents.

Disturbed by this melee, I dusted the bugs off my luggage, set the bags in the hall outside my door and closed the door. Then I tried scooping handfuls of wings and insects and throwing them into the commode in an attempt to flush them down the drain. The wingless bodies quickly disappeared in the swirl, but the wings kept rotating in the turbulence. They were so buoyant that no matter what I did, they wouldn't sink. Eventually, they filled the toilet. Frustrated, I thought of calling for a vacuum cleaner but this was Sunday night and the maids' night off. I threw up my arms. "I'm leaving this place, so why should I care!" I told the termites they were welcome to the room. After checking the room for anything I might have left,

I turned off the lights, walked into the hall, closed the door, picked up my luggage and went to the lobby.

What confronted me when I reached the lobby changed my frustration to hilarity. Amid the whooshing, deafening wails of vacuum cleaners, the bellhops, desk clerks, and concierge were in the process of trying to clear the termite deluge from their respective areas. Several guests, apparently accustomed to termite emigrations, some seated at the bar and others standing about with drinks in hand, provided encouragement and suggestions. It appeared that most often their remarks were focused at the salvation of the disconcerted insects. The desk clerk announced that the season of termite invasion had begun. He gave me a jocular apology when I turned in my key. "Forget it," I said. "Where else in the world but Kenya would nature provide such a send-off? I'm impressed." I laughed with him at the situation and wished everyone *Kwaheri* as I walked to the taxi that would take me to the airport.

AUTHOR'S NOTE

The events, people, and places I have written about in *The Malachite Lion* are real. But my readers, you must remember that the trip took place in 1987. The equator has rotated through many diurnal cycles, and the footprints I left in Kenya and the Seychelles have been obliterated by myriads of others. So some of the places I described have probably changed. Also, for a variety of reasons I have taken the liberty of changing the names of the individuals I met and interacted with on this trip to protect their privacy.

SUGGESTED HISTORICAL READINGS

Blixen, Karen. *Out of Africa.* London: Century Publishing, 1986.

Burton, Richard F. *Zanzibar; City, Island, and Coast, Volume II.* London: Tinsley Brothers, 1872.

Huxley, Elspeth. *Out in the Midday Sun.* New York: Viking, 1987.

Leakey, Richard E. *One Life: An Autobiography.* Salem: Salem House, 1983.

Miller, Charles. *The Lunatic Express.* New York: The Macmillan Company, 1971.

Mboya, Tom. *Freedom and After.* Boston: Little, Brown and Company, 1963.

Trzebinski, Errol. *The Kenya Pioneers.* New York: W. W. Norton & Company, 1985.

ABOUT THE AUTHOR

Richard Modlin, born in Toledo, Ohio, educated at the Universities of Wisconsin and Connecticut, is an Emeritus Professor of Zoology, a Fulbright Research Award recipient, and past Director of a University Honors Program. He has written over seventy scientific and natural history articles on marine and freshwater invertebrates and has named fourteen new species. His lay articles have appeared in *Sea Frontiers, Bird Watcher's Digest, Encyclopedia of Environmental Issues*, and among other magazines. He has traveled extensively throughout North and Central America, Europe, East Africa, and the islands of the Western Atlantic, Indian, and Pacific Oceans and the Mediterranean Sea. Presently, he lives in North Alabama with his wife and a cat named Bugsy.

Made in the USA
Middletown, DE
18 October 2016